3-B
학년

한국에서 유일한
중학영문법
알짜 3000제

1 ✖ Grammar Points

사진과 대표 예문만 봐도 쉽게 영문법의 개념을 이해할 수 있는 Visual Approach 도입하여 문법 설명을 시각화하였습니다. 문법 설명은 머리에 쏙쏙!! 예문과 설명은 한 눈에!! 참신한 예문과 원어민들이 실제로 사용하는 표현을 담았습니다.

2 ✖ 서술형 기초다지기

일대일로 대응되는 다양한 문제들을 구성하여 문법 개념을 확실히 이해할 수 있도록 하였습니다. 이를 통해 서술형 문제에 대비할 수 있도록 하였으며 실제 문장 구성 능력을 향상시킬 수 있도록 쓰기 영역을 강화하였습니다. 단순 문법 연습이 아닌 응용·심화 과정을 통해 기초 실력 또한 차곡차곡 쌓을 수 있습니다.

3 ✖ 이것이 시험에 출제되는 영문법이다!

어떤 문제가 주로 출제되는지를 미리 아는 것과 막연히 공부를 열심히 한 사람의 시험 성적은 하늘과 땅 차이! 12년간의 내신 만점신화를 이루어낸 저자의 비밀노트를 통해 내신문제를 출제하는 선생님들의 의도와 출제유형, 주관식과 서술형의 출제경향을 정확히 꿰뚫어 보는 눈을 키울 수 있을 것입니다.

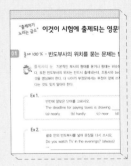

4 ✖ 기출 응용문제

실제 중학교 내신 시험에서 빈출되는 필수 문법문제와 응용문제를 수록하여 각 chapter에서 배운 문법 사항을 다양한 유형의 문제를 통해 확인하고 연습해 볼 수 있습니다.

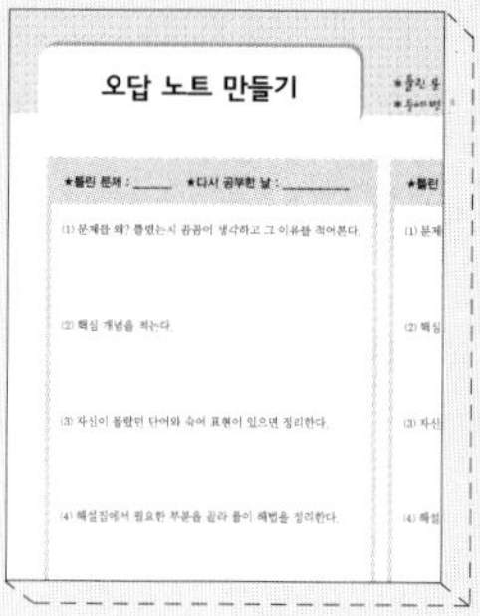
오답 노트 만들기

5 오답 노트 만들기

기출 응용문제 중 틀린 문제를 오답노트에 정리할 수 있도록 구성하였습니다. 틀린 문제의 문법 개념을 다시 확인하고 해당 문제 유형을 다시는 틀리지 않도록 스스로 공부해 볼 수 있는 코너입니다.

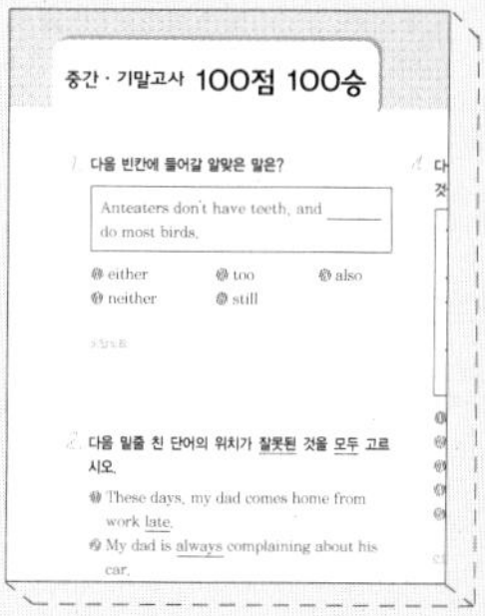
중간 · 기말고사 100점 100승

다음 빈칸에 들어갈 알맞은 말은?

Anteaters don't have teeth, and ______ do most birds.

① either ② too ③ also ④ neither ⑤ still

다음 밑줄 친 단어의 위치가 잘못된 것을 모두 고르시오.

① These days, my dad comes home from work late.
② My dad is always complaining about his car.

6 중간 · 기말고사 100점 100승

학교 시험에서 자주 나오는 빈출유형을 분석하여 출제 가능성이 가장 높은 문제 중심으로 수록하였습니다. 간단한 객관식 문제를 비롯하여 대화문과 독해문, 주관식 문제 등 다양한 문제를 풀면서 자신의 실력을 정확하게 진단해 볼 수 있습니다.

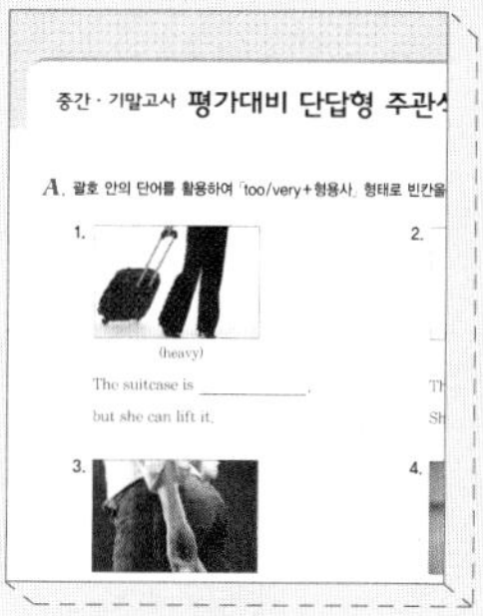
중간 · 기말고사 평가대비 단답형 주관식

A. 괄호 안의 단어를 활용하여 'too/very+형용사' 형태로 빈칸을

1. (heavy)
The suitcase is ______, but she can lift it.

7 평가대비 단답형 주관식

문법 핵심을 파악하고 어법에 맞는 문장을 직접 쓸 수 있도록 구성하여 기존의 학교 단답형 주관식 문제에 철저히 대비할 수 있습니다.

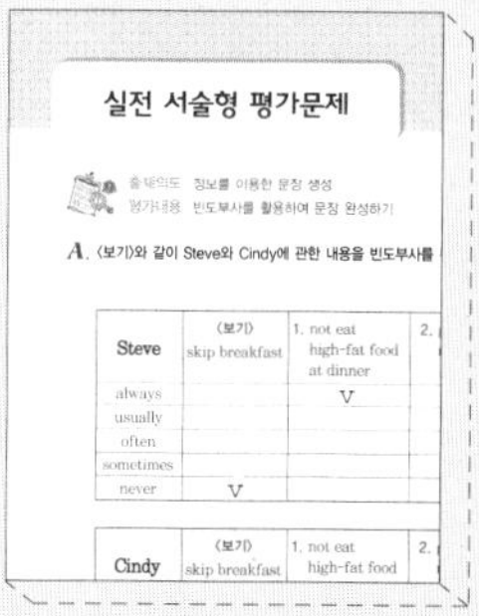
실전 서술형 평가문제

출제의도 정보를 이용한 문장 생성
평가내용 빈도부사를 활용하여 문장 완성하기

A. 〈보기〉와 같이 Steve와 Cindy에 관한 내용을 빈도부사를

Steve	〈보기〉 skip breakfast	1. not eat high-fat food at dinner
always		V
usually		
often		
sometimes		
never	V	

Cindy	〈보기〉 skip breakfast	1. not eat high-fat food

8 실전 서술형 평가문제

교육청 출제경향에 맞춘 서술형 평가대비 문제로 학생들의 사고력과 창의력을 길러줍니다. 해당 chapter에서 출제될 수 있는 서술형 문항을 개발하여 각 학교의 서술형 평가 문제에 철저히 대비할 수 있도록 하였습니다. 단순 암기에서 벗어나 직접 써보고 생각해 볼 수 있는 코너입니다.

목차

chapter 7. **일치와 화법**
(Agreement & Narration)

chapter 8. **특수 구문**
(Emphasis, Inversion, Ellipsis)

Chapter 1

부사 (Adverbs)

Unit 01 부사의 형태

1-1 부사 만들기

This sandwiches were **really** delicious.
이 샌드위치는 정말 맛있었다.
She smiled in a **friendly** way.
그녀는 정다운 모습으로 미소 지었다.

01 부사는 보통 형용사에 -ly를 붙여 만든다.

quick 빠른+ly	→ quick**ly** 빠르게	kind 친절한+ly	→ kind**ly** 친절하게
certain 확실한+ly	→ certain**ly** 확실히	fortunate 운 좋은+ly	→ fortunate**ly** 운 좋게, 다행히
sudden 갑작스러운+ly	→ sudden**ly** 갑자기	immediate 즉시의+ly	→ immediate**ly** 즉시, 당장
effective 효과적인+ly	→ effective**ly** 효과적으로	similar 비슷한+ly	→ similar**ly** 비슷하게

02 '자음+y'로 끝나는 단어: y를 i로 고치고 -ly를 붙인다.

angry 화난+ly → angr**ily** 화나게	happy 행복한+ly → happ**ily** 행복하게
easy 쉬운+ly → eas**ily** 쉽게	lucky 운 좋은+ly → luck**ily** 운 좋게도

03 -le로 끝나는 단어: e를 없애고 -y만 붙인다.

simple 간단한+y	→ simpl**y** 간단히	idle 게으른+y	→ idl**y** 게으르게
reasonable 합리적인+y	→ reasonabl**y** 합리적으로	terrible 무서운+y	→ terribl**y** 무섭게
visible 눈에 보이는+y	→ visibl**y** 눈에 보이게	comfortable 편안한+y	→ comfortabl**y** 편안하게

04 -ue로 끝나는 단어: e를 없애고 -ly를 붙인다.

true 진실의+ly → trul**y** 진실로	due 정당한+ly → dul**y** 정당하게
※ unique 독특한 → uniquely 독특하게	

05 -ll로 끝나는 단어: -y만 붙인다.

full 충분한+y → full**y** 충분히, 완전히	dull (우)둔한+y → dull**y** (우)둔하게

06 -ic로 끝나는 단어: -ical로 바꾸고 -ly를 붙인다.

basic 기초의+ally → basic**ally** 기본적으로	dramatic 극적인+ally → dramatic**ally** 극적으로

07 부사처럼 -ly로 끝나지만 형용사인 단어들이 있다. '명사+ly'의 형태이거나 원래 -ly로 끝나는 형용사들이다. 부사로 혼동하지 않도록 주의해야 한다.

costly 값비싼	friendly 정다운, 친근한	lovely 사랑스러운	lonely 외로운
ugly 추한	lively 생생한	likely 그럴 듯한	deadly 치명적인

서술형 기초다지기

정답 p. 2

Challenge 1 다음 단어를 부사로 고쳐 써 보세요.

〈일반적인 경우〉

01. quick → _____ 02. clear → _____

03. slow → _____ 04. quiet → _____

05. sudden → _____ 06. private → _____

〈자음+y로 끝나는 단어〉

07. happy → _____ 08. lucky → _____

09. heavy → _____ 10. necessary → _____

〈-le로 끝나는 단어〉

11. gentle → _____ 12. simple → _____

13. noble → _____ 14. terrible → _____

〈-ue로 끝나는 단어〉

15. true → _____ 16. due → _____

〈-ll로 끝나는 단어〉

17. full → _____ 18. dull → _____

〈-ic로 끝나는 단어〉

19. basic → _____ 20. dramatic → _____

Challenge 2 다음 괄호 안의 단어 중에서 알맞은 것을 고르세요.

01. Lucy is a (lovely / love) person. She makes people happy.

02. A (friendly / friend) attitude is important to establish a good relationship with co-workers.

03. The (ugly / ugliness) duckling thought that nobody liked him.

1-2 형용사와 모양이 똑같은 부사

We were **late** for the train.
우리는 기차 시간에 늦었다. (형용사-늦은)
We arrived a half hour **late**.
우리는 30분 늦게 도착했다. (부사-늦게)

01

형용사	부사
hard(힘든, 어려운)	hard(열심히)
fast(빠른)	fast(빠르게, 빨리)
early(이른)	early(이르게, 일찍)
late(늦은)	late(늦게)
high(높은)	high(높게, 높이)
last(마지막인)	last(마지막으로)
long(오래된, 긴)	long(오래)
right(옳은, 정확한)	right(바르게, 곧바로)
near(가까운)	near(가까이)
most(가장 많은)	most(가장 많이)

※ 형용사 good의 부사는 well이고 반대말은 각각 bad, badly이다. well이 형용사로 쓰이면
'건강한(in good health)'의 뜻이며 이때의 반대말은 ill이다.

It's the **right** answer. 그것이 정답이다. (형용사)
I'll be **right** back. 바로 돌아 올거야. (부사)

I'm sorry I'm **late**. 늦어서 미안해. (형용사)
I was up very **late** last night. 나는 지난밤 아주 늦게까지 자지 않고 있었다. (부사)

It is **hard** to believe. 그거 믿기 어려운데. (형용사)
It's raining **hard** outside. 밖에 비가 엄청나게 많이 오네. (부사)

We talked on the phone for a **long** time before starting to actually date.
우리는 실제로 데이트하기 전에 전화로 오랫동안 이야기했다. (형용사)
I arrived **long** after the party began. 나는 파티가 시작된 지 한참 후에 도착했다. (부사)

High cholesterol is a cause of heart attacks. 높은 콜레스테롤은 심장마비의 원인이다. (형용사)
My kite flew **high** up into the sky. 내 연이 하늘 높이 날았다. (부사)

서술형 기초다지기

정답 p. 2

Challenge 1 다음 밑줄 친 단어의 품사와 뜻을 쓰세요.

보기	He got up very <u>late</u> this morning.	→ 품사: __부사__ 뜻: __늦게__

01. That frog can jump very <u>high</u>.　　　　→ 품사: _____ 뜻: _____

02. She works <u>hard</u> to get promoted.　　　→ 품사: _____ 뜻: _____

03. A <u>fast</u> train is one that goes fast.　　　→ 품사: _____ 뜻: _____

04. I look forward to an <u>early</u> reply.　　　　→ 품사: _____ 뜻: _____

05. The test was very <u>hard</u>.　　　　　　　　→ 품사: _____ 뜻: _____

06. I will be able to buy a house in the <u>near</u> future.　→ 품사: _____ 뜻: _____

07. These days, my father comes home <u>late</u> from work.　→ 품사: _____ 뜻: _____

Challenge 2 다음 괄호 안의 단어를 이용하여 빈칸을 채우세요. (필요시 변형할 것)

01. The rare pictures were sold at a _____ rate. (high)

02. The driver of the car was _____ injured. (serious)

03. Our vacation was too short. The time passed very _____. (quick)

04. She is in a _____ situation. (hard)

05. Her house is very _____. (near)

06. We didn't go out because of the _____ rain. (heavy)

Challenge 3 다음 빈칸에 good 또는 well 중 알맞은 것을 써 넣으세요.

01. I play basketball, but I'm not very _____.

02. Sunny plays the piano _____.

03. The weather was very _____ while we were on vacation.

1-3 모양은 비슷하지만 뜻이 다른 부사

She worked **hard** to prepare a good meal, but her son **hardly** ate anything.
그녀는 맛있는 저녁 준비를 위해 열심히 노력했지만, 그녀의 아들은 거의 아무것도 먹지 않았다.

hard	열심히	She studied **hard** last night. 그녀는 지난밤에 열심히 공부했다.
hardly	거의 ~않는	I can **hardly** understand what he is saying. 난 그가 하는 말을 거의 이해할 수가 없다.
late	늦게	He came home **late** and missed dinner. 그는 늦게 집에 와서 저녁을 먹지 못했다.
lately	최근에	I haven't seen her **lately**. 나는 최근에 그녀를 만나지 못했다.
close	가까이	She came to me and sat **close**. 그녀는 내게 와서 가까이 앉았다.
closely	주의 깊게, 면밀히	The policeman observed his behavior **closely**. 경찰은 그의 행동을 주시했다.
high	높이, 높게	You'll have to hit the ball quite **high**. 너는 공을 아주 높이 쳐야 할 것이다.
highly	높이 평가하여, 매우	Admittedly, I think **highly** of our company's founder. 일반적으로 인정하듯, 나 역시 우리 회사 설립자를 높이 평가한다.
near	가까이	Come **near** and watch. 가까이 와서 봐라.
nearly	거의	She **nearly** fell over the cliff. 그녀는 절벽 너머로 거의 떨어질 뻔했다.
short	짧게	Her career was cut **short** by cancer. 그녀의 경력은 암으로 인해 짧게 끝났다.
shortly	곧(=soon)	The movie will begin **shortly**. 영화가 곧 시작할 것이다.
most	매우, 가장 많이	The lack of coordination at the office annoys me **most**. 사무실에서의 협동 부족이 나를 가장 많이 화나게 한다.
mostly	대체로, 주로	My co-workers are **mostly** energetic and bright college graduates. 내 동료들은 주로 활기차고 밝은 대학 졸업생들이다.
great	잘	You really have done **great** this year in terms of sales. 너는 매출 면에서 올해 정말 잘해냈다.
greatly	매우	In spite of a lack of practice, her writing has **greatly** improved. 연습 부족에도 불구하고, 그녀의 작문은 매우 향상되었다.

서술형 기초다지기

Challenge 1 다음 주어진 괄호 안의 표현 중 알맞은 것을 골라 쓰세요.

01. (late / lately)   These fans have been quite popular among tourists _____.

02. (hard / hardly)   Nancy wasn't very friendly to me at the party.
　　　　　　　　　　　　　She _____ spoke to me.

03. (hard / hardly)   I'm tired because I've been working _____.

04. (close / closely)   You had better come close to watch it _____.

05. (near / nearly)   The final day for registration drew _____.

06. (near / nearly)   The body forms _____ half its bone during the teen years.

07. (most / mostly)   Kevin is the _____ intelligent person that I've ever met.

08. (most / mostly)   They have _____ invested their money in real estate in the
　　　　　　　　　　　　　southern area.

09. (short / shortly)   She was here a minute ago. She'll probably be back _____.

10. (short / shortly)   She was wearing _____ pants as far as I remember.

11. (high / highly)   The _____ temperatures are abnormal for this time of year.

12. (high / highly)   The woman is _____ respected as an excellent doctor.

Unit 02 다양한 부사의 활용

2-1 빈도부사

A: Do you **always** eat breakfast?
당신은 항상 아침을 먹나요?
B: I **usually** don't eat breakfast.
나는 평소 아침을 먹지 않아요.

01 빈도부사는 어떤 일이 발생하는 **횟수(빈도)를 나타내는 부사**를 말한다. 빈도부사의 위치는 **be동사와 조동사 뒤, 그리고 일반동사 앞**에 쓴다.

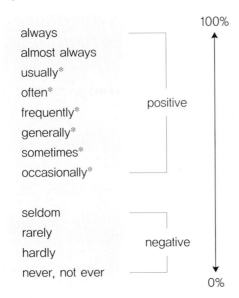

always
almost always
usually*
often*
frequently*
generally*
sometimes*
occasionally*

positive

seldom
rarely
hardly
never, not ever

negative

100%

0%

I **usually** listen to music when I'm free.
나는 시간이 나면 자주 음악을 듣는다.
She is **often** late for school.
그녀는 종종 학교에 지각한다.
You must **always** memorize English words.
너는 항상 영단어를 외워야 한다.
Ann **never** eats meal. Ann은 고기를 절대 먹지 않는다.
=Ann doesn't **ever** eat meal.

※ *표시된 빈도부사는 문장 맨 앞 또는 맨 뒤에 올 수 있다.

Sometimes I get up at 6:00. 나는 종종 6시에 일어난다.
=I get up at 6:00 **sometimes**.
Often Elena writes to her friend about Korean customs. Elena는 종종 한국 관습에 대해 친구에게 편지를 쓴다.

02 부정문에서 빈도부사는 **부정 동사 앞에 쓰고**(단 always, ever는 부정 동사 뒤), 의문문에서 빈도부사는 **항상 주어 뒤**에 쓴다.

He **usually** doesn't shave in the morning. 그는 주로 아침에 면도를 하지 않는다.
He doesn't **always** shave in the morning. 그는 항상 아침에 면도를 하지 않는다.
Does it **usually** snow in the winter? 겨울에 주로 눈이 오나요?

03 현재진행형은 빈도부사와 함께 쓰지 않으나, always는 현재진행형과 함께 쓸 수 있다. 이때는 **주어에 대한 불평이나 성가심**을 나타낸다.

Jason is never satisfied. He's **always** complaining. Jason은 절대 만족하지 않는다. 그는 항상 불평을 한다.

서술형 기초다지기

Challenge 1 괄호 안의 빈도부사를 넣어 다음 문장을 다시 써 보세요.

01. Elena writes a letter to her friend, Sofia. (sometimes)

→ _____

02. Is Mary worried about her dog? (always)

→ _____

03. The dog is happy to see Mary when she comes home. (always)

→ _____

04. She doesn't drink coffee in the morning. (usually)

→ _____

Challenge 2 괄호 안의 동사와 함께 적절한 빈도부사를 골라 빈칸을 채우세요.

| always | often/usually | sometimes | never | seldom/rarely |

> **보기**
> I watch TV in the evening five or six times a week.
> → I *often/usually watch* TV in the evening. (watch)

01. I take the bus to work once a week or once every two weeks.

→ I usually carpool to work, but I _____ the bus. (take)

02. Every time I go to a movie, I buy popcorn.

→ I _____ popcorn when I go to a movie. (buy)

03. Kevin tries to finish his homework before he goes to bed, but he usually falls asleep.

→ Kevin _____ his homework before he falls asleep and decides to go to bed. (finish)

04. My roommate eats only vegetarian food, and I like beef and chicken. We always cook separate meals.

→ My roommate _____ my meals. (eat)

2-2 too, so, either, neither

She is a Korean, and I am (a Korean), **too**.
그녀는 한국인이고, 나도 한국인이다.
= She is a Korean, and **so am I**.
She isn't a Japanese, and I'm not (a Japanese), **either**.
그녀는 일본인이 아니고, 나도 일본인이 아니다.
= She isn't a Japanese, and **neither am I**.

01

too가 긍정문의 마지막에 올 경우 '역시, 또한'이라는 동의의 의미이다. 부정문에는 '역시'라는 의미로 **either**를 쓴다.

They like Jason. I like him, **too**. (= I do, too.) 그들은 Jason을 좋아한다. 나 역시 그를 좋아한다.

She is a student. I am a student, **too**. (= I am, too.) 그녀는 학생이다. 나 또한 학생이다.

Bob went to Singapore last year. Karen went there, **too**. (= Karen did, too.)
Bob은 작년에 싱가포르로 갔다. Karen 또한 그곳에 갔다.

I don't like baseball. Paul doesn't like it, **either**. (= Paul doesn't, either.)
나는 야구를 좋아하지 않는다. Paul 또한 야구를 좋아하지 않는다.

I'm not hungry. She isn't hungry, **either**. (= She isn't, either.)
나는 배가 고프지 않다. 그녀도 배가 고프지 않다.

※ 일상 영어에서는 Me, too. 또는 Me, neither. 등으로 짧게 대답한다.

I like Sunny. – **Me, too**.   I'm not hungry. – **Me, neither**.

02

같은 표현으로 긍정문의 동의에는 「so+(조)동사+주어」를 쓰고, 부정문의 동의에는 「neither+(조)동사+주어」를 쓴다.

She is a student, and **so am I**. 그녀는 학생이고 나도 마찬가지이다.

Bob went to Seoul last year, and **so did Karen**. Bob은 작년에 서울로 갔고, Karen도 갔다.

A: Tina can drive. Tina는 운전을 할 수 있다.

B: **So can Tom**. Tom 역시 할 수 있다.

She isn't hungry, and **neither am I**. 그녀는 배가 고프지 않고 나 또한 배가 고프지 않다.

I don't like baseball, and **neither does Paul**. 나는 야구를 좋아하지 않고 Paul도 좋아하지 않는다.

A: She can't play tennis. 그녀는 테니스를 칠 줄 몰라.

B: **Neither can I**. 나도 칠 줄 몰라.

※ 두 명의 화자가 대화를 나눌 때는 So, Neither 앞에 보통 and를 쓰지 않는다.

서술형 기초다지기

Challenge 1 〈보기〉와 같이 too, so, either 또는 neither를 이용하여 문장을 완성하세요.

| 보
기 | too
so | → Bob loves her, and *James loves her, too (=James does, too)*. (James)
→ Bob loves her, and *so does James*. |

01. **either** → Kathy doesn't play tennis, and _____. (Jane)

    neither → Kathy doesn't play tennis, and _____.

02. **too** → Lisa has curly hair, and _____. (Nancy)

    so → Lisa has curly hair, and _____.

Challenge 2 다음 대화에서 B에 들어갈 말을 so나 neither를 이용한 동의의 표현으로 쓰세요.

| 보
기 | A: I'm tired.
B: *So am I.* |

01. A: I love this kind of music.

    B: _____

02. A: I didn't enjoy the movie last night.

    B: _____

03. A: I came to this city a few years ago.

    B: _____

04. A: I would like to make new friends.

    B: _____

05. A: I didn't eat breakfast this morning.

    B: _____

06. A: I can't speak Japanese.

    B: _____

2-3 too, very, enough

He is not big **enough** to wear the suit.
그는 양복을 입을 만큼 크지 않다.
The suit is **too** big for him to wear.
그 양복은 그가 입기에는 너무 크다.

01
부사 very와 too는 둘 다 '너무/아주 ~한'의 뜻이지만 이 둘은 구별해서 사용해야 한다. **too**는 '어려움이나 문제가 있어 불가능하거나 불평하는 어조'를 담고 있다. **very**는 중립적(neutral)이거나 '문제가 있지만 가능하다'라는 의미를 담고 있다.

This box is **very** heavy, but I can lift it. 이 상자는 아주 무겁지만, 나는 그것을 들 수 있다.

The shoes are **too** big for her. (→ She cannot wear them.) 그 신발은 그녀에게 너무 크다.

※ too는 부정적인 결과(negative result)를 낳는다.

This coffee is **too** hot. I can't drink it. 이 커피는 너무 뜨겁다. 나는 마실 수가 없다.

The food was **too** hot. We couldn't eat it. 그 음식은 너무 뜨거웠다. 우리는 그것을 먹을 수 없었다.

→ The food was **so** hot **that** we **couldn't** eat it.

→ The food was **too** hot **to** eat.

02
too many는 셀 수 있는 명사 앞에서 '지나치게 많은 수', **too much**는 셀 수 없는 명사 앞에서 '지나치게 많은 양'을 나타낸다. 중립적인 의미를 갖는 'a lot of'와 혼동해서 사용하면 안 된다. 'too'는 항상 문제를 암시하면서 불평하는 어조를 담고 있다.

You put **too much** salt in the soup, and I can't eat it. 네가 수프에 소금을 너무 많이 넣어서 먹을 수가 없다.

She puts **a lot of** sugar in her coffee. She likes it that way.
그녀는 커피에 설탕을 많이 넣는다. 그녀는 그렇게 먹는 걸 좋아한다.

03
enough는 형용사나 부사 뒤에 쓴다. 특히 「형용사/부사+enough+to V」의 어순일 때 enough는 '~할 정도로'의 뜻이다. '충분한'의 뜻으로도 쓰이는데 이때는 명사 앞에 온다.

He isn't <u>tall</u> **enough** to reach the shelf. 그는 선반에 닿을 정도로 키가 크지 않다.

I walked <u>quickly</u> **enough** to raise my heart rate. 나는 심박수가 올라갈 정도로 빨리 걸었다.

They can get married. They're <u>old</u> **enough**. 그들은 결혼을 할 수 있다. 그들은 나이가 충분히 들었다.

She doesn't have **enough** <u>money</u>. 그녀는 충분한 돈을 가지고 있지 않다.

서술형 기초다지기

Challenge 1 괄호 안의 단어를 활용하여 「too/very+형용사」로 문장을 완성하세요.

01.

You can't lift the box.

The box is _____. (heavy)

02.

Steve can't drive a car.

He is _____. (young)

03.

The soup is _____, (hot)

but Kelly can eat it.

04.

I can't study at night.

It is _____. (noisy)

Challenge 2 다음 문장의 빈칸에 too, too much, too many 또는 enough를 써 넣으세요.

01. I don't like the weather here. There's _____ rain.

02. I can't wait for her. I don't have _____ time.

03. There was nowhere to sit on the beach. There were _____ people.

04. You're always tired. I think you work _____ hard.

05. You don't eat _____ vegetables. You should eat some every day.

Challenge 3 〈보기〉와 같이 다음 문장을 too를 이용한 문장으로 완성하세요.

보기
I can't drink this tea. It's too hot.
→ This tea *is too hot to drink*.

01. Nobody could move the suitcase. It was too heavy.

→ The suitcase _____.

2-4 so, such

I like Sunny and Jane. They are **so** beautiful.
나는 Sunny와 Jane을 좋아한다. 그들은 매우 아름답다.
They are **such** beautiful people.
그들은 매우 아름다운 사람들이다.

01 so는 형용사와 부사 앞에서 강조하는 역할을 한다. '(그 정도로) 매우'의 뜻이다.

I didn't enjoy the movie. The story was **so** stupid. 나는 그 영화를 즐기지 못했다. 그 이야기는 시시했다.
Tell me why you're **so** upset. 왜 그렇게 화가 났는지 말해봐.

02 명사가 있을 때는 형용사 앞에 so를 쓰지 않고 **such**를 써서 형용사를 강조한다. 「such+a/an+형용사+명사」의 어순으로 쓴다. 명사가 셀 수 없는 명사이거나 복수일 경우에는 관사를 쓰지 않고 「such+형용사+명사」의 어순으로 쓴다. so와 똑같이 '(그 정도로) 매우'의 뜻이다.

It's **such a big house**. 그것은 매우 큰 집이다.
Nancy and Kevin are **such nice people**. Nancy와 Kevin은 매우 좋은 사람들이다.
I was **such a model student**. 나는 모범생이었다.
It's amazing that one company can have **such dedicated employees**.
한 회사가 그토록 헌신적인 직원들을 보유할 수 있다는 것이 놀랍다.

03 「so+형용사/부사+that~」 또는 「such+(a)+형용사+명사+that~」의 어순으로도 쓴다.

The book was **so good that** I couldn't put it down. 그 책은 너무 재미있어서 나는 눈을 뗄 수가 없었다.
It was **such a good book that** I couldn't put it down.
The iPad is **so expensive that** I can't buy it. 아이패드가 너무 비싸서 나는 그것을 살 수 없다.
It is **such an expensive iPad that** I can't buy it.
I was **so tired that** I fell asleep in the sofa. 나는 너무 피곤해서 소파에서 잠이 들었다.
It was **such nice weather that** we went to the park. 너무 좋은 날씨여서 우리는 공원에 갔다.

※ 위 두 예문의 경우 that을 생략하여 쓰기도 한다.

I was **so tired** I fell asleep.
It was **such nice weather** we went to the park.

서술형 기초다지기

Challenge 1 다음 빈칸에 so, such, 또는 such a(n)를 써 넣으세요.

보 기	It's *so* stupid of you to say so.
	It was a great party. We had *such a* good time.

01. I always feel _____ tired after I work out.

02. Everybody likes Cindy. She is _____ nice woman.

03. Everybody likes Cindy and Bob. They are _____ nice people.

04. Why were you acting _____ strangely last week?

05. Listen to her singing. She has _____ sweet voice!

06. The food at the restaurant was _____ awful. I've never eaten _____ awful food.

07. She always looks good. She wears _____ nice clothes.

Challenge 2 〈보기〉와 같이 so ~ that을 이용하여 문장을 바꿔 쓰세요.

보 기	The iPad is too expensive for me to buy.
	→ The iPad *is so expensive that I can't buy it.*

01. The woman is rich enough to travel around the world.

→ The woman is _____.

02. I was foolish enough to trust him.

→ I was _____.

03. It was too cold for us to go swimming.

→ It was _____.

2-5 still, yet, already, anymore

It was cold yesterday. It is **still** cold today.
어제는 추웠다. 오늘도 여전히 춥다.

I never go out with her **anymore**.
나는 그녀와 더 이상 만나지 않는다.

01 already는 긍정문과 놀람을 나타내는 의문문에 쓰는데 **기대했던 것보다 앞서 일어난 일**을 나타낸다. 긍정문에는 '이미', 의문문에는 놀람을 나타내는 '벌써'의 뜻이다.

All my friends were **already** there. 내 친구들은 이미 거기에 와 있었다.
Has the movie finished **already**? 영화가 벌써 끝났어?

02 yet은 주로 부정문과 의문문에서 문장 뒤에 쓴다. 부정문에서는 already의 반대의 의미로 '아직', 의문문에서는 '이미, 벌써, 이제'의 뜻이 된다.

We're not ready to leave **yet**. 우리는 아직 떠날 준비가 안 되었어.
It's 1:00 p.m. I'm hungry. I haven't eaten lunch **yet**. 오후 1시다. 배가 고픈데 난 아직 점심을 먹지 않았다.
Have they fixed the elevator **yet**? 엘리베이터를 벌써 다 고쳤나요?

03 still은 어떤 상황이나 행동이 과거부터 현재까지 이어져서 변하거나 끝나지 않은 상황을 나타낸다. 주로 문장 중간에 위치하여 긍정문과 의문문에 쓰는데 부정문에 쓸 때는 부정어 앞에 쓴다. 모두 '아직도, 여전히'의 뜻이다.

Do you **still** want to go to the concert? 너는 아직도 그 콘서트에 가고 싶니?
Your English is **still** far from perfect. 네 영어는 아직도 완벽하지 못하다.
He **still** hasn't found a steady job. 그는 아직도 안정된 직업을 찾지 못했다.

04 anymore(=any longer)는 부정문에 쓰여, 과거의 상황(행동)이 현재에는 지속되지 않는 상태를 나타낸다. '더 이상 ~하지 않다'의 의미로 문장 끝에 위치하는데 any more로 분리해서 사용할 수도 있다.

She doesn't live in Egypt **anymore**. 그녀는 더 이상 이집트에 살지 않는다.
=She doesn't live in Egypt **any longer**.
Scott doesn't work here **any more**. Scott은 더 이상 여기에서 일하지 않는다.
The bus doesn't stop here **anymore**. 그 버스는 더 이상 여기에 정차하지 않는다.
=The bus doesn't stop here **any longer**.

서술형 기초다지기

정답 p. 3

Challenge 1   다음 빈칸에 already, yet, still 또는 anymore를 써서 문장을 완성하세요.

01. It's 1:00 p.m. I'm hungry. I haven't eaten lunch _____.

02. It's 1:00 p.m. I'm not hungry. I've _____ eaten lunch.

03. If you _____ know what our goals are, then you can organize a team now.

04. If you haven't registered _____, there is _____ time to get your application in.

05. A: Has Dennis graduated _____?

    B: No. He's still in school.

06. Look! The rain has stopped. It isn't raining _____. Let's go for a picnic.

07. A: How does Bob like his job at the restaurant?

    B: He doesn't work there _____. He found a new job.

Challenge 2   다음 밑줄 친 문장에 still, yet, already 또는 anymore 중 하나를 문맥에 맞게 넣어 다시 쓰세요.

보기	Kelly lost her job a year ago and she hasn't found another job.
	→ *she hasn't found another job yet.*

01. Brian was hungry, so he ate a hamburger a few minutes ago.

    But he's hungry, so he's going to have another hamburger. → _____

02. I used to eat lunch at the cafeteria every day, but now I bring my lunch to school in a

    paper bag instead. I don't eat at the cafeteria. → _____

03. A: Do you live on Fifth Street? → _____

    B: Not anymore. I moved.

04. "Where's Maria?" – "She isn't here. She'll be here soon." → _____

Unit 03 주의해야 할 부사의 위치

3-1 「타동사+부사」의 어순

Don't chew gum and **turn off** your cell phone. (O)
껌을 씹지 말고 휴대폰을 꺼 놔라.
= Don't chew gum and **turn** your cell phone **off**. (O)
Don't chew gum and **turn** it **off**. (O)
Don't chew gum and **turn off** it. (×)

---

01 「동사+부사」로 된 동사구의 목적어가 '명사'이면, 명사는 부사 뒤에 쓰거나 동사와 부사 사이에 둘 다 쓸 수 있다. 즉, 「동사+부사+목적어(명사)」나 「동사+목적어(명사)+부사」의 어순 둘 다 가능하다.

She **put** her hat **on**. (O) 그녀는 모자를 썼다.
She **put on** her hat. (O)

02 목적어가 '대명사'일 때는 반드시 동사와 부사 사이에 써야 한다. 즉, 「동사+목적어(대명사)+부사」의 어순으로만 쓴다.

Will you **fill out** this application form? (O) 이 신청서 양식을 작성해 주시겠어요?
Will you **fill** this application form **out**? (O)
Will you **fill** it **out**? (O)
Will you **fill out** it? (×)

03 「자동사+전치사」가 하나의 **타동사 역할**을 할 경우 목적어가 명사든 대명사든 반드시 전치사 다음에 두어야 한다. 「자동사+전치사」가 하나의 타동사이므로 목적어로서 동사 뒤에 위치하는 것이다.

She **looked at** me. 그녀는 나를 쳐다보았다. ▶ 대명사 me는 look at의 목적어
She **looked at** the clock tower. 그녀는 그 시계탑을 쳐다보았다. ▶ 명사 clock tower는 look at의 목적어

※ She **looked** me **at**. (×)
※ She **looked** the clock tower **at**. (×)

서술형 기초다지기

정답 p. 3

Challenge 1 다음 괄호 안의 표현 중 올바른 것을 고르세요.

01. I turned the stove off, but soon I had to (turn on the stove / turn on it) again. It was too cold.

02. When my hair caught on fire, my brother (put out it / put it out) immediately.

03. When you visit friends' doors in Korea, you should (take your shoes off / take off them).

04. I'll (put them on / put on them) your desk.

05. I don't care (about my appearance / my appearance about) much.

Challenge 2 다음 괄호 안의 단어를 알맞은 어순으로 쓰세요.

01. He hangs up the receiver and _____. (at, looks, the wall clock)

02. I'm sorry. I'll _____ again. (it, out, check)

03. _____ if you feel cold. (your sweater, on, put)

04. The law proved ineffective in _____. (it, with, dealing)

05. Sunny _____ in her room. (her socks, took, off)

06. They are _____. (a scapegoat, for, looking)

07. Did Kevin _____ to the teacher? (them, hand, in)

08. Why did Peter _____ on the floor? (throw, it, away)

---

01 **출제 100 % - 빈도부사의 위치를 묻는 문제는 반드시 출제된다.**

 출제자의 눈 기본적인 부사의 형태를 묻거나 형태는 비슷하나 뜻이 전혀 다른 부사를 출제하기도 한다. 또한 빈도부사의 위치는 반드시 출제되는데, 조동사와 be동사 뒤, 그리고 일반동사 앞에 위치한다는 것을 명심해야 한다. 더 나아가 부정문에서는 부정어 앞에 쓰지만, always와 ever는 부정 동사 뒤에 쓴다는 것도 잊지 말아야 한다.

Ex 1.

빈칸에 알맞은 단어를 고르시오.

The deadline for paying taxes is drawing _____.

(a) nearly   (b) hardly   (c) near   (d) closely

Ex 2.

괄호 안의 빈도부사를 넣어 문장을 다시 쓰시오.

Do you watch TV in the evenings? (always)

→ _____

---

02 **출제 100 % - too와 either의 어순과 쓰임을 반드시 구별하라!**

출제자의 눈 문장 끝에서 '또한, 역시'라는 뜻으로 동의를 할 때 긍정에는 too, 부정에는 either를 쓴다. 이를 구별하는 문제나, 같은 동의의 표현인 「so+(조)동사+주어」, 「neither+(조)동사+주어」를 자주 출제한다. 또한 so는 형용사나 부사 앞에서 '강조'하는 역할을 하는데 특히 형용사를 강조하는 such의 어순이 토익이나 텝스에서도 자주 출제된다. 「such+(a/an)+형용사+명사」에서 such가 형용사를 강조하는 부사이므로 앞에 위치한다.

Ex 3.

Sales items sold out _____ quickly that the store had to close early.

(a) such   (b) so   (c) very   (d) too

Ex 4.

빈칸에 들어갈 수 없는 말은?

Human beings don't have tails, and _____.

(a) chimpanzees don't have tails, either   (b) chimpanzees don't, either

(c) neither do chimpanzees   (d) chimpanzees aren't, either

03 **출제 100 % - too와 enough를 집중적으로 공략한다!**

 출제자의 눈 too는 형용사나 부사 앞에서 '너무'라는 뜻으로 쓰여 부정적인 결과를 낳거나 문제가 있음을 암시하는 말이다. 문맥에 따라 very와 구별해서 사용해야 한다. enough는 형용사나 부사 뒤에 쓰고 '충분한'이란 뜻의 형용사로 사용하려면 명사 앞에 쓴다. too와 enough를 이용한 부분 영작이나 이 둘을 구별하는 문제, 어순을 물어보는 문제 등이 출제된다. 또한 셀 수 있는 명사에 사용하는 too many 와 셀 수 없는 명사에 사용하는 too much, 그리고 구분 없이 사용하는 a lot of를 혼동하면 안 된다. 특히 too much가 주어 자리에 올 때는 그 양이 아무리 많아도 동사는 단수 취급해야 하는 것도 잊지 말자.

Ex 5.

He isn't _____ to reach the shelf.

(a) tall enough   (b) enough tall

(c) too tall   (d) tall as enough

Ex 6.

Korea has _____ people for its limited land space.

(a) too   (b) too much   (c) a lot of   (d) too many

04 **출제 100 % - 「동사+부사」에서 목적어의 위치에 주의하라!**

 출제자의 눈 put on/off, turn on/off처럼 out, in, on, off, up, down, away, over와 같은 부사가 동사와 짝을 이뤄 동사구로 쓰이는데, 이때 목적어로 대명사가 올 경우 반드시 「동사+대명사+부사」의 어순으로만 써야 한다. 이러한 어순을 물어보는 문제는 수능에서도 출제되었고, 내신에서도 반드시 출제된다. 또한 already, still, yet, anymore 등의 부사를 의미에 따라 바르게 사용했는지를 물어보는 문제도 자주 출제된다.

Ex 7.

She loved her new dress so much that she wouldn't _____.

(a) take off it   (b) put it out   (c) put it on   (d) take it off

Ex 8.

Can you wait a few minutes? I don't want to go out _____.

(a) yet   (b) already   (c) anymore   (d) still

1. 다음 두 단어의 관계가 나머지와 <u>다른</u> 것은?

❶ free – freely   ❷ love – lovely
❸ happy – happily   ❹ certain – certainly
❺ real – really

2. 다음 글을 읽고 빈칸에 들어갈 알맞은 빈도부사를 고르시오.

> My friends like to play video games, but I don't join them because the games are too violent.
> → I _____ play video games with my friends.

❶ always   ❷ sometimes   ❸ seldom
❹ never   ❺ often

3. 다음 문장에서 enough가 들어갈 알맞은 위치는?

> She ❶ is ❷ kind ❸ to ❹ show me the way ❺.

4. 다음 중 밑줄 친 표현이 바른 것은?

❶ 그녀는 대개 버스를 타고 직장에 간다.
   → She <u>never</u> goes to work by bus.
❷ 축하해! 너의 공연은 정말 성공적이었어.
   → Congratulations! Your concert was <u>so</u> a success.
❸ 너는 더 이상 일요일에 일할 필요가 없다.
   → You don't have to work on Sunday <u>any longer</u>.
❹ 그녀는 버스를 놓쳤기 때문에 늦게 왔다.
   → She came <u>lately</u> because she missed the bus.

5. 친근한 태도는 동료들과 좋은 관계를 만드는 데 중요하다.
   → A <u>friend</u> attitude is important to establish a good relationship with co-workers.

5. 다음 중 밑줄 친 부분의 쓰임이 <u>잘못된</u> 것은?

❶ Peter lost his job two years ago and is <u>still</u> unemployed.
❷ When is Susan going on vacation?
   – She has <u>already</u> gone.
❸ Are you <u>still</u> looking for a person?
❹ I haven't finished my dinner <u>yet</u>.
❺ Kelly still works here, but Nancy doesn't work here <u>yet</u>.

6. 다음 빈칸에 공통으로 들어갈 알맞은 것은?

> · There are _____ many cars in the parking lot. (주차장에 차가 너무 많다.)
> · I forgot to bring my book to class, and the teacher did _____. (선생님도 가져 오지 않았다.)

❶ so   ❷ too   ❸ either
❹ neither   ❺ also

7. 다음 밑줄 친 단어와 바꿔 쓸 수 있는 말이 <u>잘못</u> 짝지어진 것은?

❶ Firemen put out a small fire <u>quickly</u>. (=fast)
❷ He is a <u>highly</u> successful politician. (=very)
❸ These fans have been quite popular among tourists <u>lately</u>. (=recently)
❹ It was <u>almost</u> five o'clock when she left. (=still)
❺ It rained <u>heavily</u> last night, so it is a little cold today. (=quite hard)

오답 노트 만들기

★틀린 문제 : _____ ★다시 공부한 날 : _____

(1) 문제를 왜? 틀렸는지 곰곰이 생각하고 그 이유를 적어본다.

(2) 핵심 개념을 적는다.

(3) 자신이 몰랐던 단어와 숙어 표현이 있으면 정리한다.

(4) 해설집에서 필요한 부분을 골라 풀이 해법을 정리한다.

★틀린 문제 : _____ ★다시 공부한 날 : _____

(1) 문제를 왜? 틀렸는지 곰곰이 생각하고 그 이유를 적어본다.

(2) 핵심 개념을 적는다.

(3) 자신이 몰랐던 단어와 숙어 표현이 있으면 정리한다.

(4) 해설집에서 필요한 부분을 골라 풀이 해법을 정리한다.

★틀린 문제 : _____ ★다시 공부한 날 : _____

(1) 문제를 왜? 틀렸는지 곰곰이 생각하고 그 이유를 적어본다.

(2) 핵심 개념을 적는다.

(3) 자신이 몰랐던 단어와 숙어 표현이 있으면 정리한다.

(4) 해설집에서 필요한 부분을 골라 풀이 해법을 정리한다.

★틀린 문제 : _____ ★다시 공부한 날 : _____

(1) 문제를 왜? 틀렸는지 곰곰이 생각하고 그 이유를 적어본다.

(2) 핵심 개념을 적는다.

(3) 자신이 몰랐던 단어와 숙어 표현이 있으면 정리한다.

(4) 해설집에서 필요한 부분을 골라 풀이 해법을 정리한다.

1. 다음 빈칸에 들어갈 알맞은 말은?

> Anteaters don't have teeth, and _____ do most birds.

❶ either   ❷ too   ❸ also
❹ neither   ❺ still

오답노트

2. 다음 밑줄 친 단어의 위치가 <u>잘못된</u> 것을 <u>모두</u> 고르시오.

❶ These days, my dad comes home from work <u>late</u>.
❷ My dad is <u>always</u> complaining about his car.
❸ Do you <u>still</u> want to go to the party, or have you changed your mind?
❹ She is <u>never</u> late for school.
❺ What <u>usually</u> do you do in spare time?

오답노트

3. 밑줄 친 부분의 품사가 나머지와 <u>다른</u> 것은?

❶ The girl picked up the broken doll <u>sadly</u>.
❷ You look <u>lovely</u> in that dress.
❸ He treated his friend very <u>badly</u>.
❹ My English teachers say my English is <u>quite</u> good.
❺ <u>Unfortunately</u>, you were out when we called.

오답노트

4. 다음 빈칸에 들어갈 알맞은 단어를 순서대로 나열한 것을 고르시오.

> · You have _____ said that it should not be your responsibility.
> · I haven't met anyone like you _____.
> · All his family moved to Praha. Timothy _____ lives in London.
> · We used to be good friends, but we aren't _____.

❶ yet − already − anymore − still
❷ still − yet − anymore − already
❸ anymore − still − already − yet
❹ already − yet − still − anymore
❺ anymore − still − yet − already

오답노트

5. 다음 대화의 내용을 한 문장으로 나타낼 때 빈칸에 들어갈 말이 바르게 짝지어진 것은?

> Jim   : I won't come here again.
> Sunny : I won't, either.

→ _____ Jim _____ Sunny will come here again.

❶ Either − or   ❷ Either − so
❸ Neither − or   ❹ Neither − nor
❺ Both − and

오답노트

6. 다음 빈칸에 공통으로 들어갈 말은?

> · It's _____ noisy, so I can't talk with my friends.
> · If you're _____ tired when you drive, you can fall asleep at the wheel.

❶ a lot of　　❷ too　　❸ very
❹ too much　　❺ too many

오답노트

[7-9] 〈보기〉와 같이 enough를 이용한 질문과 대답을 완성하시오. (Have you got ~?을 이용할 것)

보기	time / to go to the movie theater Q: *Have you got enough time to go to the movie theater?* A: No, *I haven't got enough time to go to the movie theater.*

7. money / to buy an iPad
Q: _____
A: No, _____ .

8. gas / to drive to Busan
Q: _____
A: No, _____ .

9. eggs / to make an omelette
Q: _____
A: No, _____ .

오답노트

10. 다음 중 밑줄 친 표현이 올바른 것은?

❶ 내 아내도 짠 음식을 좋아하지 않아.
= My wife doesn't like salty food, neither.
❷ 연습 부족에도 불구하고, 그녀의 글은 매우 향상되었다.
= In spite of a lack of practice, her writing has great improved.
❸ 그녀는 버스를 놓쳤기 때문에 늦게 왔다.
= She came lately because she missed the bus.
❹ 너는 너무 조용히 말을 한다. 나는 너의 말을 거의 들을 수가 없다.
= You're speaking very quietly. I can hard hear you.
❺ 파스타는 유명한 이탈리아 음식이고 피자도 마찬가지이다.
= Pasta is a famous Italian dish, and so is pizza.

오답노트

11. 다음 문장의 밑줄 친 부분과 바꿔 쓸 수 있는 것은?

> Christina was very sick last week, but now she is well.

❶ happy　　❷ angrily　　❸ lately
❹ good　　❺ healthy

오답노트

12. 다음 중 어법상 어색한 것을 모두 고르시오.

❶ You are already enough old to do something for our health.

❷ When my hair caught on fire, my mother put out it immediately.

❸ If you work too hard, you'll build up stress and ruin your health.

❹ It was such a beautiful day that we decided to go to the beach.

❺ She's hard to understand because she speaks so quickly.

오답노트

13. 다음 중 어법상 어색한 것을 고르시오.

❶ It was so a good book that I couldn't put it down.

❷ I was so tired that I fell asleep in the armchair.

❸ The store was so busy that it had to hire additional part-time workers.

❹ The report was too long to read all at once.

❺ The walk was very long, but the fresh air felt good.

오답노트

14. 다음 빈칸에 들어갈 말로 알맞은 것을 고르시오.

> Jane : Tom, hurry up, or we won't catch the train.
> Tom : I'm not ready, _____. Can you wait a minute, please?

❶ still   ❷ even   ❸ yet
❹ already   ❺ rarely

오답노트

15. 다음 빈칸에 들어갈 말로 알맞은 것은?

> A : Can you speak English?
> B : No, I can't. What about you?
> A : _____. But I'm going to take an English class this winter vacation.

❶ I don't, too   ❷ Me, too
❸ Me, either   ❹ Me, neither
❺ I can, either

오답노트

16. 다음 밑줄 친 부분의 뜻이 알맞게 짝지어진 것은?

> · I studied <u>hard</u> yesterday because of my English test.
> · The soil had got too <u>hard</u> and it wouldn't drain properly.
> · Sunny and Jason have only met once before. They <u>hardly</u> know each other.

❶ 열심히 – 근면히 – 거의 ~않다
❷ 딱딱한 – 근면히 – 열심히
❸ 근면히 – 열심히 – 거의 ~않다
❹ 열심히 – 딱딱한 – 거의 ~않다
❺ 딱딱한 – 열심히 – 거의 ~않다

오답노트

[17-20] 〈보기〉의 단어와 too many 또는 too much를 이용하여 다음 빈칸을 채우시오.

보기	coffee	calories	people	time

17. Some people spend _____ on the Internet.

18. If you drink _____, it can affect your sleep.

19. Children shouldn't drink so much soda because it contains _____.

20. Korea has _____ for its limited land space.

오답노트

[21-25] 빈칸에 already, still, yet 중 알맞은 것을 쓰시오.

21. A: Did you sell your car?
    B: No, I _____ have it.

22. A: Do you and Bob want to see the movie?
    B: No, we've _____ seen it.

23. A: What are you doing tonight?
    B: I don't know _____.

24. A: Do you _____ live in Vancouver?
    B: No, I live in Seoul now.

25. A: I want to tell you what happened.
    B: That's OK. I _____ know.

오답노트

26. 다음 우리말을 영어로 바르게 옮기시오. (필요한 단어는 첨가할 것)

> Tina 역시 그 질문에 대한 답을 몰랐다.
> (the answer, know, to the question)

→ _____
_____

오답노트

27. 다음 중 어법상 어색한 것을 고르시오.

❶ Their mother came to pick them up.
❷ Please fill out this registration card.
❸ He doesn't care others' interests about.
❹ Put your seat belt on before we leave.
❺ I'm looking for Mr. Donner's office.

오답노트

28. 다음 우리말과 뜻이 같도록 단어를 배열하시오.

> 방에서 나갈 때 불을 꺼 주시겠어요? (turn off, the light)

→ _____
when you leave the room?

오답노트

A. 괄호 안의 단어를 활용하여 「too/very+형용사」 형태로 빈칸을 채우시오.

1.

(heavy)

The suitcase is _____,

but she can lift it.

2.

(heavy)

The suitcase is _____.

She can't lift it.

3.

(tight)

The jeans are _____,

but she can wear them.

4.

(big)

The shoes are _____.

He can't wear them.

B. Bob은 도서관에서 Kelly를 만나 대화 도중 둘 사이의 공통점들을 발견했다. so와 neither를 이용하여 문장을 완성해 보시오.

보기	Kelly : I love this kind of music. Bob : *So do I.*

1. Kelly : I haven't seen a movie for a long time.

Bob : _____

2. Kelly : I play tennis.

Bob : _____

3. Kelly : I'm not good at making conversation.

Bob : _____

4. Kelly : I came to this city two years ago.

Bob : _____

5. Kelly : I haven't got many friends.

Bob : _____

6. Kelly : I would like to make new friends.

Bob : _____

실전 서술형 평가문제

 출제의도 정보를 이용한 문장 생성
평가내용 빈도부사를 활용하여 문장 완성하기

A. 〈보기〉와 같이 Steve와 Cindy에 관한 내용을 빈도부사를 활용한 문장으로 영작하시오.

[서술형 유형 : 8점 / 난이도 : 중]

Steve	〈보기〉 skip breakfast	1. not eat high-fat food at dinner	2. go to the movies	3. go to school on foot	4. late for school
always		V			
usually			V		
often					V
sometimes					
never	V			V	

Cindy	〈보기〉 skip breakfast	1. not eat high-fat food at dinner	2. go to the movies	3. go to school on foot	4. late for school
always	V				V
usually				V	
often			V		
sometimes		V			
not ever					

보기	*Steve never skips breakfast, but Cindy always skips breakfast.*

1. _____

2. _____

3. _____

4. _____

실전 서술형 평가문제

출제의도 so ~ that / such ~ that / too ~ to / enough to
평가내용 원인과 결과가 연관성이 있는 문장 만들기

B. 괄호 안의 표현을 이용하여 다음 두 문장을 한 문장으로 고쳐 쓰시오. [서술형 유형 : 12점 / 난이도 : 중상]

보 기	It was very cold. Tina put on two jumpers. → *It was so cold that Tina put on two jumpers.* (so ~ that)

1. Those T-shirts were very cheap. Kevin bought three of them.

→ _____ (so ~ that)

→ _____ (enough to)

2. This problem is very difficult. I can't solve it.

→ _____ (such ~ that)

3. Seoul is a big city. We can't look around it in a day.

→ _____ (such ~ that)

4. There were too many people on the bus. I couldn't find a seat.

→ _____ (so ~ that)

5. Scott walked very fast. I couldn't keep up with him.

→ _____ (so ~ that)

→ _____ (too ~ to)

6. Sally takes a lot of photographs. She has to buy a new photo album every month.

→ _____ (such ~ that)

출제의도 still, yet, already
평가내용 still, yet, already를 이용하여 문장 만들기

C. 괄호 안의 말을 이용하여 사진에 맞는 상황을 영작하시오. [서술형 유형 : 9점 / 난이도 : 중상]

보기

30 minutes ago   now (not stop)

(before) It *was raining.*
(still) *It is still raining now.*
(yet) *It hasn't stopped raining yet.*

1.

an hour ago   now (not come)

(before) They _____ .
(still) _____
(yet) _____

2.

an hour ago   now (not find)

(before) She _____ .
(still) _____
(yet) _____

3.

an hour ago   now (not finish)

(before) He _____ .
(still) _____
(yet) _____

출제의도 too, so, either, neither
평가내용 사진 묘사를 통한 동의의 표현 완성하기

D. 괄호 안의 말을 이용하여 사진에 맞는 동의의 표현을 서술하시오. [서술형 유형 : 14점 / 난이도 : 중상]

Lucy	Sunny
Jane	Nancy

보기	Lucy has curly hair, *and Jane does, too.* (=Jane has curly hair, too.) (too)

1. Lucy has curly hair, and _____. (so)

2. Sunny doesn't have curly hair, and _____. (either)

3. Sunny doesn't have curly hair, and _____. (neither)

4. Nancy is wearing glasses, and _____. (too)

5. Nancy is wearing glasses, and _____. (so)

6. Jane isn't wearing glasses, and _____. (either)

7. Jane isn't wearing glasses, and _____. (neither)

서술형 평가문제	채 점 기 준	배 점	나의 점수
A	표현이 올바르고 문법, 철자가 모두 정확한 경우	2점 × 4문항 = 8점	
B		2점 × 6문항 = 12점	
C		3점 × 3문항 = 9점	
D		2점 × 7문항 = 14점	
공통	문법, 철자가 1개씩 틀린 경우	각 문항당 1점씩 감점	
	내용과 전혀 일치하지 않거나 답을 기재하지 못한 경우	0점	

Chapter 2

비교급과 최상급
(Comparatives & Superlatives)

Unit 01 비교급과 최상급 만들기

1-1 비교급 만드는 방법

Tom's hair is shorter **than** Lucy's hair.
Tom의 머리는 Lucy의 머리보다 더 짧다.

Tigers are **more** dangerous **than** snakes.
호랑이는 뱀보다 더 위험하다.

01 형용사나 부사가 **1음절이거나 y로 끝나는 2음절어일 경우 -er**을 붙인다. -y로 끝나면 y를 i로 바꾸고 -er을 붙이고 -e로 끝나는 경우 'r'만 붙인다.

short – short**er** than	tall – tall**er** than	large – larg**er** than
easy – eas**ier** than	pretty – prett**ier** than	dirty – dirt**ier** than
cheap – cheap**er** than	wide – wid**er** than	nice – nic**er** than

※ than은 '~보다'란 뜻으로, 비교급과 항상 같이 쓰인다.

02 1음절 단어의 경우 **'단모음+단자음'으로 끝날 경우 맨 끝에 자음을 한 번 더 쓰고 -er**을 붙인다.

hot – hot**ter** than	big – big**ger** than
fat – fat**ter** than	thin – thin**ner** than

03 **2음절일 경우 대부분 형용사 앞에 more**를 쓴다. 특히 -ful, -ous, -ive, -ing(현재분사), -ed(과거분사)로 끝나는 3음절 이상의 단어에도 more를 붙인다.

famous – **more** famous than	interesting – **more** interesting than
careful – **more** careful than	expensive – **more** expensive than
shocked – **more** shocked than	tired – **more** tired than

04 **-ly로 끝나는 부사 앞에는 more**를 붙인다.(단, early는 예외: early – earlier)

slowly – **more** slowly than	quickly – **more** quickly than
beautifully – **more** beautifully than	easily – **more** easily than
fluently – **more** fluently than	

※ angry, simple, clever, friendly, gentle, quiet, common, pleasant, polite, handsome 등은 -er과 more 중 어느 것을 붙여도 괜찮지만 주로 more 비교급을 더 자주 쓴다. -er을 붙이는 단어들도 일상 영어에서는 종종 more happy, more smart처럼 more를 붙이기도 한다. 반면 only, unique, uniquely는 비교급과 최상급으로 쓰지 않는다.

서술형 기초다지기

Challenge 1 다음 형용사나 부사의 비교급을 쓰세요. (than을 반드시 쓸 것)

보기	tall	–	_taller than_	tired	–	_more tired than_

01. large   – _____

02. small   – _____

03. hot   – _____

04. slowly   – _____

05. wide   – _____

06. big   – _____

07. thin   – _____

08. boring   – _____

09. interesting   – _____

10. shocked   – _____

11. comfortable   – _____

12. complicated   – _____

13. heavy   – _____

14. lazy   – _____

15. quickly   – _____

16. fluently   – _____

17. pretty   – _____

18. cheap   – _____

19. pleasing   – _____

20. easily   – _____

21. amazing   – _____

22. energetic   – _____

1-2 최상급 만드는 방법

Antarctica is **the cold**est place in the world.
남극대륙은 세계에서 가장 추운 곳이다.

Tokyo is **the most** crowded city in the world.
도쿄는 세계에서 가장 혼잡한 도시이다.

01 최상급도 비교급을 만드는 방법과 같다. 우리말은 '더 예쁜, 가장 예쁜'이란 말에서 형용사 '예쁜'은 그대로 두고 단어 앞에 '더'와 '가장'이란 말을 붙여서 비교급과 최상급을 만든다. 하지만 영어는 이러한 기능이 없어서 형용사에 '-er'을 붙이거나 '-est'를 붙여서 비교급과 최상급을 만든다.

규칙 변화	원급 (~한/하게)	비교급 (더 ~한/하게)	최상급 (가장 ~한/하게)
① 대부분의 경우: 형용사, 부사 끝에 -est를 붙임	long strong fast	longer stronger faster	the long**est** the strong**est** the fast**est**
② -e로 끝나는 경우: -st를 붙임	large wise late	larger wiser later	the large**st** the wise**st** the late**st**
③ 「자음+y」로 끝나는 경우: y를 i로 고치고 -est를 붙임	happy pretty dirty	happier prettier dirtier	the happ**iest** the prett**iest** the dirt**iest**
④ 「단모음+단자음」으로 끝나는 경우: 마지막 자음을 한 번 더 쓰고 -est	big hot sad	bigger hotter sadder	the big**gest** the hot**test** the sad**dest**
⑤ -full, -less, -ive, -ous, -ing(현재분사), -ed(과거분사)로 끝나는 2음절 단어나 3음절 이상의 단어, -ly로 끝나는 부사 앞: 형용사, 부사 앞에 most를 붙임	famous difficult carefully interesting expensive easily	more famous more difficult more carefully more interesting more expensive more easily	the **most** famous the **most** difficult the **most** carefully the **most** interesting the **most** expensive the **most** easily

※ 최상급 앞에는 주로 정관사 'the'를 쓴다. 학교 문법에서는 부사가 최상급일 때 'the'를 쓰지 않는다고 하지만 반드시 그런 것은 아니다. 부사의 최상급에 'the'를 쓸 때도 있고 일상 영어에서는 형용사나 부사의 최상급에도 'the'를 쓰지 않을 때도 있다.

서술형 기초다지기

Challenge 1 다음 단어의 비교급과 최상급을 쓰세요. (than은 쓰지 말 것)

보기	happy – *happier* – *happiest*	kind – *kinder* – *kindest*

01. difficult – _____ – _____ **02.** high – _____ – _____

03. tired – _____ – _____ **04.** heavy – _____ – _____

05. fat – _____ – _____ **06.** cold – _____ – _____

07. hot – _____ – _____ **08.** large – _____ – _____

09. interesting – _____ – _____ **10.** short – _____ – _____

11. funny – _____ – _____ **12.** lucky – _____ – _____

13. poor – _____ – _____ **14.** popular – _____ – _____

15. easy – _____ – _____ **16.** frequent – _____ – _____

17. brightly – _____ – _____ **18.** sad – _____ – _____

19. depressed – _____ – _____ **20.** crowded – _____ – _____

21. attractive – _____ – _____ **22.** healthy – _____ – _____

1-3 불규칙 변화형

Ji-sung Park is **the best** known Korean soccer player in the world.
박지성은 세계에서 가장 잘 알려진 한국인 축구선수이다.

01 비교급과 최상급의 불규칙 변화

원급	비교급	최상급
good 좋은	better 더 좋은	the best 가장 좋은
well 잘, 건강한	better 더 잘	(the) best 가장 잘하는
bad 나쁜	worse 더 나쁜	the worst 가장 나쁜
ill 병든, 건강이 나쁜	worse 더 병든, 더 건강이 나쁜	the worst 가장 건강이 나쁜
many (수) 많은	more 더 많은	the most 가장 많은
much (양) 많은	more 더 많은	the most 가장 많은
few (수) 적은	fewer 더 적은	the fewest 가장 적은
little (양) 적은	less 더 적은	the least 가장 적은

This MP3 player is **better** than that one. 이 MP3 플레이어가 저것보다 더 좋다.
She was **the worst** singer of the three. 세 명 중에 그녀가 가장 노래를 못했다.

02 비교급과 최상급이 두 개이고, 그 의미가 다른 경우도 있다.

원급	비교급	최상급
old	older (나이) 더 늙은, 더 오래된	the oldest 가장 나이가 많은
	elder (서열) 손위의	the eldest 가장 손위의
late	later (시간) 더 늦은	the latest 가장 늦은, 최근의
	latter (순서) 뒤쪽의, 후반의	the last 가장 마지막의
far	farther (거리) 더 먼	the farthest (거리가) 가장 먼
	further (정도) 더욱, 한층	the furthest (정도가) 가장 많이

The **latter** part of the movie is very exciting. 이 영화의 후반부는 매우 흥미진진하다.
Especially, I would never forget **the last** scene. 특히, 나는 마지막 장면을 절대 잊지 못할 거야.
Pluto is **the farthest** planet from the Sun. 명왕성은 태양으로부터 가장 멀리 있는 행성이다.

서술형 기초다지기

정답 p. 5

Challenge 1 다음 단어의 비교급과 최상급을 쓰세요.

01. good – _____ – _____

02. well – _____ – _____

03. bad – _____ – _____

04. ill – _____ – _____

05. old(나이) – _____ – _____

06. old(손위) – _____ – _____

07. many – _____ – _____

08. much – _____ – _____

09. late(순서) – _____ – _____

10. far(거리) – _____ – _____

11. far(정도) – _____ – _____

12. late(시간) – _____ – _____

13. little – _____ – _____

14. few – _____ – _____

Challenge 2 다음 괄호 안의 단어를 이용하여 빈칸을 완성하세요.

01. My friend and I both jog. I run _____ than my friend. (far)

02. Who's a _____ soccer player – you or your brother? (good)

03. People who exercise a lot are in _____ shape than people who don't. (good)

04. If you have any _____ questions, don't hesitate to ask. (far)

05. I like my new apartment, but it is _____ away from school than my old apartment was. (far)

06. He is less clever than his _____ brother. (old)

07. He is the _____ student I've ever taught. (good)

Unit 02 비교급

2-1 비교급의 쓰임

Summer is **hotter than** Spring.
여름이 봄보다 더 덥다.

In Korea, soccer is **more** popular **than** baseball.
한국에서 축구는 야구보다 더 인기가 많다.

01 비교급은 **두 명의 사람이나 사물을 놓고 서로 비교**하는 것으로, 「비교급＋than＋비교 대상」처럼 비교 대상 앞에 than을 쓴다. 비교 대상은 같거나 같은 종류여야 한다.

The blue jacket is **cheaper than** the white one. 푸른색 자켓이 하얀색 자켓보다 더 싸다.
Last month's test was **harder than** this one is. 지난달 시험은 이번 달 시험보다 더 어려웠다.
I can speak English **more** fluently **than** my brother. 나는 형보다 더 유창하게 영어를 할 수 있다.

02 격식을 갖추는 영어(formal English)에서는 **than 뒤에 주격** 대명사를 쓰지만 **일상 영어(informal English)에서는 목적격**을 더 많이 쓴다.

She's taller **than I am.** ▶ Formal
→ She's taller **than me.** 그녀는 나보다 더 키가 크다. ▶ Informal

I can play soccer better **than he can.** ▶ Formal
→ I can play soccer better **than him.** 나는 그보다 축구를 더 잘할 수 있다. ▶ Informal

※ 주어의 인칭과 시제에 따라 일반동사 대신 do/does/did를 쓰거나 또는 생략할 수 있다. 조동사도 마찬가지이다.
I study harder **than she does.** ▶ Formal → I study harder **than her.** 나는 그녀보다 더 열심히 공부한다.
I got up earlier **than she did.** ▶ Formal → I got up earlier **than her.** 나는 그녀보다 더 일찍 일어났다.

03 than 뒤에는 절(「주어＋동사」가 있는 문장)을 쓸 수 있고, 구(단어＋단어)를 쓸 수도 있다.

The movie was better **than I expected.** 그 영화는 내가 기대했던 것보다 더 좋았다.
Taking the train is more expensive **than driving a car.** 기차를 타는 것이 차를 운전하는 것보다 더 비용이 든다.

04 비교급 앞에 'the'를 붙이지 않는 것이 원칙이지만, **비교 범주가 둘인 경우(of the two), 서로 알고 있는 정해진 것을 가리키므로 정관사 'the'를 비교급 앞에 쓴다.**

Steve is **the** taller **of the two.** 둘 중에 Steve가 더 키가 크다.
I like Kevin and Bob, but Bob is **the** smarter **of the two.**
나는 Kevin과 Bob을 좋아하지만 Bob이 둘 중에서 더 똑똑하다.

서술형 기초다지기

Challenge 1 다음 괄호 안의 단어를 이용하여 문장을 완성하세요.

Nancy		Jason
10살		18살
25kg		50kg

01. Jason is _____ Nancy. (old)

02. Jason is _____ Nancy. (heavy)

Challenge 2 다음 빈칸에 들어갈 단어를 아래에서 찾아 알맞은 형태로 써 넣으세요.

early	interesting	few	popular	easy

보기 In the U.S., basketball is *more popular than* soccer.

01. My sister was exhausted from the long flight. She went to bed _____ usual.

02. Children learn sports _____ adults.

03. Do you think soccer is _____ football?

04. A basketball team has _____ players _____ a baseball team.

Challenge 3 다음 문장을 읽고 〈보기〉와 같이 비교급을 이용한 문장으로 다시 쓰세요.

보기 My brother is really tall. I'm just medium height.
→ He's *taller than I am. / He's taller than me.* (tall)

01. I can reach the top shelf of the bookcase. Tom can only reach the shelf next to the top.

→ I _____. (high)

2-2 비교급 강조 / less+원급+than

He looks **much** younger than his girlfriend.
그는 그의 여자 친구보다 훨씬 더 어려 보인다.

The shopping mall was **less** crowded **than** usual.
쇼핑몰은 평소보다 덜 붐볐다.

01 **비교급 바로 앞에서 비교급을 강조할 때** much, a lot(=far), still, even, a little bit, a little(=slightly) 등을 써서 '훨씬/약간 더 ~한/하게'란 뜻을 나타낸다.

Canada is **much** bigger than France. 캐나다는 프랑스보다 훨씬 더 크다.
Lucy is **a little** older than Peter – she's 18 and he's 17. Lucy는 Peter보다 좀 더 나이 들었다
  – 그녀는 18살이고 그는 17살이다.

The iPad was **much** more expensive than I expected. 아이패드는 내가 예상했던 것보다 훨씬 더 비쌌다.
Sunny did the work **a lot**(=far) better than I did. Sunny는 나보다 그 일을 훨씬 더 잘했다.

※ very는 형용사나 부사의 비교급을 강조하지 못하고 원급만 강조한다.

I didn't sleep at all last night. I'm **very** tired today. 나는 어젯밤 전혀 잠을 자지 못했다. 오늘 너무 피곤하다.
She bought a **very** expensive car. 그녀는 매우 비싼 차를 샀다.

02 「less+형용사/부사+than」은 '두 명의 사람이나 사물 중 어느 하나가 더 낫다'를 나타내는 **비교급과 반대로** '~보다 더 ~ 하지 못하다'란 뜻의 열등비교 구문이다. 일상 영어에서는 주로 원급비교(as ~ as)에 not을 붙인 'not as[so]~ as'를 더 자주 쓴다.

The actor is **less** popular **than** the actress. 그 남자 배우는 그 여배우보다 인기가 많지 않다.
=The actor isn't **as[so]** popular **as** the actress.
=The actress is **more** popular **than** the actor.

The MP3 player is **less** expensive **than** the digital camera. MP3 플레이어는 디지털 카메라보다 덜 비싸다.
=The MP3 player isn't **so[as]** expensive **as** the digital camera.
=The MP3 player is **cheaper than** the digital camera.
=The digital camera is **more** expensive **than** the MP3 player.

※ less 뒤에는 형용사나 부사의 원급을 써야 한다. 2음절 이상인 형용사라고 해도 'less more expensive'처럼 쓰지 않는다.

서술형 기초다지기

정답 p. 6

Challenge 1 다음 사진을 보고 괄호 안의 단어를 이용하여 빈칸에 알맞은 말을 쓰세요.

〈보기〉   **01.**    **02.**   **03.**

> **보기** Brian is *much taller than* Jane. (tall, much)

01. The iPhone is _____ the MP3 player. (expensive, a little bit)

02. She is _____ her husband. (thin, even)

03. The cheetah is _____ the deer. (fast, a lot)

Challenge 2 다음 우리말과 뜻이 같도록 괄호 안의 말을 이용하여 비교급 문장으로 완성하세요.

01. 농구선수들은 축구선수들보다 키가 훨씬 더 크다. (even, tall, soccer players)

→ Basketball players are _____.

02. 이 파란 가방이 저 빨간 배낭보다 훨씬 더 가볍다. (that red backpack, a lot, light)

→ This blue bag is _____.

03. 그녀는 나보다 훨씬 더 일본어를 잘한다. (me, good, far)

→ She speaks Japanese _____.

Challenge 3 다음 문장을 less ~ than을 이용한 열등비교 문장으로 바꿔 쓰세요.

01. Tom is not as kind as Jane.

→ _____

02. She doesn't feel so tired as her father.

→ _____

03. Basketball games aren't as exciting as soccer games.

→ _____

2-3 비교구문을 이용한 표현

Laptops are becoming smaller and smaller.
노트북들이 점점 더 작아지고 있다.

The longer she waits, **the angrier** she gets.
그녀는 오래 기다리면 기다릴수록 더 화가 난다.

01 '점점 더 ~하다'란 의미의 「비교급＋and＋비교급」은 계속해서 변화하는 것을 강조하기 위해 사용한다.

Life in the modern world is becoming **more and more** complex. 현대 세계의 삶은 점점 더 복잡해져 가고 있다.
When I get excited, my heart beats **faster and faster**. 내가 흥분했을 때, 내 심장은 점점 더 빨리 뛴다.
She got **less and less** interested in his story. 그녀는 그의 이야기에 점점 더 흥미를 잃었다.

02 「the＋비교급, the＋비교급」은 '~하면 할수록 더 ~하다'의 뜻으로, **상호 연관을 갖고 변화하고 있음을 보여** 준다. 앞의 내용이 '조건이나 원인', 뒤의 내용이 '결과'에 해당된다.

The older he grew, **the more** obstinate he became. 그는 나이가 들면 들수록, 고집이 더 세졌다.
The higher prices rose, **the more** money the workers asked for.
물가가 오르면 오를수록 노동자들은 임금 인상을 요구했다.
The warmer the weather is, **the better** I feel. 날씨가 따뜻해지면 따뜻해질수록 나는 더 기분이 좋아진다.

03 no more than(＝only)은 '단지, 겨우', not more than(＝at most)은 '기껏해야, 많아야', much more는 '훨씬(한층) 더 ~하다'란 뜻의 관용 표현이다.

He owns **no more than** three pairs of shoes. 그는 신발이 딱 세 켤레뿐이다.
She spent **not more than** 100 dollars. 그는 기껏해야 100달러를 썼다.
Modern technology makes our living **much more** convenient.
현대 과학기술은 우리 생활을 훨씬 더 편리하게 만든다.

04 -or로 끝나는 형용사인 senior, junior, superior, inferior와 동사 prefer는 **비교 대상 앞에 than 대신 to를** 쓴다.

Nancy **prefers** chocolate ice cream **to** vanilla. Nancy는 바닐라 아이스크림보다 초콜릿 아이스크림을 더 좋아한다.
Tom is three years **senior to** Bob. Tom은 Bob보다 3살 더 많다.
The new version of this 3D game is far **superior to** the old one.
이 3D 게임의 새 버전은 이전 것보다 훨씬 더 우수하다.

서술형 기초다지기

Challenge 1 「비교급+and+비교급」 표현을 이용하여 다음 문장의 빈칸을 완성하세요.

> 보기
> It's becoming *harder and harder* to find a job. (hard)

01. The world is getting _____. (small)

02. Air pollution is becoming _____. (serious)

03. She studies Japanese very hard. Her Japanese is getting _____. (good)

04. My bags seemed to get _____. (heavy)

05. As I waited for my interview, I became _____. (nervous)

Challenge 2 다음 문장을 〈보기〉와 같이 「the+비교급, the+비교급」을 이용하여 바꾸어 쓰세요.

> 보기
> If you study hard, you learn a lot.
> → *The harder you study, the more you learn.*

01. If the fruit is fresh, it tastes good.

    → _____

02. If we climb the mountain high, the wind blows hard.

    → _____

03. As the size of cell phones becomes smaller, the prices get higher.

    → _____

Challenge 3 다음 우리말과 의미가 같도록 빈칸을 완성하세요.

01. 그는 겨우 10달러 밖에 없다.

    → He has _____ 10 dollars.

02. 그는 기껏해야 10달러를 가지고 있다.

    → He has _____ 10 dollars.

최상급

3-1 최상급의 활용

Susan is tall. Susan은 키가 크다.
Tom is taller than Susan. Tom은 Susan보다 더 키가 크다.
Peter is taller than Tom. Peter는 Tom보다 더 키가 크다.
Peter is **the tallest** of the three. Peter가 셋 중에서 가장 키가 크다.

Susan / Tom / Peter

01 최상급은 셋 이상의 명사를 비교할 때 쓴다. 「the+최상급」으로 쓰고 **셋 이상의 사람이나 사물 중에서 '(누가 /무엇이) 가장 ~한'이란 뜻으로** 사용된다. 부사의 최상급에도 정관사 the를 쓴다. 단, 가족이나 친구와 말을 할 때 또는 일상 영어에서는 종종 형용사와 부사의 최상급에 the를 쓰지 않는다.

What is **the longest** river in the world? 세상에서 가장 긴 강이 무엇입니까?
She is **the most popular** actress in Korea. 그녀가 한국에서 가장 인기있는 여배우이다.

02 최상급 뒤에는 **비교 범위를 정해 주는 말로 in이나 of가** 온다. 범위를 나타내는 in(~안에서) 뒤에는 장소나 단체인 단수 명사(this class, the world, my family 등)를 쓰고, of(~중에서) 뒤에는 복수 명사(all the students, all the cities, four seasons 등)를 쓴다. 형용사절을 써서 최상급의 명사를 수식하기도 한다.

What's the highest mountain <u>in Korea</u>? 한국에서 가장 높은 산은 무엇이니?
He is the funniest boy **of** all the children. 그는 모든 아이들 중에서 가장 재미있는 소년이다.
It is the most informative documentary <u>that I've ever seen</u>.
그것은 내가 본 것 중에서 가장 유익한 다큐멘터리이다.

03 이미 앞에서 명사가 제시되어 있어 말하지 않아도 **앞뒤 문맥상 그 내용을 미루어 짐작하거나 알 수 있는 경 우에는 형용사의 최상급 뒤에 있는 명사를 쓰지 않을 때도 있다.** 그러나 항상 명사를 생략할 수 있는 것은 아 니다.

There are four seasons in Korea. Summer is **the hottest (season)** of all.
한국에는 사계절이 있다. 여름이 그 중에서 가장 더운 계절이다.
The blue whale is **the biggest (animal)** of all animals. 흰긴수염고래가 모든 동물 중에 가장 크다.

04 **'가장 ~하지 않는'이란 뜻의 'the least'는** the most와는 반대의 의미를 나타내지만 일상 영어에서는 잘 쓰 지 않는다. the least 뒤에는 원급을 쓴다.

Sunny is **the least tall** student in her class. Sunny는 그녀의 학급에서 가장 키가 크지 않은 학생이다.
→ Sunny is **the shortest** student in her class. ▶ more common

서술형 기초다지기

정답 p. 6

Challenge 1 괄호 안의 단어를 최상급 형태로 바꾸고, in 또는 of 중 알맞은 것을 고르세요.

01. The blue whale is (big) _____ (in / of) all animals.

02. The giraffe is (tall) _____ animal (in / of) the world.

03. Who is (good) _____ student (in / of) the class?

04. The elephant is (big) _____ (in / of) all the animals on land.

05. People think the tiger is the king and (strong) _____ (in / of) the animals.

06. Sortex is (expensive) _____ restaurant (in / of) Paris.

Challenge 2 다음 빈칸에 최상급을 써서 문장을 완성하세요.

> 보기
> That movie was really boring. It was _the most boring_ movie I've ever seen.

01. It's a very cheap restaurant. It's _____ _____ _____ in town.

02. She's a very intelligent student. She is _____ _____ _____ _____ in the class.

03. The Nile is a very long river. It's _____ _____ _____ in the world.

04. He's a very dangerous criminal. He is _____ _____ _____ _____ in the country.

Challenge 3 다음 상황을 읽고 〈보기〉와 같이 「최상급 ~ ever」 형태의 문장을 영작하세요.

> 보기
> You've just been to the movies. The movie was really boring. You tell your friend:
> That's _the most boring movie I've ever seen_. (boring, see, movie)

01. You're drinking green tea with a friend. It's really delicious. You say:

This is _____. (good, green tea, taste)

02. You're talking to a friend about Cindy. Cindy is very smart. You tell your friend about her:

She is _____. (smart, person, meet)

3-2 최상급의 다양한 쓰임

Seoul is **one of the largest cities** in the world.
서울은 세계에서 가장 큰 도시들 중 하나이다.
Seoul is **larger than any other city** in Korea.
서울은 한국에서 다른 어떤 도시보다 더 크다.

01 「one of the+최상급+복수 명사」는 '가장 ~한 것 중의 하나'라는 뜻으로 쓰인다.

The Taj Mahal is **one of the most beautiful buildings** in the world.
타지마할은 세상에서 가장 아름다운 건물 중 하나이다.

One of the best students in this class is Mary. 이 학급에서 가장 우수한 학생 중 한 명은 Mary이다.

It was **one of the worst experiences** I've ever had. 그것은 내가 겪었던 가장 나쁜 경험들 중 하나이다.

02 원급과 비교급을 이용하여 최상급의 의미를 나타낼 수 있다.

No (other) ~ as[so]+원급+as
=No (other) ~ 비교급+than
=비교급+than any other+단수 명사
=비교급+than (all) the other+복수 명사

Nancy is the tallest girl in her class. Nancy는 그녀의 반에서 가장 키가 큰 소녀이다.
=**No (other)** girl is **as[so] tall as** Nancy in her class.
=**No (other)** girl is **taller than** Nancy in her class.
=Nancy is **taller than any other girl** in her class.
=Nancy is **taller than (all) the other girls** in her class.

Tokyo is **the largest** city in Japan. 도쿄는 일본에서 가장 큰 도시이다.
=**No (other)** city is **as[so] large as** Tokyo in Japan.
=**No (other)** city is **larger than** Tokyo in Japan.
=Tokyo is **larger than any other city** in Japan.
=Tokyo is **larger than (all) the other cities** in Japan.

서술형 기초다지기

Challenge 1 〈보기〉와 같이 「one of+최상급+the+복수 명사」를 이용하여 문장을 완성하세요.

> **보기**
> a beautiful country in the world
> → Costa Rico is *one of the most beautiful countries in the world.*

01. a large city in the world

→ Seoul is _____ .

02. a serious problem in Korea

→ Yellow dust is _____ .

03. an old player on his team

→ Michael Jordan was _____ .

04. a tall basketball player in the world

→ Yao Ming is _____ .

05. a hard thing I've ever done

→ Running a marathon was _____ .

Challenge 2 다음 최상급 문장을 괄호 안의 지시대로 고쳐 쓰세요.

01. Mt. Everest is the highest mountain in the world. (No other ~ as+원급+as)

→ _____

02. Bill Gates is the richest man in the world. (비교급+than any other+단수 명사)

→ _____

03. Yu-na Kim is the most attractive athlete in Korea. (비교급+than the other+복수 명사)

→ _____

04. Canada is the biggest country in the world. (No other ~ 비교급+than)

→ _____

Unit 04 원급과 기타 비교 표현

4-1 원급을 이용한 비교 표현

Kevin and Peter are twins.
Kevin과 Peter는 쌍둥이다.

Kevin is 170cm. Peter is 170cm.
Kevin은 170센티미터이다. Peter도 170센티미터이다.

Kevin is **as** tall **as** Peter.
Kevin은 Peter만큼 키가 크다.
(= Kevin and Peter are the same height.)

---

01 비교급은 둘 중 어느 하나가 더 크거나, 더 잘 생겼다 등으로 표현하지만 **원급비교는 두 명의 사람이나 두 개의 사물을 두고 서로 같거나 비슷하다고 표현**하는 말이다. 원급비교는 「as+형용사/부사의 원급+as」로 쓰고 '~만큼 ~한'으로 해석한다. 이 때 첫 번째 as는 큰 의미가 없고 두 번째 as를 '~만큼'으로 해석한다.

I love her **as** much **as** you (do). 나도 당신만큼 그녀를 사랑한다.
Lisa is **as** busy **as** Jason (is). Lisa는 Jason만큼 바쁘다.

---

02 원급비교의 부정 표현은 as 앞에 'not'을 붙여 「not as[so]+형용사/부사의 원급+as」로 쓰는데 '~만큼 ~하지 않다'라는 뜻이다. 원급비교의 부정은 「비교급+than」으로 바꾸어 쓸 수 있다.

Ben isn't **as** tall **as** Nancy. Ben은 Nancy만큼 키가 크지 않다.
→ Ben is **shorter than** Nancy.
→ Nancy is **taller than** Ben.

Autumn is **not as** cold **as** winter. 가을은 겨울만큼 춥지 않다.
→ Autumn is **warmer than** winter.
→ Winter is **colder than** Autumn.

---

03 「A ~ 배수사+as+형용사/부사의 원급+as+B(비교 대상)」는 'A는 B보다 몇 배나 ~하다'의 의미이다.

My grandfather is **four times as** old **as** I (am). 할아버지는 나보다 4배나 더 나이가 많다.
This bridge is **three times as** long **as** that one. 이 다리는 저것보다 3배나 더 길다.
The population of Seoul is **twice as** large **as** that of our city. 서울의 인구는 우리 도시의 인구에 2배이다.

---

04 「as+원급+as possible」은 '가능한 ~한/하게'의 뜻으로, 「as+원급+as+주어+can/could」로 바꾸어 쓸 수 있다. 'not so much A as B'는 'A라기보다는 오히려 B이다'의 뜻이다.

Please let me know the result **as** soon **as possible**. 가능한 한 빨리 그 결과를 알려주세요.
= Pleas let me know the result **as** soon **as** you **can**.

He is **not so much** a poet **as** a novelist. 그는 시인이라기보다는 오히려 소설가이다.

서술형 기초다지기

Challenge 1   다음 문장을 as ~ as 또는 not as[so] ~ as를 이용하여 한 문장으로 만드세요.

보기	Peter is famous. Steve is famous. → Peter is *as famous as Steve (is)*.

01. A river isn't big. An ocean is very big.

→ A river _____.

02. Kelly isn't very busy at all. Jason is very busy.

→ Kelly _____.

03. I was tired. Sunny was very tired.

→ I _____.

Challenge 2   다음 원급의 부정 표현은 비교급으로, 비교급은 원급 부정 표현으로 바꾸어 쓰세요.

01. This car is more expensive than that motorcycle.

→ That motorcycle _____.

02. Jason speaks Korean more fluently than I do.

→ I _____.

03. Cindy's hair isn't as long as Karen's.

→ Karen's hair _____.

Challenge 3   다음 우리말과 뜻이 같도록 빈칸에 알맞은 말을 쓰세요.

01. 그는 가능한 한 천천히 말했다. (slowly)

→ He spoke _____ _____ _____ _____.

02. 아프리카는 유럽보다 4배나 넓다. (large)

→ Africa is _____ _____ _____ _____ _____ Europe.

4-2 알아두어야 할 기타 비교 표현 (1)

Jane has a red car. Bob has a red car.
Jane은 빨간색 차를 가지고 있다. Bob은 빨간색 차를 가지고 있다.

Jane's car is **the same** color **as** Bob's.
Jane의 차는 Bob의 자동차와 똑같은 색이다.

Their cars are **the same**.
그들의 차는 똑같다.

---

01 the same, similar, different는 유사함과 차이를 나타내는 말로 형용사처럼 쓰인다. 형용사처럼 쓰이기 때문에 명사 앞이나 연결동사인 be동사 뒤에 위치한다. 단, **same은 형용사지만 the와 함께 쓴다.**

Tom and Peter have **the same** cell phones. Tom과 Peter는 똑같은 휴대전화를 갖고 있다.
Tom's cell phone and Peter's cell phone are **the same**. Tom과 Peter의 휴대전화는 똑같다.

Sunny and Jane have **similar** bags. Sunny와 Jane은 비슷한 가방을 가지고 있다.
Sunny's bag and Jane's bag are **similar**. Sunny와 Jane의 가방은 비슷하다.

Steve and Scott have **different** characters. Steve와 Scott은 다른 성격을 가지고 있다.
Steve's character and Scott's character are **different**. Steve와 Scott의 성격은 다르다.

---

02 the same, similar, different는 서로 다른 전치사를 써서 「**the same as**+비교 대상」, 「**similar to**+비교 대상」, 「**different from**+비교 대상」으로 쓴다.

My bicycle is **the same as** yours. 내 자전거는 네 것과 똑같다.

It's very **similar to** Choosuk in Korea. 그것은 한국의 추석과 비슷하다.

Football is not **the same as** soccer. Football is **different from** soccer.
풋볼은 축구와 똑같지 않다. 풋볼은 축구와 다르다.

---

03 「the same+명사+as」의 형태로 **the same과 as 사이에 명사를 자주 쓴다**. 반대말인 「not the same+명사+as」는 형용사와 부사를 이용한 비교급으로 나타낼 수 있다.

Erick has the same **ability** as his teammates. Erick은 그의 팀 동료들과 같은 능력을 가졌다.
=Erick and his teammates have **the same ability**.

A soccer ball is the same **shape** as a volleyball. 축구공은 배구공과 똑같은 모양이다.
=A soccer ball and a volleyball are **the same shape**.

He's not the same **age** as his wife. 그는 그의 아내와 나이가 같지 않다.
→ His wife is **older**. 그의 아내가 더 나이가 들었다.

Kathy is not the same **weight** as Cindy. Kathy는 Cindy와 체중이 같지 않다.
→ Cindy is **fatter**. Cindy가 더 뚱뚱하다.

서술형 기초다지기

정답 p. 7

Challenge 1 다음 빈칸에 as, to 또는 from을 넣고 불필요한 경우에 X 표시를 하세요.

01. An orange is different _____ a grapefruit.

02. Gold is similar _____ silver. They are both valuable metals.

03. Kathy's hair style and mine are similar _____.

04. Teenage culture is different _____ adult culture.

05. John's and Mike's cars are different _____.

06. This car is not the same price _____ that car.

07. My bicycle and your bicycle are the same _____.

Challenge 2 「(not) the same ~ as」를 이용하여 문장을 만드세요.

> **보기**
> a soccer ball / a volleyball (shape)
> → *A soccer ball is the same shape as a volleyball.*

01. a golf ball / a tennis ball (size)

→ _____

02. a baseball player / a basketball player (height)

→ _____

03. "flour" / "flower" (has / pronunciation)

→ _____

Challenge 3 빈칸에 the same (as), similar (to), 또는 different (from)를 넣어 문장을 완성하세요.

01. Christina and Brian both come from Canada. In other words, they come from _____ country.

02. You and I don't agree. Your ideas are _____ mine.

03. These shoes are not _____ size _____ those shoes. These shoes are smaller.

04. "Meet" and "meat" are homonyms; i. e. they have _____ pronunciation.

4-3 알아두어야 할 기타 비교 표현 (2)

A soccer player **looks like** a rugby player. 축구선수는 럭비선수처럼 보인다.
A soccer player doesn't **dress like** a football player. 축구선수는 미식축구선수처럼 옷을 입지 않는다.
A soccer player and a rugby player **look alike**. 축구선수와 럭비선수는 비슷해 보인다.
A soccer player and a football player don't **dress alike**. 축구선수와 미식축구선수는 옷을 비슷하게 입지 않는다.

01 비슷함을 나타내는 단어인 like와 alike가 있다. **like는 전치사로 반드시 뒤에 명사와 함께 쓰이고, alike는 형용사나 부사로 쓰이므로 보어처럼 동사 뒤**에만 온다.

You **look like** your sister. 너는 너의 언니와 닮아 보인다.

→ You and your sister **look alike**. 너와 너의 언니는 비슷해 보인다.

It **sounds like** thunder. 그것은 천둥처럼 들린다.

The twins **look alike**. 그 쌍둥이는 비슷해 보인다.

※ 주로 감각을 나타내는 동사 look, sound, smell, taste, feel, seem과 자주 쓰인다.

02 like와 alike는 act, sing, dress, think, talk 등의 동사들과 자주 쓰인다. like는 반드시 뒤에 명사를 쓰고 alike는 명사와 함께 쓰지 않고 동사 뒤에만 쓴다.

She doesn't **dress like** her sister. 그녀는 그녀의 언니처럼 옷을 입지 않는다.

Karen and Cindy **dressed alike**. Karen과 Cindy는 비슷하게 옷을 입었다.

They are watching him **act like** a fool. 그들은 남자가 바보짓 하는 것을 보고 있다.

Most four-year-olds **act alike**. 대부분의 4살짜리들은 비슷하게 행동한다.

03 「be동사+like+명사」 또는 「be동사+alike」로 유사함을 나타낸다.

My pen **is like** your pen. 내 펜은 너의 펜과 비슷하다.

My pen and your pen **are alike**. 내 펜과 너의 펜은 비슷하다.

※ look like는 사람의 신체적인 외모를 나타내고 「be동사+like」는 내적인 특성을 나타낸다.

Eric **looks like** an athlete. He's tall and strong. Eric은 운동선수처럼 보인다. 그는 키가 크고 힘이 세다.

Eric **is like** his teammates. He has a lot of experience. Eric은 팀 동료들과 비슷하다. 그는 많은 경험을 갖고 있다.

서술형 기초다지기

정답 p. 7

Challenge 1   다음 빈칸에 like와 alike 중 알맞은 것을 골라 써 넣으세요.

> **보기** Twins look *alike*.

01. My mother and my father rarely argue because they think _____.

02. My daughter is only 16 years old, but she acts _____ an adult. She's very responsible and hard-working.

03. You and I have similar ideas. In other words, your ideas are _____ mine. Our ideas are _____.

04. This laptop doesn't look _____ the one I ordered.

05. Children in private schools usually wear a uniform. They dress _____.

06. Dogs don't look _____ cats at all. Dogs are very friendly. Cats are more distant.

07. My children learned English very quickly. Now they sound _____ Americans. They have no accent at all.

Challenge 2   빈칸에 like, alike, similar (to) 또는 different (from)를 써서 문장을 완성하세요.

01. Soccer players don't look _____ football players at all.

02. Kevin swims _____ a fish. He never wants to come out of the water.

03. Americans and people from England don't sound _____. They have different accents.

04. A: How do you like the spaghetti sauce I made? I tried to make it exactly _____ yours.
    B: I can tell. Your sauce is very _____ the one I make, but I think it's missing one spice.

05. The English spoken in the United States is only slightly _____ the English spoken in Britain, Canada, and Australia.

06. Some people think my sister and I are twins. We look _____ and talk _____, but our personalities are quite _____.

01 출제 100 % – 원급, 비교급, 최상급의 기본에 충실하자.

 출제자의 눈 비교급 형태를 묻는 것은 1, 2학년 때 많이 출제되고 3학년 때는 비교급 불규칙 변화형을 물어보는 문제가 많이 출제된다. 비교급 뒤에 than을 다른 단어로 틀리게 해 놓기도 한다. than 대신 'to'를 쓰는 senior, junior, superior, inferior, prefer 등도 반드시 알아두자. 원급비교에서는 as ~ as를 써야 하는데 두 번째 as를 틀리게 하거나, as와 as 사이에는 형용사와 부사의 원급을 써야 하는데 비교급을 슬쩍 갖다놓기도 한다. 최상급에서 정관사 the를 빼놓고 실수를 유발하는 문제도 출제된다.

Ex 1.

다음 단어들의 비교급이 <u>잘못된</u> 것은?

(a) heavy – heavier   (b) good – better

(c) little – fewer   (c) much – more

Ex 2.

My pencil isn't so long as yours.

=My pencil is _____ yours.

(a) shorter to   (b) as long as   (c) not shorter than   (d) shorter than

02 출제 100 % – 최상급의 의미를 나타내는 원급과 비교급 표현을 알아두자.

 출제자의 눈 원급비교의 부정을 비교급으로 나타내거나 원급과 비교급으로 최상급의 의미를 나타내는 표현에 대해 묻는다. 서로 의미가 같은지 다른지 물어보는 객관식 문제가 출제되거나, 문장 하나를 주고 같은 의미가 되도록 부분 영작하는 문제로 자주 출제된다. 그리고 비교급을 강조하는 much, still, far, a lot 등과 very를 구분하는 문제도 많이 출제된다. less ~ than에서 less 뒤에는 원급을 써야 하므로 비교급이나 최상급을 쓰지 않도록 조심하자.

Ex 3.

밑줄 친 부분이 의미하는 것은?

<u>Nothing is more important than courage</u> for the captain.

(a) courage is very important

(b) courage is not so important as anything else

(c) courage is not more important than anything else

(d) courage is the most important

03 출제 100% - 비교구문을 이용한 표현은 부분 영작과 서술형으로 출제된다.

 출제자의 눈 「the+비교급, the+비교급」과 「비교급+and+비교급」은 우리말을 주고 영작하거나 문장을 주고 같은 의미의 비교구문을 완성하는 문제가 반드시 출제된다. 또한 배수를 나타내는 「배수사+as+형용사/부사의 원급+as」 형태를 묻는 문제도 출제될 수 있다. 마지막으로 '가능한 ~한/하게'의 뜻인 'as ~ as possible'을 부분 영작하거나 「as ~ as+주어+can/could」로 바꿔 쓰거나 같은 의미를 고르는 문제가 출제된다.

Ex 4.

두 문장의 의미가 같도록 빈칸에 알맞은 말을 쓰시오.
As we study harder, our grades become better.
= _____ we study, _____ our grades become.

04 출제 100% - 원급, 비교급, 최상급을 이용한 서술형 문제를 대비하라.

 출제자의 눈 원급, 비교급, 최상급은 단답형 주관식 또는 서술형으로 출제하기에 가장 좋은 문제이다. 특히 최상급에서 주의할 점은 more 대신 most를 써야 하는 것과 「one of+the+최상급+복수 명사」에서 복수 명사를 단수 명사로 틀리게 해놓는 문제가 출제된다. 「one of+the+최상급+복수 명사」가 주어로 쓰일 때 동사는 반드시 단수 동사를 써야 하는 것도 알아두자. 또한 원급과 비교급을 이용해서 최상급을 만드는 부분 영작이나 같은 의미 또는 틀린 의미를 고르는 문제도 출제된다.

Ex 5.

두 문장이 같은 뜻이 되도록 빈칸에 알맞은 말을 쓰시오.
He is the tallest boy in his class.
He is _____ than any _____ _____ in his class. (3단어로)

Ex 6.

다음 우리말을 영어로 옮겨 쓰시오.
· 그녀는 한국에서 가장 유명한 여배우 중 한 명이다. (actress, Korea, famous)
→ _____

1. 다음 밑줄 친 부분과 같은 의미의 문장을 만들 때, 빈칸에 들어갈 알맞은 말은?

> A : What was so great about him?
> B : No one in the world can swim faster than him.
> (=He is _____ swimmer in the world.)

❶ fast   ❷ faster   ❸ the fastest
❹ slower   ❺ the slowest

2. 빈칸에 들어갈 알맞은 말을 한 단어로 쓰시오.

> When you eat fewer calories _____ you use, your body uses the stored calories.

3. 다음 빈칸에 들어갈 말이 바르게 짝지어진 것은?

> The _____ expensive the hotel, the _____ the service.
> (호텔이 비싸면 비쌀수록 서비스가 더 좋다.)

❶ many – good   ❷ much – more
❸ more – better   ❹ most – well
❺ best – best

[4-5] 다음 우리말과 뜻이 같도록 괄호 안의 말을 이용하여 문장을 완성하시오.

4. 파리에 사는 것이 Seattle에 사는 것보다 훨씬 더 좋다고 생각한다. (far, good)

> → I think that living in Paris is _____ _____ _____ living in Seattle.

5. 이 빨간 가방은 저 파란 배낭보다 훨씬 더 가볍다. (a lot, light)

> → This red bag is _____ _____ _____ _____ that blue backpack.

6. 다음 두 문장의 의미가 같도록 빈칸에 알맞은 말을 쓰시오.

> She borrowed a wedding dress as cheaply as possible.
> = She borrowed a wedding dress as cheaply as _____ _____.

7. 두 문장이 같은 뜻이 되도록 빈칸에 알맞은 말을 쓰시오.

> As the size of computers becomes smaller, the prices get higher.
> = _____ the size of computers becomes, _____ the prices get.

8. 다음 중 〈보기〉의 내용과 일치하지 않는 것은?

> | 보 기 | A : ₩1,000 | B : ₩1,500 |
> |---|---|---|
> | | C : ₩2,000 | D : ₩1,200 |

❶ A is the cheapest of the four.
❷ D is more expensive than A.
❸ B is as cheap as D.
❹ C is the most expensive of the four.
❺ C is twice as expensive as A.

9. 다음 빈칸에 들어갈 말이 바르게 짝지어진 것은?

> · Ted isn't quite as _____ as Tina.
> · The harder you study, the _____ you will learn.

❶ old – many   ❷ older – much
❸ old – more   ❹ older – more
❺ oldest – more

오답 노트 만들기

※ 틀린 문제에는 빨간색으로 V표시를 한다.
※ 두세 번 정도 반복해서 복습하고 완전히 알 때에만 O표를 한다.

★틀린 문제 : _____   ★다시 공부한 날 : _____

(1) 문제를 왜? 틀렸는지 곰곰이 생각하고 그 이유를 적어본다.

(2) 핵심 개념을 적는다.

(3) 자신이 몰랐던 단어와 숙어 표현이 있으면 정리한다.

(4) 해설집에서 필요한 부분을 골라 풀이 해법을 정리한다.

★틀린 문제 : _____   ★다시 공부한 날 : _____

(1) 문제를 왜? 틀렸는지 곰곰이 생각하고 그 이유를 적어본다.

(2) 핵심 개념을 적는다.

(3) 자신이 몰랐던 단어와 숙어 표현이 있으면 정리한다.

(4) 해설집에서 필요한 부분을 골라 풀이 해법을 정리한다.

★틀린 문제 : _____   ★다시 공부한 날 : _____

(1) 문제를 왜? 틀렸는지 곰곰이 생각하고 그 이유를 적어본다.

(2) 핵심 개념을 적는다.

(3) 자신이 몰랐던 단어와 숙어 표현이 있으면 정리한다.

(4) 해설집에서 필요한 부분을 골라 풀이 해법을 정리한다.

★틀린 문제 : _____   ★다시 공부한 날 : _____

(1) 문제를 왜? 틀렸는지 곰곰이 생각하고 그 이유를 적어본다.

(2) 핵심 개념을 적는다.

(3) 자신이 몰랐던 단어와 숙어 표현이 있으면 정리한다.

(4) 해설집에서 필요한 부분을 골라 풀이 해법을 정리한다.

1. 다음 두 문장이 같은 뜻이 되도록 빈칸에 알맞은 말을 쓰시오.

> Nothing is more important than time.
> =Time is _____ important thing of all.
> = _____ is as _____ as time.

오답노트

2. 다음 빈칸에 알맞은 단어를 쓰시오.

> 그는 우리나라에서 가장 유명한 가수 중에 한 명이다.
> → He is _____ of the most famous singers in our country.

오답노트

3. 다음 밑줄 친 우리말을 영어로 알맞게 표현한 것은?

> In my dream, I saw a balloon which was 집만큼 큰 (집채만 한).

❶ like a house as big   ❷ as big as a house
❸ as a house like big   ❹ as a house as big
❺ as big a house as

오답노트

4. 다음 밑줄 친 부분의 쓰임이 **틀린** 것은?

❶ Lisa studied as much as Thomas did.
❷ The sky seems to be getting darker and darker.
❸ The score was three times higher than everyone expected.
❹ This city is alike my hometown. Both are quiet and conservative.
❺ That is the highest building in Seoul.

오답노트

5. 다음 우리말을 영어로 고칠 때 빈칸에 알맞은 단어를 써 넣으시오.

> 나는 Peter만큼 빨리 달릴 수 없다. (fast)
> =I can't run _____ Peter.

오답노트

6. 다음 빈칸에 들어갈 알맞은 말을 고르시오.

> In this party, you can eat _____.
> (이 파티에서, 네가 원하는 만큼 많이 먹을 수 있다.)

❶ as large as you want
❷ as big as you want
❸ as much as you want
❹ as much you want as
❺ as you want as

오답노트

7. 다음 괄호 안의 단어의 형태가 바르게 짝지어진 것은?

· This stone is three times as (heavy) as that one.
· Sunny received the (high) mark in the class.
· The less you complain, the (happy) everyone else will be.

❶ heavier – higher – happier
❷ heavy – high – happy
❸ heavy – highest – happy
❹ heaviest – highest – happiest
❺ heavy – highest – happier

오답노트

8. 다음 빈칸에 들어갈 수 없는 말은?

Well, I think the world will be _____ better. Medical science will help people enjoy good health and long life.

❶ even   ❷ far   ❸ still
❹ very   ❺ much

오답노트

9. 다음 문장의 빈칸에 알맞지 않은 것은?

This mountain is _____ higher than your father's building.

❶ lots of   ❷ still   ❸ far
❹ even   ❺ much

오답노트

10. 다음 중 어법상 잘못된 것을 고르시오.

❶ Rats are much smaller than cats.
❷ Kevin is older of all the teachers in school.
❸ This chair isn't as comfortable as that sofa.
❹ The Nile is one of the longest river in the world.
❺ I prefer watching TV to playing outside.

오답노트

11. 다음 빈칸에 들어갈 말로 알맞은 것은?

If you eat _____ calories than you consume, your body will burn the fat and use their energy.

❶ little   ❷ few   ❸ less
❹ least   ❺ fewer

오답노트

12. 다음 문장의 밑줄 친 부분과 바꾸어 쓸 수 있는 것은?

He went home full tear to tell them the news as soon as he could.

❶ he can   ❷ can   ❸ able
❹ possible   ❺ possibility

오답노트

13. 〈보기〉의 밑줄 친 even과 의미가 같은 것은?

> | 보 기 | He studies English <u>even</u> harder than his classmates. |
> |---|---|

❶ <u>Even</u> though he was born in England, he is a Korean boy.

❷ They did not <u>even</u> know what kind of company they wanted.

❸ He <u>even</u> said that his wife was crazy.

❹ Kathy walks <u>even</u> faster than her boyfriend.

❺ Murder was a big social problem <u>even</u> in ancient times.

오답노트

14. 빈칸에 들어갈 말이 바르게 짝지어진 것은?

> 날씨가 시원해질수록, 나는 기분이 더 좋아진다.
> → _____ the weather is, _____ I feel.

❶ Cool − good

❷ Cooler − better

❸ The cool − the good

❹ The cooler − the better

❺ The coolest − the best

오답노트

15. 다음 빈칸에 공통으로 들어갈 단어를 고르시오.

> Some love to come to L.A. because _____ is more exciting than Disneyland. Others like to visit Seoul because _____ is more attractive than old palaces.

❶ L.A.   ❷ no other thing   ❸ everyone
❹ Seoul   ❺ all

오답노트

16. 다음 문장과 같은 의미가 되도록 빈칸을 완성하시오.

> Jejudo is the biggest island in Korea.
> = _____ _____ island in Korea is _____ big _____ Jejudo.

오답노트

17. 다음 두 문장의 의미가 같도록 빈칸에 알맞은 단어를 쓰시오.

> As the prices are higher, we will buy less.
> = _____ the prices are, _____ we will buy.

오답노트

18. 다음 빈칸에 공통으로 들어갈 말을 쓰시오.

> · _____ more popular the restaurant became, _____ more crowded it got.
> · This is _____ hardest situation we've ever faced.

오답노트

19. 다음 중 밑줄 친 부분과 의미가 같은 것은?

> A : What was so great about her?
> B : No one was stronger than her.

❶ She was the weakest woman.
❷ Everyone was as strong as her.
❸ She was the strongest of all.
❹ She was not so strong as you.
❺ No one was not so strong as her.

오답노트

20. 다음 괄호 안의 단어를 이용하여 우리말과 같은 뜻이 되도록 빈칸에 알맞은 말을 쓰시오.

> 보통, 남자가 여자보다 맛과 냄새에 덜 민감하다.
> = Usually men are _____ to tastes and smells _____ women. (sensitive)

오답노트

21. 다음 질문에 대한 대답으로 알맞지 않은 것은?

> Which is the tallest building in Korea?

❶ The 63 building is the tallest in Korea.
❷ No building in Korea is as tall as the 63 building.
❸ The 63 building is not as tall as any other building in Korea.
❹ The 63 building is taller than any other building in Korea.
❺ No building in Korea is taller than the 63 building.

오답노트

22. 다음 대화의 빈칸에 들어갈 수 없는 말은?

> A : Did you hear the news?
> B : What news?
> A : Tae-Hwan Park made a new Korean record in the 200m race yesterday.
> B : Does that mean _____?
> A : Of course.

❶ he is the fastest swimmer in Korea
❷ no one in Korea can swim faster than him
❸ he can swim as fast as the other swimmer in Korea
❹ he can swim faster than any other swimmer in Korea
❺ no one in Korea can swim as fast as he

오답노트

A. 다음 그림에 맞게 비교급과 최상급 문장을 완성하시오.

1. The golf ball is _____ _____ the baseball.

2. The soccer ball is _____ _____ the baseball.

3. The soccer ball is _____ _____ the golf ball.

4. The soccer ball is _____ _____ of all.

B. 〈보기〉와 같이 「a little/much+비교급」을 이용하여 문장을 영작하시오.

보기	Kevin is 16. Lucy is 14. → Kevin *is a little older than Lucy.*

1. Susan's mother is 50. Her father is 60.

   → Susan's mother _____.

2. Peter is an excellent soccer player. I'm not very good.

   → Peter _____.

3. Today the temperature is 12 degrees Celsius. Yesterday it was 10 degrees.

   → It's _____.

C. 다음 그림을 보고 원급, 비교급, 최상급 표현을 완성하시오.

| Hotel A | Hotel B | Hotel C | Hotel D |
| built in 1955 | built in 1990 | built in 2007 | built in 1990 |

1. The Hotel A is _____ of the four. (old)

2. The Hotel B is _____ the Hotel D. (old)

3. The Hotel C is _____ the Hotel B. (new)

4. The Hotel C is _____ of the four. (new)

D. 다음 우리말과 뜻이 같도록 빈칸에 알맞은 말을 쓰시오.

• 한글은 세계에서 가장 좋은 언어이다. (good)

→ Hangeul is _____ _____ language in the world.

→ Hangeul is _____ _____ _____ _____ language in the world.

→ _____ other language in the world is _____ _____ Hangeul.

→ _____ other language in the world is _____ _____ _____ Hangeul.

E. 다음 상황에 어울리도록 빈칸에 「the+비교급, the+비교급」 문장을 완성하시오.

1. The party got noisy next door. I got angry.

→ I had a terrible time getting to sleep last night. My neighbors were having a loud party. _____ _____ it got, _____ _____ I got. Finally, I hanged on the wall and told them to be quiet.

2. Bob talked very fast. I became confused.

→ Bob was trying to explain some complicated physics problems to help me prepare for an exam. He kept talking faster and faster. _____ _____ he talked, _____ _____ confused I became.

실전 서술형 평가문제

 출제의도 원급, 비교급, 최상급
평가내용 사람, 사물을 비교하여 문장 서술하기

A. 〈보기〉와 같이 주어진 형용사/부사를 이용하여 비교 문장을 만드시오.   [서술형 유형 : 18점 / 난이도 : 중하]

sofa A	＊＊＊
sofa B	＊＊
sofa C	＊

comfortable

> **보기**
> sofa B / sofa A
> → *Sofa B is not as comfortable as sofa A.*

1. sofa B / sofa C

→ _____

2. sofa C / of all

→ _____

Tom	runs 100 meters in 11 seconds
Mike	runs 100 meters in 12 seconds
John	runs 100 meters in 13 seconds
Jason	runs 100 meters in 13 seconds

fast

3. Tom / run / of all

→ _____

4. Mike / run / Jason

→ _____

5. John / run / Jason

→ _____

Sunny	＊＊＊
Cindy	＊＊
Maria	＊

carefully

6. Maria / drive / Sunny

→ _____

7. Cindy / drive / Maria

→ _____

8. Sunny / drive / of the three

→ _____

9. Maria / drive / of the three

→ _____

출제의도 원급, 비교급, 최상급

평가내용 사람, 사물을 비교하여 문장 서술하기

B. 〈보기〉와 같이 빈칸에 「비교급＋비교급」으로 문장을 완성하시오.　　　　[서술형 유형 : 8점 / 난이도 : 하]

| tired　　good　　cold　　loud　　discouraged |

> **보기**　He studies English very hard. His English is getting *better and better*.

1. As the ambulance came closer to us, the siren became _____.

2. As we continued traveling north, the weather got _____. Eventually, everything we saw was frozen.

3. Jason has been looking for a job for a month and still hasn't been able to find one. He is getting _____.

4. We stayed up all night to work on our geology project. We became _____ as the night wore on, but we stayed awake and finally finished in time for class.

C. 〈보기〉와 같이 「the＋비교급, the＋비교급」을 이용하여 문장을 만드시오.　　　　[서술형 유형 : 4점 / 난이도 : 중상]

> **보기**　Bob talked very fast. I became confused.
> → Bob was trying to explain some complicated physics problems to help me prepare for an exam. He kept talking faster and faster. *The faster he talked, the more confused I became.*

1. I became bored. She talked.

→ I met a strange woman at a party last night. I tried to be interested in what she was saying, but _____.

2. My eyes get tired. I look at a computer screen.

→ I spend a long time each day looking at a computer screen. My eyes get very tired.

_____

출제의도 same, similar, different

평가내용 유사와 차이를 나타내는 형용사로 문장 서술하기

D. 다음 집의 모양을 보고 same, similar, different를 이용한 비교 문장을 최소한 6개 만드시오.

[서술형 유형 : 12점 / 난이도 : 중]

House 1

House 2

House 3

House 4

보기	House 1 is similar to House 4.

1. _____

2. _____

3. _____

4. _____

5. _____

6. _____

서술형 평가문제	채 점 기 준	배 점	나의 점수
A	표현이 올바르고 문법, 철자가 모두 정확한 경우	2점×9문항=18점	
B		2점×4문항=8점	
C		2점×2문항=4점	
D		2점×6문항=12점	
공통	문법, 철자가 1개씩 틀린 경우	각 문항당 1점씩 감점	
	내용과 전혀 일치하지 않거나 답을 기재하지 못한 경우	0점	

Chapter 3

수동태 (Passive Voice)

1-1 수동태의 기본 개념 및 형태

John Pemberton **invented** Coca-Cola in 1886.
John Pemberton이 1886년에 코카콜라를 발명했다.
Coca-Cola **was invented** in 1886.
코카콜라는 1886년에 발명되었다.

01 수동태는 행위의 주체에 관심이 있는 것이 아니라, **행위를 받는 대상에 관심**이 있다. 즉, 행위를 받는 대상이 문장의 중심(주어)이 되어 이를 주어로 쓰고 동사를 「be동사+p.p.」로 쓴다.

능동태(주어가 ~ 하다)	수동태(주어가 ~당하다/받다/되다)
J.K. Rowling **wrote** the Harry Potter series. J.K. Rowling이 해리포터 시리즈를 썼다. Graham Bell **invented** the telephone in 1876. 그레이엄 벨이 1876년에 전화기를 발명했다.	The telephone **was invented** in 1876. 전화기는 1876년에 발명되었다. The telephone **was invented** by Graham Bell in 1876. 전화기는 1876년 그레이엄 벨에 의해 발명되었다.
책을 쓴 행위자가 중요해서 능동태 문장을 썼다. 이러한 능동태는 그 행위가 전달되는 대상(목적어)이 반드시 있다.	수동태는 누가 그것을 했는가보다는 행위 자체에 중요성을 둔다. 수동태는 주어를 강조하기 때문에 행위가 전달되는 목적어가 존재하지 않는다. 보통 「by+행위자(목적격)」가 없는 경우가 많다.

시제	능동태	수동태
현재시제	He **fixes** the car.	The car **is fixed** by him.
현재진행	He **is fixing** the car.	The car **is being fixed** by him.
현재완료	He **has fixed** the car.	The car **has been fixed** by him.
과거시제	He **fixed** the car.	The car **was fixed** by him.
과거진행	He **was fixing** the car.	The car **was being fixed** by him.
과거완료	He **had fixed** the car.	The car **had been fixed** by him.
미래시제 will	He **will fix** the car.	The car **will be fixed** by him.
미래시제 be going to	He **is going to fix** the car.	The car **is going to be fixed** by him.
미래완료	He **will have fixed** the car.	The car **will have been fixed** by him.

서술형 기초다지기

정답 p. 9

Challenge 1 다음 능동태 문장을 수동태로 바꿔 쓰세요.

보 기	Peter broke the window. → *The window was broken by Peter.*

01. Thomas Edison invented the electric light bulb.

→ _____

02. Millions of tourists visit the Eiffel Tower every year.

→ _____

03. Bob is painting the door.

→ _____

04. Somebody has stolen my purse.

→ _____

05. She will paint the house.

→ _____

06. He is repairing the car.

→ _____

07. Tom is going to send the letter.

→ _____

08. They have not cleaned the classroom.

→ _____

09. They will have finished the work by this time next week.

→ _____

10. The Romans built the Colosseum in Rome.

→ _____

1-2 by+행위자(목적격) / 수동태를 쓰지 않는 경우

The telephone was invented **by Alexander Graham Bell**.
전화기는 알렉산더 그레이엄 벨에 의해 발명되었다.

01 행위자를 중심으로 할 때는 능동태 문장을 선호하지만 **수동태 문장이 보다 효과적인 의미를 전달할 수 있는 경우**에는 수동태를 쓴다.

① 어떤 행위를 **누가 했는지 모르거나, 누가 했는지 안다고 해도 중요하지 않은 경우**에는 「by+행위자(목적격)」를 쓰지 않는다.

My sweater **was made** in Korea. 내 스웨터는 한국에서 만들어졌다.
The office **is cleaned** every day. 그 사무실은 매일 청소된다.

② 행위자가 **일반인이거나, 언급하지 않아도 뻔히 아는 경우**에는 「by+행위자(목적격)」를 쓰지 않는다. 실제로 수동태 문장 중 약 80%는 행위의 주체를 쓰지 않는다.

English **is spoken** almost all over the world. 영어는 거의 전 세계에서 사용된다.
I **was invited** to Mary's birthday party. 나는 Mary의 생일파티에 초대받았다.

③ 수동태에서 「by+행위자(목적격)」는 **주어를 강조하면서도 행위자가 중요**하거나 추가적인 정보로 사용할 때 쓴다.

The Eiffel Tower was designed **by Gustave Eiffel**. 에펠탑은 Gustave Eiffel에 의해 디자인되었다.
These books were written **by Shakespeare**. 이 책들은 세익스피어에 의해 쓰여졌다.

02 목적어를 갖지 못하는 **자동사**나 목적어를 갖는다 하더라도 **상태동사**인 have, resemble, fit, suit, lack 등은 **수동태로 쓰지 못한다**.

She **has** a nice car. 그녀는 멋진 차를 가지고 있다.
→ A nice car is had by her. (×)

Kathy **resembles** her father. Kathy는 아버지를 닮았다.
→ Her father is resembled by Kathy. (×)

서술형 기초다지기

정답 p. 9

Challenge 1 괄호 안의 단어들을 이용하여 수동태 문장을 완성하세요.

01. _____ (in 1920, this house, built)

02. _____ (the office, clean, yesterday)

03. _____ (hundreds of people, injure, in the accident)

04. _____ (my car, steal, a few days ago)

05. _____ (soccer, play, in most countries of the world)

06. _____ (how many languages, speak, in Canada)

Challenge 2 밑줄 친 동사를 자동사와 타동사로 구별하고, 수동태가 가능한 문장은 바꿔 쓰세요.

| 보기 | Kevin <u>broke</u> the window. | → | _____타동사_____ |
| | → *The window was broken by Kevin.* | | |

01. We <u>stayed</u> in a hotel. → _____

→ _____

02. An accident <u>happened</u> at the corner of Third and Main. → _____

→ _____

03. The president of the company <u>conducted</u> the interview. → _____

→ _____

04. Research scientists will <u>discover</u> a cure for AIDS someday. → _____

→ _____

1-3 4형식과 5형식 동사의 수동태

I gave Jane a new calendar.
나는 Jane에게 새 달력을 주었다.
→ **Jane** was given a new calendar by me.
  Jane은 내게 새 달력을 받았다.
→ **A new calendar** was given to Jane by me.
  새 달력이 나에 의해서 Jane에게 주어졌다.

01 목적어가 두 개인 **4형식 문장**은 **2개의 수동태 문장이 가능**하다. 주로 사람을 나타내는 간접목적어를 주어로 사용하고, 직접목적어가 수동태의 주어가 되는 경우 대부분의 수여동사는 간접목적어 앞에 to를 쓴다. 하지만 buy, make, get, find, build는 for를 쓴다. 영국식 영어에서는 to나 for를 생략한다.

I gave her a gold ring.
나는 그녀에게 금반지를 주었다.

→ **She** was given a gold ring by me.
→ **A gold ring** was given **to** her by me.

My mother bought me the scarf.
엄마가 내게 그 스카프를 사주셨다.

→ **The scarf** was bought **for** me by my mother.

02 buy, make, write, cook, read, sell, send, hand, explain, suggest는 **직접목적어만을 주어로 하여 수동태**를 만든다. 간접목적어를 주어로 쓰면 어색한 문장이 된다.

I sold him **my old car** for $500. 나는 그에게 내 헌 차를 500달러에 팔았다.

→ **My old car** was sold to him for $500. 내 헌 차가 그에게 500달러에 팔렸다.

He explained **the history of the building** to us. 그는 우리에게 그 건물의 내력에 대해 설명했다.

→ **The history of the building** was explained to us. 그 건물의 내력이 우리에게 설명되었다.

→ We were explained the history of the building by him. (×)

※ explain, suggest는 3형식으로만 사용되는 동사여서 간접목적어가 없고, 따라서 (직접)목적어만을 주어로 수동태를 만든다.

03 **5형식 문장**을 수동태로 만들 때 **목적어가 한 개이므로 목적어를 주어**로 쓰고, 목적격 보어인 명사, 형용사, 분사, to부정사 등은 「be동사+p.p」 뒤에 그대로 이어서 쓴다.

Her parents made **her** a doctor. 그녀의 부모는 그녀를 의사로 만들었다.

→ **She** was made a doctor by her parents.

You must keep **the door** closed. 너는 그 문을 닫아두어야 한다.

→ **The door** must be kept closed (by you).

The teacher allowed **me** to go home. 선생님은 내가 집에 가는 걸 허락했다.

→ **I** was allowed to go home by the teacher.

We saw John **walk** with the actress at the park. 우리는 John이 그 여배우와 공원에서 걷고 있는 것을 보았다.

→ John was seen **to walk** with the actress at the park.

※ 지각동사나 사역동사가 쓰인 5형식 문장에서 목적격 보어인 동사원형은 수동태로 전환될 때 to부정사로 바뀐다.

서술형 기초다지기

정답 p. 10

Challenge 1 다음 문장을 한 가지 또는 두 가지 형태의 수동태로 만드세요.

01. They gave Kathy the Best Actress award.
    - →
    - →

02. My father bought me this birthday cake.
    - →
    - →

03. The teacher explained the topic to the children.
    - →
    - →

04. The waitress showed me the bill.
    - →
    - →

Challenge 2 다음 5형식 문장을 수동태로 바꿔 써 보세요.

01. I saw her dancing like a mad person.
    - →

02. They elected him their leader.
    - →

03. The doctor made me stop smoking.
    - →

04. She always makes me happy.
    - →

05. The manager forced us to work over time everyday.
    - →

1-4 조동사의 수동태 / 준동사의 수동태 / get+p.p.

Animals in danger should be protected.
위험에 처한 동물들은 보호되어야 한다.

I don't like to be punished.
나는 벌 받는 것을 좋아하지 않는다.

01 조동사 뒤에는 동사원형을 써야 하므로 be동사의 원형인 be를 그대로 써서 「조동사+be+p.p.」로 수동태를 만든다.

This homework **must be finished** by tomorrow. 이 숙제는 내일까지 끝마쳐져야 한다.

The room **will be cleaned** later. 그 방은 나중에 청소될 것이다.

The same mistake **should not be made** again. 똑같은 실수가 다시는 있어선 안 된다.

02 to부정사의 to 뒤에는 동사원형(be)이 와야 하므로 **부정사의 수동태는** 「to be+p.p.」의 형태로 수동태를 만든다.

We started **to respect** her. 우리는 그녀를 존경하기 시작했다.

→ She started **to be respected** (by us). 그녀는 우리에게 존경받기 시작했다.

I hope **to be selected** for the school soccer team. 나는 학교 축구팀에 선발되기를 희망한다.

03 수동태는 「be동사+p.p.」 형태이고 **be동사의 동명사형은 being이므로, 동명사의 수동태는** 「being+p.p.」이다.

I hate **being treated** like a child. 나는 어린애처럼 취급받는 것이 싫다.

Loving is more precious than **being loved**. 사랑하는 것은 사랑받는 것보다 더 귀중하다.

She doesn't like **being asked** to make a speech. 그녀는 연설해 달라는 요청을 받는 걸 싫어한다.

04 수동태(be동사+p.p.)에서 be동사 대신 get을 쓰기도 하는데 주로 대화체에서 **계획되지 않았거나 예상치 못한 일, 그리고 불공평한 행위를 강조**하기 위해 사용한다.

Our dog **got run** over by a car. 우리 개가 자동차에 치었다. ▶ 뜻밖의 사고

She **got awarded** a big prize. 그녀는 큰 상을 받았다. ▶ 예상치 못한 일

He has misgivings about **getting fired**. 그는 해고당할 것을 불안해 하고 있다.

※ 위 모든 상황에 get 대신 be동사를 써도 상관없다.

서술형 기초다지기

정답 p. 10

Challenge 1 · 다음 문장을 수동태 문장으로 바꾸어 쓰세요.

01. We should save energy.

→ _____

02. Someone must fix our car before we leave for Seattle.

→ _____

03. Will Kevin sing the national anthem in the opening ceremony?

→ _____

04. We should recycle bottles and paper.

→ _____

05. If the river floods, water could destroy the village.

→ _____

Challenge 2 · 다음 괄호 안의 표현 중 알맞은 것을 고르세요.

01. Go to a fairly quiet place where you are not likely to (disturb / be disturbed).

02. I wanted the project (to finish / to be finished) by Monday.

03. If I were a genius, I would not mind (being treated / treating) like one.

04. I stopped (to be smoked / to smoke) and found out I had no lighter.

05. The thief was afraid of (seeing / being seen) by the police.

Challenge 3 · 〈보기〉의 단어 중 알맞은 것을 골라 「get+p.p.」의 문장으로 빈칸을 채우세요.

보기				
	ask	irritate	break	hurt

01. The vase _____ when I bumped into the table.

02. She _____ when the subway is late.

03. There was a fight at the party, but nobody _____.

04. People always want to know what my job is. I often _____ that question.

1-5 동사구의 수동태 / 명사절 목적어의 수동태

The poor girl was laughed at by her.
그 불쌍한 소녀는 그녀에 의해 비웃음을 당했다.

It is said that stress causes 99% of all illnesses.
스트레스는 모든 질병의 99%를 야기시킨다고 한다.

01 동사에 부사나 전치사가 이어져 하나의 동사 역할을 하는 것을 동사구라고 한다. 이때 동사구가 있는 문장은 **동사구를 하나의 동사처럼 취급하여 동사만 「be동사+p.p.」로 고치고 부사나 전치사는 그대로 쓴다.**

A car **ran over** my puppy yesterday. 자동차가 어제 내 강아지를 치었다.

→ My puppy **was run over** by a car yesterday. 내 강아지는 어제 자동차에 치였다.

The children **looked up to** the teacher. 그 아이들은 그 선생님을 존경했다.

→ The teacher **was looked up to** by the children. 그 선생님은 아이들에 의해 존경을 받았다.

※ 수동태로 자주 쓰이는 동사구

do away with : ~을 제거하다   catch up with : ~을 따라 잡다   put up with : ~을 참다

take care of(=look after) : ~을 돌보다   depend/rely on : ~을 신뢰하다   run over : (차가) ~을 치다

pay attention to : ~에 주의를 기울이다

02 목적어가 명사절일 경우, **가주어 it을 사용하여 수동태**로 만든다. that절 안의 주어를 문장의 주어로 써서 수동태를 만들 경우 **that절 안의 동사는 to부정사로 바뀐다.**

Many people **believe that** music **is** art. 많은 사람들이 음악은 예술이라고 믿는다.

→ **It is believed** that music **is** art.

→ Music is believed **to be** art. ▶ that절 안의 주어를 문장의 주어로 쓴 경우 be동사(is)는 to be로 쓴다.

We **expect that** the strike will **end** soon. 우리는 파업이 곧 끝날 것이라고 예상합니다.

→ **It is expected** that the strike will **end** soon.

→ The strike is expected **to end** soon.

They **say** that he **was** a brave soldier as a young man. 그는 젊은 시절 용감한 군인이었다고 사람들이 말한다.

→ It is said that he **was** a brave soldier as a young man.

→ He is said **to have been** a brave soldier as a young man.

※ 주절의 시제보다 앞선 시제일 경우 완료부정사 「to have+p.p.」를 쓴다.

서술형 기초다지기

정답 p. 10

Challenge 1 다음 문장을 수동태로 바꾸어 쓰세요.

01. People laughed at him.

→ _____

02. My sister looked after the dog.

→ _____

03. She takes good care of my baby.

→ _____

04. A foreign company took over our bank.

→ _____

Challenge 2 다음 문장을 It ~ that과 that절의 주어를 문장 전체 주어로 하는 두 개의 수동태로 완성하시오.

> 보기
>
> Everyone knows that she believes in ghosts.
> → *It is known that she believes in ghosts.*
> → *She is known to believe in ghosts.*

01. They say that she is a very sincere person.

→ _____

→ _____

02. People believe that the politician took a bribe.

→ _____

→ _____

03. They believe that the company will lose money this year.

→ _____

→ _____

1-6 by 이외의 전치사를 쓰는 수동태

The Seoul Tower **is** well **known to** the tourists.
서울타워는 여행객들에게 잘 알려져 있다.

01 수동태에서 행위자를 나타낼 때 '**by**' **이외의 다른 전치사가 쓰이는 경우**가 많으니 숙어처럼 외워두는 게 좋다.

She **is interested in** painting. 그녀는 그림에 흥미가 있다.

Water **is composed of** hydrogen and oxygen. 물은 수소와 산소로 이루어져 있다.

She **is satisfied with** her mediocre income. 그녀는 평범한 수입에 만족하고 있다.

※기타 수동태의 관용적 표현

be covered with : ~로 뒤덮이다	be married to : ~와 결혼하다
be filled with : ~로 가득 차 있다	be involved in : ~와 관련이 있다
be based on : ~에 근거를 두다	be known to : ~에게 알려져 있다
be known for : ~로 유명하다	be known as : ~로서 알려져 있다
be known by : ~을 보면 알 수 있다	be concerned about : ~에 대해 걱정하다
be occupied with/in : ~에 종사하다	be engaged in : ~에 종사하다
be devoted to : ~에 헌신하다, 전념하다	be absorbed/lost in : ~에 몰두하다, 열중하다
be made of : ~로 만들어지다 (모양만 바뀜)	be made from : ~로 만들어지다 (성질이 바뀜)

02 수동태로 자주 쓰이는 표현

The author **was born in** 1975. 그 저자는 1975년에 태어났다.

Our hotel **is located on** a beautiful lake. 우리 호텔은 아름다운 호수변에 위치하고 있다.

The square **is crowded with** people. 그 광장은 사람들로 붐빈다.

When the accident happened, many people **were injured**. 사고가 발생했을 때, 많은 사람들이 다쳤다.

03 **형태는 능동태이지만 수동태의 의미를 나타낼 수 있다.** 이 경우에는 보통 well, easily 등의 부사(구)를 수반한다.

These books still **sell** well. 이 책들은 여전히 잘 팔린다.

"A Brief History of Time" by Stephen Hawking **reads** well. 스티븐 호킹의 "시간의 역사"는 잘 읽힌다.

Jeju oranges **peel** well. 제주 감귤은 껍질이 잘 벗겨진다.

Who is to **blame**(=to be blamed) for the accident? 그 사고로 인해 비난받아야 할 사람은 누구인가?

This material doesn't **dye** well. 이 재료는 염색이 잘 안 된다.

This bread doesn't **cut** easily. 이 빵은 쉽게 잘라지지 않는다.

서술형 기초다지기

정답 p. 10

Challenge 1 다음 빈칸에 들어갈 알맞은 말을 〈보기〉에서 골라 쓰세요.

보기					
	with	about	to	of	in

01. This chair is made _____ iron.

02. The professor is devoted _____ astronomy.

03. You should be satisfied _____ what you have.

04. I'm interested _____ English and mathematics.

05. She is concerned _____ the results of the examination.

Challenge 2 다음 괄호 안의 단어를 이용하여 수동태 문장이 되도록 빈칸을 완성하세요.

01. She was not very _____ _____ the service in the restaurant. (satisfy)

02. Paper is _____ _____ wood and other things. (make)

03. Many people are very _____ _____ the destruction of the rainforests. (concern)

04. She seems to have got _____ _____ the man against her will. (marry)

Challenge 3 다음 우리말과 뜻이 같도록 빈칸에 알맞은 수동태 표현을 만드세요.

01. 우리 학교는 축구팀이 유명하다.

→ Our school _____ _____ _____ its soccer team.

02. 그 캐나다 작가는 한국사람들에게 알려져 있지 않다.

→ That Canadian writer is not _____ _____ Koreans.

03. 탁자 위에 있는 지갑은 가죽으로 만들어졌다.

→ The wallet on the table _____ _____ _____ leather.

04. 와인은 포도로 만들어진다.

→ Wine _____ _____ _____ grapes.

01 출제 100 % - 동작을 하느냐 당하느냐 그것이 문제로다!

 출제자의 눈 능동태 문장을 주고 수동태로 고치는 문제를 집중적으로 출제한다. 3형식 문장은 물론이고 4형식과 5형식 문장도 수동태로 고치는 연습을 충분히 해두어야 한다. 문장의 빈칸에 능동태 문장이 와야 할지 수동태 문장이 와야 할지 고르는 문제를 출제할 수도 있다. 동사의 대상인 목적어가 없거나, by와 같은 단어가 뒤에 따라오면 수동태임을 의심해 봐야 한다.

Ex 1.

다음 문장을 수동태로 바꿀 때 빈칸에 알맞은 말을 쓰시오.
The teacher allowed her to go home.
→ _____ home by the teacher.

02 출제 100 % - 능동태의 시제에 따라 be동사의 시제와 수의 일치를 점검하라!

 출제자의 눈 진행, 완료, 미래시제를 수동태로 고칠 때 목적어가 주어로 이동하므로 목적어에 따라 be동사를 결정해야 한다. 또한 조동사가 있는 수동태를 고치거나 동사구를 수동태로 고칠 때 실수하지 않도록 조심해야 한다. 수동태로 쓸 수 없는 자동사 belong to, (dis)appear, seem, look, remain, suffer from, happen, occur, take place는 수동으로 해석되어 수동태로 착각하기 쉬우나 모두 자동사여서 수동태로 쓸 수 없다. 이를 be+V-ed로 바꿔 놓고 틀린 것을 고르는 문제가 수능, 토익, 텝스에서도 출제된다. 특히, consist of(~로 구성되다)는 자동사여서 be consisted(X)로 쓸 수 없기 때문에 이를 수동태로 고칠 때는 타동사 make up of(~로 구성하다)의 수동태인 be made up of(=be composed of)로 써야 한다. die(자동사), kill(타동사)의 수동태는 be killed로 쓴다.

Ex 2.

다음을 수동태 문장으로 바꿀 때 빈칸에 알맞은 말을 쓰시오.
Kevin will put off the schedule of the wedding.
→ The schedule of the wedding _____ by Kevin.

Ex 3.

Water _____ hydrogen and oxygen.
(a) is consisted of   (b) consists   (c) is made up of

03 출제 100 % - 명사절, 부정사, 동명사가 수동의 의미로 쓰일 경우

 출제자의 눈 목적어가 명사절인 경우 it ~ that 또는 that절 안의 주어를 문장의 주어로 하여 수동태로 고칠 수 있다. 이중에서 that절 안의 주어를 문장의 주어로 쓸 경우에 that절의 동사는 반드시 'to부정사'로 고치는 것을 잊지 말아야 한다. to부정사의 수동태는 「to be+p.p.」나 「to have been+p.p.」(본동사보다 시제가 앞설 경우)를 쓴다. 동명사의 수동태(being+p.p.)의 경우 과거분사(p.p.) 대신 명사나 동사원형을 써 놓고 틀린 것을 고르라는 문제가 나온다. 특히, 전치사 뒤에 동명사의 수동태가 올 때는 「전치사+being+p.p.」의 형태임에 유의하자.

Ex 4.

제시된 주어로 시작하는 수동태를 완성하시오.
They say that she works 12 hours a day.
→ She _____.

Ex 5.

Having received over eighty percent of the vote, she became the first woman _____ as a mayor in Korea.
(a) to elect   (b) to have been elected   (c) to be elected

04 출제 100 % - by 이외의 전치사, 4형식의 수동태, 지각/사역동사의 수동태

 출제자의 눈 수동태라고 하여 행위자를 나타낼 때 무조건 전치사 by를 쓰지 않는다. 표현에 따라 by 대신 at 또는 in과 같은 전치사를 쓸 수 있다는 것을 알아두자. 4형식을 수동태로 고칠 때 직접목적어를 주어로 할 경우 간접목적어 앞에 대부분 전치사 'to'를 쓰지만 buy, make, get, find, build와 같은 동사는 전치사 to 대신 'for'를 사용할 줄 아는지 물어본다. 특히, 사역동사나 지각동사를 수동태로 만들 경우 목적격 보어 자리에 있던 원형동사는 to부정사로 바뀐다는 사실도 반드시 알아두자.

Ex 6.

제시된 주어로 시작하는 수동태를 완성하시오.
The teacher made us finish our homework.
→ We _____.

[1-2] 다음 빈칸에 들어갈 알맞은 것을 고르시오.

1.

> This present was bought _____ me by my father.

❶ at ❷ to ❸ by
❹ for ❺ with

2.

> Spanish _____ in most Latin American countries.

❶ speaks ❷ spoke
❸ is speaking ❹ will be spoken
❺ is spoken

3. 다음 중 밑줄 친 부분이 어법상 틀린 것은?

❶ Koreans are taught not to smoke in front of elder people.
❷ Ice cream was brought by him yesterday.
❸ Someone was seen by Mary near the window.
❹ To be honest, I was watching TV last night.
❺ Left-handed people are not consider normal in this country.

4. 다음 빈칸에 들어갈 말이 알맞게 짝지어진 것은?

> Animals are _____ killed for quick money.
> Five books have _____ sold for a week.

❶ having – being ❷ had – been
❸ having – had ❹ been – being
❺ being – been

5. 다음 밑줄 친 부분 중 그 쓰임이 어색한 것은?

❶ Water is composed of hydrogen and oxygen.
❷ The mountain was covered in much snow.
❸ Sunny was satisfied with the result.
❹ What kind of car are you interested in?
❺ She seems to have got married to the man against her will.

6. 수동태로 바꿀 때 다음 빈칸에 알맞은 말을 쓰시오.

> We must not throw waste from factories into the sea.
> → Waste from factories _____ _____ _____ _____ into the sea.

7. 수동태로 바꿀 때 다음 빈칸에 알맞은 것은?

> They will send a letter to my parents.
> → A letter _____ to my parents by them.

❶ was send ❷ will send
❸ is sent ❹ will be sent
❺ will be sending

8. 다음 중 수동태로 잘못 고친 문장을 고르시오.

❶ The teller at the bank gave Jane a new calendar.
  =A new calendar was given to Jane by the teller at the bank.
❷ The doctor made me take a rest in the sick room.
  =I was made to take a rest in the sick room by the doctor.
❸ His father bought the boy a Nintendo DS.
  =The boy was bought a Nintendo DS by his father.
❹ We can see stars at night.
  =Stars can be seen at night.
❺ He is reading a book.
  =A book is being read by him.

오답 노트 만들기

★틀린 문제 : _____ ★다시 공부한 날 : _____

(1) 문제를 왜? 틀렸는지 곰곰이 생각하고 그 이유를 적어본다.

(2) 핵심 개념을 적는다.

(3) 자신이 몰랐던 단어와 숙어 표현이 있으면 정리한다.

(4) 해설집에서 필요한 부분을 골라 풀이 해법을 정리한다.

★틀린 문제 : _____ ★다시 공부한 날 : _____

(1) 문제를 왜? 틀렸는지 곰곰이 생각하고 그 이유를 적어본다.

(2) 핵심 개념을 적는다.

(3) 자신이 몰랐던 단어와 숙어 표현이 있으면 정리한다.

(4) 해설집에서 필요한 부분을 골라 풀이 해법을 정리한다.

★틀린 문제 : _____ ★다시 공부한 날 : _____

(1) 문제를 왜? 틀렸는지 곰곰이 생각하고 그 이유를 적어본다.

(2) 핵심 개념을 적는다.

(3) 자신이 몰랐던 단어와 숙어 표현이 있으면 정리한다.

(4) 해설집에서 필요한 부분을 골라 풀이 해법을 정리한다.

★틀린 문제 : _____ ★다시 공부한 날 : _____

(1) 문제를 왜? 틀렸는지 곰곰이 생각하고 그 이유를 적어본다.

(2) 핵심 개념을 적는다.

(3) 자신이 몰랐던 단어와 숙어 표현이 있으면 정리한다.

(4) 해설집에서 필요한 부분을 골라 풀이 해법을 정리한다.

1. 다음을 수동태 문장으로 바꾸었을 때 어법상 <u>틀린</u> 것은?

   ❶ Elise asked me to clean the kitchen.
   → I was asked to clean the kitchen by Elise.
   ❷ The dentist instructed my daughter to brush her teeth well.
   → My daughter was instructed to brush her teeth well by the dentist.
   ❸ The manager forced us to work over time everyday.
   → We were forced to work over time everyday by the manager.
   ❹ I often heard Tom play the piano.
   → Tom was often heard play the piano by me.
   ❺ My sister gave me a wallet for Christmas.
   → I was given a wallet by my sister for Christmas.

   오답노트

2. 다음 문장을 수동태로 바꿀 때 빈칸에 적절한 표현은?

   They are teaching Taekwondo in an increasing number of high schools.
   → Taekwondo _____ in an increasing number of high schools.

   ❶ will be taught   ❷ will teach
   ❸ are teaching   ❹ is being taught
   ❺ is been teach

   오답노트

3. 다음 괄호 안의 단어를 빈칸에 넣을 때 올바른 형태는?

   He _____ go into the movie theater yesterday. (see)

   ❶ saw   ❷ was seen
   ❸ was seen to   ❹ can be seen to
   ❺ is seeing to

   오답노트

4. 다음 중 어법상 <u>잘못된</u> 문장은?

   ❶ Her life was thrown into the unknown.
   ❷ She was glad to have been called into the meeting by her boss.
   ❸ This is the first one to be called a computer.
   ❹ Wilson was taken by his parents care of.
   ❺ She was called a big mouth.

   오답노트

5. 다음 문장을 수동태로 바꿀 때 빈칸에 알맞은 말을 쓰시오.

   They believe that she is very rich.
   → She _____ very rich.

   오답노트

6. 다음 빈칸에 들어갈 말이 바르게 짝지어진 것은?

· Calcutta, India, is known _____ many people as the home of Mother Teresa.
· The glasses were filled _____ water, each one at a different level.

❶ of − from
❷ with − to
❸ to − with
❹ in − at
❺ at − with

오답노트

9. 다음 글의 밑줄 친 부분 중 쓰임이 틀린 것은?

Long ago it ❶ was not so easy to get books as it is today, for they ❷ were all writing by hand. When you ❸ remember how long you take ❹ to write a page or even a line, you ❺ will understand how much patience and toil went to the making of books.

오답노트

7. 다음 두 문장의 뜻이 같도록 빈칸을 채우시오.

The school will hold the Arts Festival in April.
= The Arts Festival _____ _____ _____ by the school in April.

오답노트

[10-11] 다음 빈칸에 알맞은 단어를 쓰시오.

10. Wine _____ grapes.
(와인은 포도로 만들어진다.)

11. He _____ everyone in the town.
(그는 그 마을의 모든 사람에게 알려져 있다.)

오답노트

8. 다음 빈칸에 들어갈 말이 바르게 짝지어진 것은?

· Some advice was offered _____ him by me.
· Sunny asked a question _____ Wilson.
· The MP3 player was bought _____ Kathy by her boyfriend.

❶ for − of − to
❷ to − for − of
❸ for − to − of
❹ of − to − for
❺ to − of − for

오답노트

12. 다음 문장을 수동태로 고칠 때 올바른 것은?

What do you call the car in English?

❶ What did you called the car in English?
❷ What were you called the car in English?
❸ What are you called the car in English?
❹ What was the car called in English?
❺ What is the car called in English?

오답노트

13. 다음 문장을 수동태로 바꾸어 쓰시오.

My mother has baked the cherry cake.
→ The cherry cake _____
by my mother.

오답노트

14. 다음 문장을 수동태로 바르게 바꾼 것은?

Wilson has not seen her since last year.

❶ She did not seen by Wilson since last
year.

❷ She did not been seen by Wilson since
last year.

❸ She was not been seen by Wilson since
last year.

❹ She had not been seen by Wilson since
last year.

❺ She has not been seen by Wilson since
last year.

오답노트

15. 다음 각 문장을 수동태로 바꾼 것 중 바르지 <u>못한</u>
것은?

❶ They put off the game because of the
rain.
→ The game was put off because of the
rain.

❷ Everyone looked forward to the game.
→ The game was looked forward to by
everyone.

❸ We heard the ghost sing a song.
→ The ghost was heard to sing a song
by us.

❹ Mr. Rice is teaching our class today.
→ Our class is being taught by Mr. Rice
today.

❺ Someone must send this letter
immediately.
→ This letter must sent immediately.

오답노트

16. 다음 문장을 수동태로 <u>잘못</u> 바꾼 것은?

❶ Should the government control cell
phone use?
→ Should cell phone use be controlled by
the government?

❷ People speak English in New Zealand.
→ English is spoken in New Zealand.

❸ Everybody knows the fact.
→ The fact is known to everybody.

❹ They say that she is a famous actress.
→ She is said to be a famous actress.

❺ The teacher made the students memorize
a lot of English words.
→ The students were made memorize a
lot of English words by the teacher.

오답노트

17. 다음 문장을 수동태로 바꿀 때 어법상 틀린 것은?

❶ Wilson cannot finish the project in time.
→ The project cannot be finished in time by Wilson.

❷ World War I made Coca-Cola popular outside the US.
→ Coca-Cola was made popular outside the US by World War I.

❸ They have performed the play many times.
→ The play has been performed many times.

❹ All the students in the classroom look up to the teacher.
→ The teacher is looked up to by all the students in the classroom.

❺ Somebody saw you talking on the phone.
→ You were seen to talking on the phone.

오답노트

[18-19] 다음 글을 읽고 물음에 답하시오.

Chopsticks ❶ were developed about 5,000 years ago in China. People ❷ cooked their food in large pots, and hasty eaters then broke tiny branches off trees to pick out the hot food. By 400 B.C., food was chopped into small pieces so ❸ it could cook quickly. The pieces of food were small enough that knives ❹ were not needed at the dinner table. People ❺ were advised to use chopsticks instead of knives at the table because knives would remind them of killing animals. By A.D. 500, chopstick use had spread to other countries.

18. 다음 젓가락에 관한 설명 중 윗글의 내용과 일치하는 것을 고르시오.

❶ 초기에는 동물의 뼈로 만들었다.
❷ 뜨거운 음식을 집는 데 사용하였다.
❸ 한때 왕족과 귀족들만 사용하였다.
❹ 고기 요리를 대접할 때 사용하였다.
❺ 사냥 도구로도 사용하였다.

오답노트

19. 윗글의 밑줄 친 부분 중 어법상 틀린 것은?

_____

오답노트

20. 다음 문장을 어법상 바르게 고친 것은?

The Japanese say that Dokdo is part of Korea.

❶ Dokdo is being said to be part of Korea.
❷ Dokdo is said to be part of Korea.
❸ Part of Korea is said to be Dokdo by the Japanese.
❹ The Japanese are said that Dokdo is part of Korea.
❺ Korea says that Dokdo is parted of the Japanese.

오답노트

_A._ 다음 문장을 수동태로 고쳐 다시 쓰시오.

1. Mr. Kevin is teaching our class today.

→ Our class _____ by Mr. Kevin today.

2. Someone must send this letter immediately.

→ This letter _____ immediately.

3. Somebody has cleaned the room.

→ The room _____ .

4. I didn't realize that somebody was recording our conversation.

→ I didn't realize that _____ .

5. People cannot control the weather.

→ The weather _____ .

_B._ 괄호 안의 표현을 사용하여 다음 대화를 완성하시오. (단, 수동태 문장으로 완성할 것)

1. A: Who invented the telephone? (Alexander Graham Bell)

B: _____

2. A: Who designed the Eiffel Tower? (Gustave Eiffel)

B: _____

3. A: How often is the office cleaned? (every day)

B: _____

실전 서술형 평가문제

정답 p. 12

 출제의도 be + 과거분사
평가내용 실생활에서 수동태 문장 활용하기

A. 사진의 내용과 일치하도록 주어진 표현을 이용하여 수동태 문장을 만드시오.　　[서술형 유형 : 8점 / 난이도 : 중하]

1.

(cook / Nancy)

2.

(wash / Scott)

3.

(clean / the children)

4.

(water / Tiffany)

1. Lunch _____ .

2. The bus _____ .

3. The room _____ .

4. The flowers _____ .

실전 서술형 평가문제

출제의도 be+과거분사
평가내용 수동태로 문장 전환하기

B. 〈보기〉와 같이 수동태가 가능한 문장은 수동태로 고치고 수동태로 고칠 수 없는 문장에는 "No change"라고 쓰시오.

[서술형 유형 : 14점 / 난이도 : 중상]

보기	 German immigrants introduced the hamburger to the United States. → *The hamburger was introduced to the United States by German immigrants.*

1. People believe that the word "hamburger" appeared in 1834 on the menu of Delmonico's restaurant in New York.

→ _____

2. The McDonald brothers opened the first McDonald's restaurant in California in 1949.

→ _____

3. The restaurant served only three things: hamburgers, French fries, and milkshakes.

→ _____

4. Ray Kroc bought the restaurant.

→ _____

5. Since then, the company has opened over 25,000 McDonald's restaurants around the world.

→ _____

6. People eat more than 40 million hamburgers every day.

→ _____

7. Ray Kroc became a millionaire.

→ _____

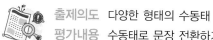 출제의도 다양한 형태의 수동태
평가내용 수동태로 문장 전환하기

C. 다음 문장을 수동태는 능동태로, 능동태는 수동태로 바꿔 쓰시오.　　　　[서술형 유형 : 16점 / 난이도 : 중하]

1. You can use a dictionary during the test.

→ _____

2. Your phone bill must be paid.

→ _____

3. People have seen the president on TV many times.

→ _____

4. You are not allowed by the teacher to use your books during a test.

→ _____

5. When are wedding gifts opened by the bride and groom?

→ _____

6. People expect you to learn English in the U.S.

→ _____

7. You have been told by the teacher to write a composition.

→ _____

8. We think that the prisoner escaped by climbing over a wall.

→ _____

출제의도 미래를 나타내는 수동태
평가내용 be going to로 수동태 서술하기

D. 다음 그림을 보고 〈보기〉와 같이 'be going to'를 이용한 수동태 문장을 만드시오.

[서술형 유형 : 10점 / 난이도 : 중]

보기	driver / take / to hospital → *The driver is going to be taken to hospital.*

1. car / repair / ?

_____

2. witnesses / interview / the police / ?

_____

3. the people / rescue / firefighters

_____

4. cars / remove

_____

5. the fire / put out

_____

서술형 평가문제	채 점 기 준	배 점	나의 점수
A	표현이 올바르고 문법, 철자가 모두 정확한 경우	2점×4문항=8점	
B		2점×7문항=14점	
C		2점×8문항=16점	
D		2점×5문항=10점	
공통	문법, 철자가 1개씩 틀린 경우	각 문항당 1점씩 감점	
	내용과 전혀 일치하지 않거나 답을 기재하지 못한 경우	0점	

Chapter 4

접속사 (Conjunctions)

Unit 01 등위접속사

1-1 and, but, or, so

We stayed at home **and** watched TV.
우리는 집에 있으면서 TV를 봤어.

It started to rain, **so** she opened her umbrella.
비가 오기 시작해서 그녀는 우산을 폈다.

01 접속사는 형태와 기능이 같은 **단어와 단어, 구와 구, 그리고 문장(절)과 문장(절)을 연결시켜 주는 역할**을 한다. 등위접속사 and(~와, 그리고), but(그러나, 하지만), or(또는, 혹은)은 단어와 구, 절을 대등하게 연결한다. 두 단어를 연결할 때는 쉼표(,)를 쓰지 않지만 세 개 이상의 단어를 연결할 때는 각 단어 뒤와 접속사 앞에 쉼표를 써준다.

Wilson puts milk, sugar, **and** lemon in his tea. Wilson은 그의 차에 우유, 설탕 그리고 레몬을 넣는다.
We all enjoyed singing **and** dancing at the party. 우리는 모두 파티에서 노래와 춤을 즐겼다.
Do you want iced tea **or** hot tea? 차가운 차를 드실래요, 뜨거운 차를 드실래요?

02 문장(절)과 문장(절)을 연결할 때는 접속사 앞에 쉼표를 쓴다. 단, 앞 문장이 짧은 경우에는 쉼표를 쓰지 않아도 좋다.

We can go fishing, **or** we can just stay home. 우리는 낚시하러 가거나 그냥 집에 있어도 된다.
He is poor **but** she is rich. 그는 가난하지만 그녀는 부자다.
A doctor can prescribe medicine, **but** a nurse cannot prescribe medicine.
의사는 약을 처방할 수 있지만, 간호사는 약을 처방할 수 없다.

03 등위접속사 so(=therefore 그래서), for(=because 왜냐하면), yet(=but 그러나)은 **문장과 문장만 연결**시키며, 접속사 앞에 항상 쉼표를 쓴다. so는 앞 문장의 동작이나 생각의 결과를 나타낸다.

I was tired, **so** I went to bed early. 나는 피곤해서 일찍 잠을 잤다.
　원인　　　　　　　결과
They don't like him, **for** he lies too much. 그들은 그가 거짓말을 너무 많이 하기 때문에 그를 싫어한다.
He was my close friend, **yet** he wouldn't help me. 그는 내 절친한 친구였지만 나를 도우려 하지 않았다.

서술형 기초다지기

Challenge 1 다음 빈칸에 and, but 또는 or 중 알맞은 것을 쓰세요.

> **보기** I washed my shirt, *but* it didn't get clean.

01. We need to eat fruit _____ vegetables for good health.

02. Would you like some water _____ some fruit juice?

03. I've studied English for ten years, _____ I can't speak English very well.

04. I bought some paper, a greeting card, _____ some envelopes.

05. Soccer _____ baseball are popular sports.

06. Which would you prefer? Would you like to play tennis _____ basketball Saturday morning?

Challenge 2 다음 문장을 읽고 빈칸에 so, for, yet 중 알맞은 것을 쓰세요.

01. My stomachache got really bad, _____ I took some medicine for it.

02. He is a kindhearted man, _____ it is strange that no one specially likes him.

03. We can go to the movies, _____ we have no classes today.

Challenge 3 다음 빈칸에 접속사 but 또는 so 중 알맞은 것을 쓰세요.

01. It began to rain, _____ he opened his umbrella.

02. It began to rain, _____ he didn't open his umbrella.

03. My friend lied to me, _____ I still like and trust her.

04. My friend lied to me, _____ I don't trust her anymore.

05. The weather was cold, _____ we didn't go fishing.

06. The weather was cold, _____ we went fishing anyway.

Unit 02 상관접속사

2-1 상관접속사의 종류

She is from Korea. I am from Korea.
→ **Both** she **and** I are from Korea.
그녀와 저는 둘 다 한국인이에요.

01 **both A and B : 'A와 B 둘 다(부가 additive)'**의 뜻으로 주어 자리에 쓸 때 동사의 수는 복수형으로 쓴다.

Both Eric **and** his wife are coming here. Eric과 그의 아내가 여기에 오고 있다.
Both whales **and** humans are mammals. 고래와 사람은 둘 다 포유동물이다.

02 **either A or B : 'A와 B 둘 중에 하나(양자택일 alternative)'**의 뜻이다. 주어 자리에 쓸 때 동사의 수는 B에 일치시켜야 한다.

Either bus **or** taxi **is** available from the airport. 공항에서 버스 또는 택시 이용이 가능하다.
Kathy is now **either** in London **or** in Paris. Kathy는 지금 런던이나 파리 중 어느 한 곳에 있다.

03 **neither A nor B : 'A도 B도 ~아닌(양자부정 negative)'**의 뜻으로 주어 자리에 쓸 때 동사의 수는 B에 일치시켜야 한다. 「not ~ either A or B」로 바꿔 쓸 수 있다.

Jack **neither** knows her **nor** wants to get to know her.
Jack은 그녀를 알지도 못하고, 알게 되기를 원하지도 않는다.

Neither Mary **nor** her bother **is** going to come tonight. Mary도 그녀의 오빠도 오늘 밤에 오지 않을 것이다.
=**Not either** Mary **or** her brother **is** going to come tonight.

04 **not only A but (also) B : 'A뿐만 아니라 B도(B를 강조)'**의 뜻이다. 주어 자리에 쓸 때 동사의 수는 B에 일치시켜야 한다. also를 생략하고 but만 쓰는 경우도 많으며 'B as well as A'와 같은 의미이다.

Comfortable living conditions include **not only** chemical and physical cleanliness, **but also** privacy. 안락한 삶의 조건이란 화학적이고 물리적인 청결함뿐만 아니라 개인의 사생활도 포함된다.
She is **not only** smart **but (also)** lovely. 그녀는 영리할 뿐만 아니라 사랑스럽기까지 하다.
=She is lovely **as well as** smart.

05 **not A but B : 'A가 아니라 B'**란 뜻으로 B에 수를 일치시킨다.

Wilson goes to the library **not** to study **but** to sleep. Wilson은 도서관에 공부하러 가는 것이 아니라 자러 간다.
Do **not** hate her, **but** try to understand her. 그녀를 미워하지 마라, 오히려 그녀를 이해하려고 노력해라.

서술형 기초다지기

정답 p. 13

Challenge 1 다음 두 문장이 같은 의미가 되도록 빈칸에 알맞은 말을 쓰세요.

01. Kelly can speak Korean. She can speak Japanese.

→ Kelly can speak _____ Korean _____ Japanese.

02. The man cannot be a suspect. That old lady cannot be a suspect, either.

→ _____ the man _____ that old lady can be a suspect.

03. I'm going to major in sociology, or I'm going to major in economics.

→ I'm going to major in _____ sociology _____ economics.

Challenge 2 「not only ~ but also」와 「as well as」를 이용하여 같은 뜻이 되도록 문장을 만드세요.

보기	He is not only poor but also lazy.
	= *He is lazy as well as poor.*

01. The scientist is famous in foreign countries as well as in Korea.

= _____

02. The gift shop not only offered discounts but (also) gave away small souvenirs.

= _____

03. Some other countries as well as the United States use English as their first language.

= _____

Challenge 3 다음 빈칸에 알맞은 상관접속사를 넣으세요.

01. In many countries bicycles are used for _____ work _____ pleasure, by grown-ups as well as children.

02. The object of learning a foreign language is to learn _____ the language itself, _____ something about the life and character of the nation.

Unit 03 명사절 접속사

3-1 명사절로 쓰이는 that

That smoking can cause lung cancer **is a fact.**
= It is a fact **that** smoking can cause lung cancer.
흡연이 폐암을 유발한다는 것은 사실이다.

01 「that+주어+동사」의 한 덩어리가 문장에서 명사 자리인 **문장 맨 앞의 주어 자리와 동사 뒤의 목적어나 보어 자리에 위치**하여 명사 역할을 할 때 이를 **명사절**이라고 한다. '~라는 것이, ~라는 것은'의 의미이다.

That Ji-sung Park is a great soccer player is true. 박지성이 훌륭한 축구선수라는 것은 사실이다.
▶ 주어(명사) 자리＝명사절

= **It is true that** Ji-sung Park is a great soccer player.

That he is alive is certain. 그가 살아 있는 것이 확실하다. ▶ 주어(명사) 자리＝명사절
= It is certain that he is alive.

※ 영어는 주어가 길면 핵심 동사가 멀어지기 때문에 it을 쓰고 모두 뒤로 보낸다. to부정사와 마찬가지로 가주어, 진주어라고 한다.

02 동사 뒤에는 (대)명사가 위치하는 자리지만, 「주어+동사」를 쓰려면 명사절을 써야 한다. **명사절이 목적어로 사용될 경우 명사절을 이끄는 접속사 that은 자주 생략**한다. '~(라)고, ~하는 것을'로 해석한다.

I think **that** women can be better politicians than men.
나는 여성이 남성들보다 뛰어난 정치인이 될 수 있다고 생각한다. ▶ 목적어(명사) 자리＝명사절

Long ago, people believed the earth was flat.
옛날 사람들은 지구가 평평하다고 믿었다. ▶ believed와 the earth 사이에 that 생략

Many people know (that) smoking has something to do with lung cancer.
많은 사람들은 흡연이 폐암과 관련이 있다는 것을 안다.

03 be동사 뒤에는 명사나 형용사가 위치하는 자리지만 「주어+동사」를 쓰려면 명사절을 써야 한다. 보어절에 쓰이는 명사절 접속사 that은 생략하지 않는다.

The problem is **that** I often feel lonely at night. 문제는 내가 밤에 종종 외롭다는 것이다. ▶ 보어(명사) 자리＝명사절
The rumor is **that** she has been fired. 그 소문은 그녀가 해고당했다는 것이다.
His main complaint is **that** he has too much work to do. 그의 주된 불평은 할 일이 너무 많다는 것이다.

서술형 기초다지기

Challenge 1 다음 두 문장을 연결해서 that과 it으로 시작하는 문장을 각각 하나씩 쓰세요.

보기	Yu-na Kim is a great figure skater. That's true. → *That Yu-na Kim is a great figure skater is true.* → *It is true that Yu-na Kim is a great figure skater.*

01. Drug abuse can damage a person's health. That's a widely known fact.

→ _____

→ _____

02. He won the first prize. It is hardly surprising.

→ _____

→ _____

Challenge 2 다음 문장에서 명사절 접속사 that이 생략된 곳에 V 표시를 하세요.

보기	We know ᵛour parents will always love us.

01. Last night I dreamed I was at my aunt's house.

02. Did you notice Wilson wasn't in class yesterday?

03. Experts point out a labor shortage is a serious problem that could slow down the development of our economy.

Challenge 3 다음 문장을 괄호 안의 표현을 이용하여 〈보기〉와 같이 완성하세요.

보기	People can live without water. (don't believe) → I *don't believe that people can live without water.*

01. Computers will have emotions. (think / don't think)

→ I _____ .

3-2 의문사로 시작하는 명사절(간접의문문)

I don't know **her address**. 나는 그녀의 주소를 모른다.
▶ 명사가 목적어 역할

I don't know. + Where does she live?
→ I don't know **where she lives**. 나는 그녀가 어디에 사는지 모른다.
▶ 명사절이 목적어 역할

---

01 의문사가 있는 문장(절)이 문장의 주어 또는 목적어, 보어 자리에서 명사 역할을 할 수 있는데 이때 의문사절은 **직접의문문의 어순이 아닌「의문사+주어+동사」의 어순**이다. 이를 **간접의문문**이라고도 부르며 의문사의 의미를 해석하여 '～지(는, 를)'로 해석한다.

When did they leave? 그들은 언제 떠났니?

→ Do you know **when they left**? 그들이 언제 떠났는지 아니? ▶ 직접의문문의 did가 없어지므로 left로 과거 표시

Why is Kevin absent? Kevin은 왜 결석하니?

→ I wonder **why Kevin is absent**. 나는 Kevin이 왜 결석하는지 궁금하다.

What did she say? 그녀가 뭐라고 했니?

→ Could you tell me **what she said**? 그녀가 무엇을 말했는지 말해 줄래?
▶ 직접의문문의 did가 없어지므로 said로 과거 표시

02 직접의문문에서 조동사로 쓰인 do, does, did는 간접의문문에서 '주어+동사'의 어순이 되기 때문에 없어지고 대신 **주어에 따라 동사의 수와 시제를 일치**시킨다. 의문사 자신이 주어인 경우에는「의문사+동사」의 어순으로 쓴다.

I wonder. + How **did** she learn to play the guitar?

→ I wonder how she **learned** to play the guitar. 나는 그녀가 어떻게 기타 치는 법을 배웠는지 궁금하다.

Could you tell me? + Who is coming to the party?

→ Could you tell me **who is coming** to the party? 누가 파티에 오는지 말해 주겠니?

03 think, believe, guess, suppose, imagine 등과 같이 생각과 관련된 동사의 경우 **의문사를 문장 맨 앞으로 보낸다.**

Do you think? + What will they do next?

→ Do you think **what they will do** next?

→ **What** do you think **they will do** next? 그들이 다음에는 뭘 할 거라고 생각하니?

Do you guess? + How old is she?

→ Do you guess **how old she is**?

→ **How old** do you guess **she is**? 그녀가 몇 살이라고 추측하니?

서술형 기초다지기

정답 p. 13

Challenge 1 　다음 대화의 직접의문문을 명사절로 바꾸어 빈칸을 완성하세요.

> **보기**
> A: How does Wilson go to school?
> B: I don't know *how Wilson goes to school*.

01. A: Why is the sky blue?

　　B: I don't know _____.

02. A: How old is your grandfather?

　　B: I don't know _____.

03. A: How often does the bell ring at a time?

　　B: I don't know _____.

Challenge 2 　〈보기〉와 같이 직접의문문과 간접의문문을 이용하여 문장을 완성하세요.

> **보기**
> A: Where *did Kathy eat* (Kathy, eat) dinner yesterday?
> B: I don't know where *she ate* (she, eat) dinner yesterday.

01. A: Where _____ (Tom, go) last night?

　　B: I'm sorry. I didn't hear what _____ (you, say).

　　A: I want to know where _____ (Tom, go) last night.

Challenge 3 　다음 두 문장을 한 문장으로 고쳐 다시 쓰세요.

01. Do you think? + Where can I park my car?

　　→ _____

02. Do you think? + Who will be the next president?

　　→ _____

03. Do you think? + What is the most typical Korean dish?

　　→ _____

3-3 if와 whether로 시작하는 명사절

Is Karen at home?
Karen은 집에 있니?
Do you know **if[whether]** Karen is at home?
Karen이 집에 있는지 없는지 아니?

01 의문사가 없는 직접의문문은 if나 whether를 사용하여 간접의문문으로 만드는데 문장에서 주어, 목적어, 보어 역할을 한다. 간접의문문은 항상 「if/whether+주어+동사」의 어순을 쓰고 if와 whether는 '~인지 아닌지'로 해석한다.

I don't know. + Did I lock the door?

→ I don't know **if** I locked the door. 나는 문을 잠갔는지 안 잠갔는지 모르겠다. ▶ 명사절이 목적어 역할

Is she rich? + It is not important to me.

→ **Whether** she is rich or not is not important to me. 그녀가 부자인지 아닌지는 내게 중요하지 않다.
　　▶ 명사절이 주어 역할

02 '~인지 아닌지'의 명사절이 문장 맨 앞에 올 경우 whether를 쓴다. 동사 바로 뒤에는 whether와 if를 둘 다 쓰지만 일상 영어에서는 if를 더 많이 쓴다. 조건의 부사절을 이끄는 접속사 if와의 구별은 if 바로 앞에 동사가 자리하고 있으면 명사절 if임을 기억하자.

Whether we succeed is not important. 우리가 성공하느냐 아니냐는 중요하지 않다.

I will check **if** the movie is playing. 내가 그 영화가 상영 중인지 아닌지 확인해 볼게.

I'll back you up **if** you need support. 지원이 필요하면 내가 널 도와줄게. ▶ 부사절 접속사 if

I don't know **whether** she likes me **or** hates me. 그녀가 날 좋아하는지 싫어하는지 모르겠다.

I can't tell **whether or not** an e-mail message is spam. 이메일 메시지 하나가 스팸 메일인지 아닌지 모르겠다.

※ 'whether A or B', 'whether or not'은 쓸 수 있지만 'if A or B', 'if or not'은 쓰지 않는다. 또한 if 명사절은 주어 자리에도 올 수 없고 전치사 다음에도 올 수 없다.

I'm confused **about whether** we should invite everyone in the class. ▶ about if ~ (×)
우리가 학급의 모든 사람을 초대해야 하는지 아닌지 혼란스럽다.

서술형 기초다지기

정답 p. 13

Challenge 1   다음 직접의문문을 if나 whether를 이용한 명사절로 바꿔 보세요.

> **보기**
> Is Tom coming?
> → I wonder *if[whether] Tom is coming*.

01. Did I turn off the gas?

   → I'm not sure _____ .

02. Is Tiffany here today?

   → Can you tell me _____ ?

03. Did Kevin go to work yesterday?

   → I wonder _____ .

04. Do the passengers come out here?

   → Can you tell me _____ ?

Challenge 2   〈보기〉와 같이 명사절 접속사 if를 사용하여 문장을 완성하세요.

> **보기**
> A: Do penguins ever get cold?
> B: That's an interesting question. I don't know *if penguins ever get* cold.

01. A: Can I drive the car to the store, Dad?

   B: Are you serious? Of course not! Why do you ask _____ to the store?

     You haven't passed your driver's test.

02. A: Are you going to be in your office later today?

   B: What? Sorry. I didn't hear you.

   A: I need to know _____ in your office later today.

03. A: Has Kelly already left the party?

   B: Sorry, it's so noisy here. I didn't catch that.

   A: I need to know _____ the party.

3-4 그외 자주 사용하는 명사절 that

It is true that a cat is not able to taste sweet things. 고양이가 단맛을 모른다는 것은 사실이다.

A: Is she from Korea? 그녀는 한국인인가요?
B: I think **so**. (so = that she is from Korea)
그런 거 같아요.

---

01 「be+형용사/과거분사」 뒤에 that명사절을 쓴다. 주로 감정을 나타내는 형용사가 등장하며 that절은 감정을 일으킨 원인을 나타내며 '~해서'라는 의미이다. 일상 영어에서는 that을 생략한다.

be afraid	be delighted	be happy	be proud
be terrified	be amazed	be disappointed	be horrified
be sad	be thrilled	be angry	be fortunate
be impressed	be shocked	be worried	be aware
be furious	be lucky	be sure	be convinced
be glad	be pleased	be surprised	It is true/a fact

I **am disappointed** (**that**) I failed the test. 나는 그 시험에 떨어져서 실망스럽다.
I'm **afraid** (**that**) I can't come to your party. 유감스럽지만 난 네 파티에 갈 수가 없어.
I'm **sure** (**that**) water pollution is bad for animals. 난 수질오염이 동물들에게 해롭다고 확신해.

---

02 Yes/No 의문문의 대답으로 think, believe, hope, guess 등의 동사 뒤에는 **that절의 내용을 반복하지 않고, 대신에 so를 쓴다.** 단, know와 sure 뒤에는 so를 쓰지 않는다.

A: Does Sunny live in Singapore? Sunny가 싱가포르에 사니?
B: I believe **so**. 그런 것 같아. (so = that Sunny lives in Singapore)
▶ 확실할 때는 Yes/No로 대답 (Yes, she does. / No, she doesn't.)

A: Romeo and Juliet married at the end. 로미오와 줄리엣은 결국 결혼했어.
B: Yes, I **know**. 응, 나도 알아.

---

03 확실하지 않은 부정 대답은 'don't think so / don't believe so'로 쓰고, hope, guess는 각각 'hope not, guess not'으로 쓴다.

A: Is Wilson married? Wilson이 결혼했니?
B: I **don't think so**. / I **don't believe so**. 그렇지 않다고 생각해. / 그렇지 않으리라 봐.
A: Did you fail the test? 그 시험에 떨어졌니?
B: I **hope not**. 그러지 않길 바래. (not = that I didn't fail the test)

서술형 기초다지기

정답 p. 13

Challenge 1　다음 문장을 괄호 안의 표현을 이용하여 〈보기〉와 같이 완성하세요.

보기	There is a town called Chicken in Alaska. (be surprised) → *I am surprised that there is a town called Chicken in Alaska.*

01. I missed class yesterday.

(be sorry) → _____

02. The peace conference failed.

(was disappointed) → _____

03. Women live longer than men.

(It is a fact) → _____

04. Men laugh longer, more loudly, and more often than women.

(was not aware) → _____

Challenge 2　다음 대화에 나온 so와 not의 의미를 that명사절로 풀어서 다시 쓰세요.

보기	A: Is Kathy going to be home tonight? B: I think so. → *I think that Kathy is going to be home tonight.*

01. A: Is rice the chief food for half the people in the world?

B: I believe so. → _____

02. A: Will your flight be canceled because of the bad weather in Seoul?

B: I hope not. → _____

03. A: Is Brian going to be at the meeting?

B: I hope so. → _____

04. A: Is the library open on Sunday?

B: I believe so. → _____

Unit 04 부사절

4-1 시간을 나타내는 부사절 (1)

When I went out, it was raining.
내가 밖에 나갔을 때, 비가 내리고 있었다.
= It was raining when I went out.

01 시간의 부사절을 이끄는 접속사 **when, as, while**이 과거의 비교적 긴 시간을 나타내는 과거진행형과 함께 쓸 때는 모두 같은 의미이다. 주절에는 과거시제를 쓰고, 부사절에는 이미 진행되고 있었던 동작을 과거진행형으로 쓴다.

When I was sitting in the garden, it suddenly began to rain.
　　　이미 진행 중인 동작 → 과거진행　　　　　　　중간에 끼어든 짧은 동작 → 과거
=**As** I was sitting in the garden, it suddenly began to rain.
=**While** I was sitting in the garden, it suddenly began to rain.
내가 정원에 앉아 있던 중에 갑자기 비가 내리기 시작했다.

02 when, as, while이 서로 다른 의미로 사용될 때 약간의 의미 차이가 있다.

① when(~할 때, ~ 할 때마다): **인생의 어느 한 시점이나 기간**을 뜻할 때 사용한다.

　When I was a child, I wanted to be Superman. 어렸을 때 나는 슈퍼맨이 되고 싶었다.

② while(~하는 동안에, ~하는 사이에): **비교적 긴 시간에 걸쳐 동시에 일어나는 일**에 사용한다.

　While he lived in Canada, he had a hard life. 캐나다에서 사는 동안 그는 힘든 삶을 살았다.

③ as(~할 때, ~함에 따라): **두 가지 동작이 동시에 변화하고 있음**을 나타낼 때 사용한다. as soon as (=on+V-ing)는 '~하자마자'의 뜻이다.

　As she got older, she looked more like her grandmother.
　그녀는 나이를 먹어감에 따라 점점 할머니와 닮아갔다.

03 또 다른 시간의 접속사로는 before(~하기 전에), after(~한 후에), since(~한 이래로, 이후로)가 있다. 특히 since는 주로 완료시제에 쓰여 '~이래로'의 뜻을 나타낸다.

Make sure to turn off the TV **before** you go to bed. 잠자리에 들기 전에 반드시 TV를 꺼라.

04 until과 by the time은 둘 다 '~할 때까지'의 의미이나, **until은 동작이나 상태가 계속**될 때 쓰고 **by the time은 완료의 기한**을 나타낼 때 쓴다.

Don't ever leave me **until** I die. 죽는 날까지 날 떠나지 마세요.
I will have finished my work **by the time** you come home. 당신이 집에 올 때까지 나는 그 일을 끝낼 거예요.

서술형 기초다지기

정답 p. 14

Challenge 1 다음 빈칸에 when, while, until, since, as soon as 중 알맞은 것을 써 넣으세요.

01. 내가 TV를 보는 동안 아내는 요리를 하고 있었다.

→ My wife was cooking _____ I was watching TV.

02. 우리 할아버지는 20살에 미국으로 왔다.

→ My grandfather came to the U.S. _____ he was 20 years old.

03. 도둑을 보자마자 우리는 경찰을 불렀다.

→ _____ we saw the thief, we called the police.

04. 그녀는 결혼한 이후로 여기에 살고 있다.

→ She has lived here _____ she married.

05. 나는 아빠가 내게 소리를 지를 때까지 일어나지 않았다.

→ I didn't wake up _____ my dad screamed at me.

Challenge 2 다음 두 문장을 〈보기〉와 같이 괄호 안의 접속사를 이용하여 한 문장으로 완성하세요.

보기	I arrived home. My dad was brushing his teeth. (when)
	→ *When I arrived home, my dad was brushing his teeth.*

01. I made some friends. I was staying in Seattle. (while)

→ _____

02. We got closer to downtown. The bus became more crowded. (as)

→ _____

03. We reached home. It was quite dark. (by the time)

→ _____

04. She was listening to the radio. Someone knocked on the door. (while)

→ _____

4-2 시간을 나타내는 부사절 (2)

When walking home, I happened to meet a ghost.
집에 가고 있을 때 나는 귀신을 봤다.

After they graduate from university, they will get a good job.
대학을 졸업한 후에, 그들은 좋은 직업을 갖게 될 것이다.

01 부사절의 내용을 강조하기 위해 부사절을 문장 처음에 쓰는 경우가 많다. 하지만 핵심내용은 주절이 담고 있어서 주절을 먼저 쓰고 부사절을 뒤에 써도 그 의미는 변하지 않는다. 이 때 **시간의 부사절의 주어가 주절의 주어와 같을 때 부사절의 주어를 없애고 동사를 -ing로 바꾸어 부사구로 줄여 짧고 빠르게 의미를 전달하는 방법이 있다.** 하지만 시간의 전후가 혼동이 될 수 있어 시간의 접속사는 생략하지 않는 것이 좋고, 부사절의 시제가 사라져 주절의 내용으로 시제를 예측할 수밖에 없는 단점이 생긴다.

While I was walking down the street, I met a strange woman. 길을 가다가 나는 이상한 여자를 만났다.
=**While walking down the street**, I met a strange woman.
▶ 부사절과 주절의 주어(I)가 같으므로 부사절의 주어를 생략하고 be동사(was)도 뜻에 큰 영향을 주지 않으므로 생략한다.

After Bob finished the work, he went to a movie. 일을 끝낸 후에 Bob은 영화를 보러갔다.
=**After finishing the work**, Bob went to a movie.
▶ 부사절에 쓰인 동일한 주어 Bob을 생략할 때 주절의 주어 he를 Bob으로 고쳐 쓴다.

02 **시간의 부사절이 미래를 나타내더라도 부사절에서는 미래시제를 쓰지 않고** 현재시제로 미래를 나타낸다. 미래완료의 경우에는 현재완료를 써서 미래를 나타낸다.

When it **stops** raining, we'll go out. 비가 그칠 때, 우리는 밖으로 나갈 거야.
Please close the windows **before** you **go** out. 밖에 나가기 전에 창문을 닫아 주세요.
Can I borrow it **after** you **have finished**? 네가 사용한 후에 내가 빌릴 수 있을까?

※ before, after, until 등은 전치사와 접속사 두 가지 모두로 쓰인다.

Who are you going to meet **after school**? 방과 후에 누구 만날 거니? ▶ 전치사 after
=Who are you going to meet **after school is over**? ▶ 접속사 after

03 for와 during은 둘 다 '~동안에'라는 뜻이지만, **for는 얼마 동안인지 구체적인 시간의 단위가 오고, during 은 시간의 단위가 아닌 기간을 나타내는 명사가 온다.**

She lived in Chicago **for three years**. 그녀는 시카고에서 3년 동안 살았다.
What will you do **during the summer vacation**? 이번 여름 휴가 동안에 무엇을 할 거니?

서술형 기초다지기

정답 p. 14

Challenge 1 다음 문장의 부사절을 「접속사+V-ing」 형태로 줄여 쓰세요.

> **보기**
> While she was waiting for her son, she read a magazine.
> → *While waiting for her son, she read a magazine.*

01. When the thief saw the police, he turned and ran away.

→ _____

02. I shut off the lights before I left the room.

→ _____

03. After I had met the movie star in person, I understood why she was so popular.

→ _____

04. After my daughter graduates from university, she's going to get a good job.

→ _____

Challenge 2 다음 두 문장을 괄호 안의 접속사를 이용하여 다시 쓰세요.

> **보기**
> I will retire. I will play tennis. (when)
> → *When I retire, I will play tennis.*

01. She will finish her homework. She's going to go to the movies. (after)

→ _____

02. I will call Kevin tomorrow. I'll ask him to come to my party. (when)

→ _____

03. Nancy will get home tonight. She's going to read the history book. (after)

→ _____

04. I will be 25 years old. I will get married. (when)

→ _____

Tina is hungry **because** she didn't have breakfast.
Tina는 아침을 먹지 않았기 때문에 배가 고프다.

= Tina didn't have breakfast, **so** she is hungry.
Tina는 아침을 먹지 않아서 배가 고프다.

01 because, as, since는 '~때문에'라는 의미로 원인을 나타내는 부사절을 이끄는 접속사이다. because는 듣는 사람이 잘 알지 못하는 이유를 나타내고, as나 since는 말하는 사람과 듣는 사람 모두가 이미 알만한 원인을 나타낸다.

As it was a national holiday, all the banks were closed. 공휴일이었기 때문에 모든 은행이 문을 닫았다.

Since you look tired, you'd better take a rest. 피곤해 보이니 너는 쉬는 게 좋겠다.

Because the movie was so sad, I turned on the waterworks. 영화가 너무 슬퍼서 나는 눈물을 흘렸다.

02 since는 완료시제와 함께 쓰이지 않을 때는 이유를 나타내고, because는 듣는 사람이 잘 알지 못하는 이유를 말하므로 이유를 묻는 why에 대한 대답으로 because를 쓴다. **because of, due to, thanks to는 뒤에 명사(구)를 써서 이유를 강조하는 부사구를 만든다.** now that(~이니까)도 since와 비슷한 의미로 쓰인다.

We had to postpone the conference **due to** the weather. 우리는 날씨 때문에 회담을 취소해야 했다.

She quit the job **because of** her health. 그녀는 건강상의 이유로 직장을 그만두었다.

I finished the work **thanks to** her help. 그녀의 도움 덕분에 나는 그 일을 끝냈다.

Now (that) we are all here, let's begin the meeting. 우리 모두 여기에 모였으니까, 회의를 시작합시다.

03 부사절과 주절의 주어가 같을 때, 부사절임을 먼저 알리면서 주절의 내용을 빠르게 전달하기 위해 부사절의 주어를 없애고 동사를 현재분사(V-ing)로 바꾸어 부사구로 줄여 쓸 수 있다. **주절만으로 인과 관계를 알 수 있으므로 접속사도 생략**할 수 있지만 시제가 사라지는 단점이 있다.

Because Alice **was** sick, she was absent yesterday.

→ **Being** sick, Alice was absent yesterday. 아팠기 때문에 Alice는 어제 결석했어.

As she **didn't know** what to do, she came to ask for my advice.

→ **Not knowing** what to do, she came to ask for my advice.
뭘 해야 할지 몰라서 그녀는 나의 조언을 구하러 왔다.

※ 부정문인 경우 부정하는 내용(V-ing) 바로 앞에 not을 쓴다.

서술형 기초다지기

정답 p. 14

Challenge 1 〈보기〉와 같이 because와 so를 이용하여 두 문장을 한 문장으로 만드세요.

보기	We have no classes on weekends. We can go skiing every Saturday. → *Because we have no classes on weekends, we can go skiing every Saturday.* → *We have no classes on weekends, so we can go skiing every Saturday.*

01. They didn't have time. They didn't go for a drive.

→ _____

→ _____

02. I was sick. I went to bed early last night.

→ _____

→ _____

Challenge 2 다음 문장의 부사절을 V-ing 형태의 부사구로 짧게 줄여 쓰세요.

보기	Because she was honest, she was liked by many people. → *Being honest, she was liked by many people.*

01. As we had no food at home, we decided to go out to eat.

→ _____

02. Because Brian was tired, he went to bed early last night.

→ _____

Challenge 3 다음 괄호 안의 표현 중 알맞은 것을 고르세요.

01. (Since / Due to) inclement weather, Flight 65, bound for New York, will be postponed until tomorrow.

02. I've just heard on the news that the airport is closed (because of / because) the fog.

03. (Thank you / Thanks to) his invention, many people live better lives.

4-4 조건의 부사절

If you **go** out without a coat, you'll get a cold.
코트를 입지 않고 밖에 나가면 감기에 걸릴 거야.

Sunny's parents said they'd buy her a car **only if** she graduated.
Sunny의 부모님은 그녀가 졸업을 하기만 하면 차를 사 주겠
다고 말했다.

---

01 if는 조건의 부사절을 이끄는데 **조건의 부사절 안에서는 현재시제가 미래를 대신**한다. unless는 '∼아니라면'의 뜻으로 if ∼ not으로 바꿔 쓸 수 있다. 단, unless 부사절에 부정문을 쓰지 않도록 조심하자.

If I **have** time tomorrow, I will visit you. 내일 시간이 있다면, 너를 방문할게.

Let's go to the movies **if** you **aren't** too tired. 네가 너무 피곤하지 않으면, 영화 보러 가자.

=Let's go to the movies **unless** you are **too** tired.

02 **변하지 않는 진리나, 항상 사실적인 일**에도 조건의 부사절을 쓴다.

If the temperature falls below zero, water freezes and becomes ice.
온도가 0℃ 이하로 떨어지면 물이 얼어 얼음이 된다. ▶ 진리

If you water plants, they grow. 네가 식물에 물을 주면, 식물들은 자란다. ▶ 사실

03 기타 조건을 나타내는 접속사: **only if**(∼할 때에만), **in case**(∼의 경우에 대비해서), **as[so] long as**(∼ 하는 한)

In case it rains, I'll take an umbrella. 비가 올 경우에 대비해서 나는 우산을 가져갈 거다.

=**Whether** it rains **or not**, I'll take an umbrella.
　▶ 비가 오든지 안 오든지 상관없이 만약을 위해서 우산을 가지고 다니겠다는 의미

If it rains, I'll take an umbrella. 비가 온다면, 우산을 가져갈 거다.

=**Only if** it rains, I'll take an umbrella.
▶ 비가 오는 경우에만 우산을 가지고 간다는 의미

You can use my car **as[so] long as** you drive carefully. 네가 운전을 조심하는 한 내 차를 사용할 수 있다.

=You can use my car, but you must drive carefully.

I shall never forget your kindness **as long as** I live. 내가 살아 있는 한 당신의 은혜를 결코 잊지 않겠습니다.

서술형 기초다지기

정답 p. 14

Challenge 1   다음 문장을 접속사 if를 이용한 조건의 부사절로 〈보기〉와 같이 다시 쓰세요.

> 보기
> I will be healthy. I will continue to work for the rest of my life.
> → *If I am healthy, I will continue to work for the rest of my life.*

01. My parents will need help. I'll take care of them.

    → _____

02. I won't have money. I will get help from the government.

    → _____

Challenge 2   다음 빈칸에 in case 또는 if를 구별해서 써 보세요.

01. I bought some candles _____ the electricity goes out.

02. Let's not go to the park _____ it rains tomorrow.

03. I wrote down her address and phone number _____ I should forget it.

04. You can call me at the hotel _____ you need to contact me.

Challenge 3   다음 문장을 〈보기〉와 같이 only if 부사절을 이용하여 다시 쓰세요.

> 보기
> You can't play tennis there unless you are a member.
> → *You can play tennis there only if you are a member.*

01. We can't start the project unless our boss approves it.

    → _____

02. The alligator won't attack you unless you move suddenly.

    → _____

4-5 양보와 대조를 나타내는 부사절

Although it rained a lot, they went out for a walk.
비가 많이 오는데도 불구하고, 그들은 산책을 나갔다.
In spite of(=Despite) the rain, they went out for a walk.
비가 내리는데도 불구하고, 그들은 산책을 나갔다.

01

though, although, even though는 예상치 못한 결과를 나타내는 양보의 부사절을 이끈다. 모두 '~임에도 불구하고'라는 의미로 주절을 강조한다. 일상 영어에서는 though를 많이 쓰고 even though는 though보다 더 강한 양보의 의미를 나타낸다.

Although it rained a lot, we enjoyed our vacation. 비가 많이 왔는데도 불구하고, 우리는 휴가를 즐겼다.
She didn't get the job **though** she was extremely qualified.
그녀는 정말 자격이 되는데도 불구하고 그 일자리를 얻질 못했다.
We went out **although** it was raining. 우리는 비가 오고 있는데도 불구하고 밖에 나갔다.
I missed the bus. Tom gave me a ride, **though.** 나는 버스를 놓쳤어. 하지만 Tom이 차를 태워 주었어.
(=I missed the bus. However Tom gave me a ride.)

※ though가 문장 맨 마지막에 오면 '그러나(but)'의 뜻이 된다.

02

even if는 조건이나 가정의 내용이 오고, (al)though, even though는 기정사실이 온다.

The shop owner hired her **even though** she had a record.
그 가게 주인은 그녀가 전과자임에도 불구하고 그녀를 고용했다. ▶ 그녀가 전과자인 것은 기정사실
Even if I starve to death, I won't steal. 굶어 죽을지라도 도둑질은 안 한다. ▶ 굶어 죽는 것은 가정

03

while과 whereas는 두 가지 생각이 대조를 이루는 경우에 사용하는데 이들이 이끄는 절은 문장 중간에 와도 항상 쉼표(,)를 쓴다. whereas는 주로 문어체에 자주 쓴다.

Some people are generous, **while** others are selfish. 어떤 사람들은 너그러운 반면에 다른 사람들은 이기적이다.
Whales are mammals, **whereas** sharks are fish. 고래는 포유류인 반면, 상어는 어류이다.

04

in spite of, despite는 (al)though, even though와 같은 뜻을 가진 전치사이다. 전치사의 특성상 반드시 뒤에 (대)명사나 동명사를 써야 한다.

In spite of the heavy traffic, we arrived on time. 교통체증에도 불구하고 우리는 제시간에 도착했다.
=**Although** the traffic was bad, we arrived on time.
I couldn't sleep **despite** being very tired. 매우 피곤한데도 불구하고 나는 잠을 잘 수가 없었다.
=I couldn't sleep **even though** I was very tired.

서술형 기초다지기

정답 p. 14

Challenge 1 빈칸에 though, in spite of, because, because of, whereas 중 하나를 넣으세요.

01. I've just heard on the news that the airport is closed _____ the fog.

02. _____ I was tired, I decided anyway to stay up and finish my homework.

03. I'm a vegetarian, _____ my sisters and brothers are meat-eaters.

04. _____ having a university degree, Nancy can't find a job.

05. You should not despise a man _____ he is poor.

Challenge 2 〈보기〉와 같이 다음 문장을 괄호 안의 표현을 이용하여 한 문장으로 고쳐 쓰세요.

보기	I couldn't sleep. I was tired. (despite) → *I couldn't sleep despite being tired.*

01. Ostriches have wings. They can't fly. (even though)

    → _____

02. He looks about forty. His wife looks about twenty. (whereas)

    → _____

03. We live on the same street. We hardly ever see each other. (despite)

    → _____

04. He didn't get the job. He was extremely qualified. (in spite of)

    → _____

05. Some children are spoiled. Others are well-behaved. (while)

    → _____

06. We had planned everything carefully. A lot of things went wrong. (although)

    → _____

이것이 시험에 출제되는 영문법이다!

01 출제 100% - 등위접속사의 앞뒤 문맥을 파악하라!

출제자의 눈 앞뒤 문장 관계를 파악한 후 알맞은 등위접속사를 고르는 문제가 기본적으로 출제되고, 특히 등위접속사를 기준으로 앞뒤에 동일한 문장성분이 온다는 점에 유의해야 한다. 명사는 명사, 형용사는 형용사, 부정사는 부정사, 동명사는 동명사, 분사는 분사끼리 대등하게 연결되어야 하는데 이를 틀리게 해놓고 고르는 문제가 출제된다. 주어 자리에 'A and B'를 주고 동사를 복수형으로 쓸 줄 아는지를 묻는 문제도 출제된다.

Ex 1.

Reading is the act of interpreting printed and _____ words.

(a) wrote　　(b) written　　(c) writing　　(d) to write

Ex 2.

Reading develops the powers of imagination _____ inner visualization.

(a) but　　(b) or　　(c) so　　(d) and

02 출제 100% - 상관접속사는 부분 영작으로 출제한다.

출제자의 눈 both A and B, either A or B, neither A nor B, not only A but (also) B에서 각각 and, or, nor, but을 틀리게 해놓거나 both, either, neither, but also를 구별하는 문제가 출제된다. 특히, 수의 일치문제에 대비해야 하는데 위의 상관접속사가 주어로 쓰일 경우 both A and B를 제외하고 모두 B에 수를 일치시켜야 한다. 상관접속사를 이용한 부분 영작 문제를 출제하는데, 특히 not only ~ but also를 as well as로 바꿔 영작하는 문제가 자주 출제된다.

Ex 3.

Either mom _____ dad will come and pick me up since it's raining.

(a) and　　(b) both　　(c) nor　　(d) or

Ex 4.

다음 문장을 as well as로 고쳐 쓰시오.

She visited not only France but also Germany.

＝She _____ .

03 출제 100% - 간접의문문은 반드시 서술형으로 출제한다.

 출제자의 눈 명사절을 이끄는 접속사 that은 대명사 that 및 관계사 that과 구별해야 하는데 시험에서 이를 자주 물어본다. that이 명사절 접속사로 쓰일 때는 문장 맨 앞 또는 동사 바로 뒤에 위치할 때이다. 또한 의문사가 있는 직접의문문을 주고 간접의문문으로 영작하게 하는 문제도 반드시 출제된다. 의문사가 없을 때는 if나 whether를 이용해서 간접의문문을 만드는 것에 주의하자. 특히, 의문사가 주어 역할을 할 경우 「의문사(주어)+동사」의 어순이 된다는 것도 기억해 두자.

Ex 5.

밑줄 친 that과 용법이 같은 것은?

One problem with MP3 files is that they can break an artist's copyright.

(a) I saw the musician that electrified the audience on TV last night.

(b) Last night I dreamed that I was on the top of a mountain along.

Ex 6.

밑줄 친 직접의문문을 간접의문문으로 바꿔 다시 쓰시오.

Is Sunny here today?

→ Can you tell me _____ ?

04 출제 100% - 간접의문문의 어순은 무조건 「접속사+S+V」의 어순이다.

 출제자의 눈 문장 중간에 의문사가 나오는 경우 그 뒤는 무조건 「주어+동사」의 어순이 되어야 한다. 이 어순이 바뀌면 어법상 틀린 문장이다. How가 '얼마나'란 의미로 형용사나 부사를 수식할 경우 간접의문문에서 「how+형용사/부사+주어+동사」의 어순이 된다. 만약 주절의 동사가 think, consider, suppose, expect, imagine, believe, guess일 때는 의문사를 문장 맨 앞으로 보내, 「의문사+do you think[consider…]+주어+동사」의 어순으로 만든다.

Ex 7.

다음 문장에서 어법상 틀린 부분을 바르게 고쳐 쓰시오.

A father took his son to the country to show him how can people be poor.

_____

05 출제 100 % - 시간의 접속사의 의미를 확실히 알아두자.

 출제자의 눈 알맞은 시간의 접속사를 고르라는 기본 문제로 출발하여 as soon as를 on+V-ing로 고치는 주관식 문제도 출제 가능성이 높다. 또한 until과 by the time의 쓰임을 물어보는 문제도 출제 가능하다. until은 동작이나 상태가 계속될 때 쓰고, by the time은 완료의 기한을 나타낼 때 쓴다. as, since, because는 앞 문장이 결과, 뒤 문장이 원인을 나타낸다. 앞뒤 문장을 비교하여 알맞은 접속사를 고르는 문제가 출제된다. 시간의 부사절을 부사구로 짧게 고치는 단답형 주관식 문제도 언제나 출제 가능하다.

Ex 8.

밑줄 친 부분을 같은 의미가 되도록 빈칸을 완성하시오.

I'll help you with your assignment <u>as soon as I finish</u> washing the dishes.

→ I'll help you with your assignment _____ _____ washing the dishes.

Ex 9.

I will wait _____ you come back.

(a) by the time   (b) now that   (c) since   (d) until

06 출제 100 % - 시간과 조건의 부사절 안에 있는 시제를 조심하라.

 출제자의 눈 시간(when, after 등), 조건(if, unless, only if, in case)의 부사절에서는 현재시제를 써서 미래를 나타낸다. 따라서, 미래의 의미라도 will, shall과 같은 미래를 나타내는 조동사를 써서는 안 된다. 미래완료 또한 will을 뺀 현재완료(have+p.p.)로 미래를 나타낸다. 단, 시간이나 조건을 나타내는 접속사가 '명사절'로 사용될 경우에는 will을 사용한다. 이 둘을 혼동케 하는 고난이도 문제가 출제될 수 있다.

Ex 10.

I wonder if Jessica _____ Bob's proposal.

(a) accepts   (b) will accept   (c) has accepted   (d) will have accepted

Ex 11.

Before Olivia _____ for work this morning, she's going to lock the door.

(a) will leave   (b) had left   (c) will have left   (d) leaves

07 출제 100% – **접속사인지 전치사인지 조심하라!**

 출제자의 눈 because of, due to, owing to(~때문에), thanks to, in spite of, despite는 모두 뒤에 절이 아닌 명사(구)가 와야 한다. 명사(구)를 쓰지 않고 절을 쓰도록 유인하는 함정 문제가 출제된다. 또는 역으로 「주어+동사」가 있는 절이면 접속사 because, (al)though를 고르라고 물어보기도 한다. for와 during도 뒤에 명사(구)가 오지만 절을 쓰려면 '~동안에'의 표현인 접속사 while을 적절히 구별해서 사용할 줄 알아야 한다.

Ex 12.

Rail services were shut down _____ cold winter weather.

(a) due to   (b) because   (c) while   (d) in spite of

Ex 13.

_____ our efforts, we failed to win the prize.

(a) Even though   (b) Although   (c) Despite   (d) Owing to

08 출제 100% – **부사절에서는 시제 문제를 빼놓을 수 없다.**

 출제자의 눈 since가 '~때문에(이유)'가 아닌 '~이래로, ~이후로(시간)'의 뜻으로 부사절을 이끌 때, 주절에는 완료시제를 쓴다. since 부사절은 당연히 '(과거 어느 시점) 이래로'란 의미이므로 과거시제를 써야 한다. 반면, when은 과거의 한 시점이나 기간을 나타내므로 when이 이끄는 부사절은 물론 주절에도 과거시제를 쓴다. 한편, 시간의 부사절을 이끄는 when, while, as가 '~하는 중에'의 의미로 쓰일 때는 앞서 진행 중이었던 동작은 부사절 안에서 과거진행형으로 쓰고, 도중에 끼어들어 짧은 시간 동안 행해진 동작은 과거시제를 쓴다. 이 시제를 서로 혼동케 하는 문제가 출제될 수 있다.

Ex 14.

Wilson has studied Korean _____ he _____ a student.

(a) since – is   (b) when – was   (c) since – was   (d) when – is

Ex 15.

Tom and Jessica _____ in the street when it started to rain.

(a) walked   (b) are walking   (c) walking   (d) were walking

1. 다음 빈칸에 공통으로 들어갈 알맞은 접속사는?

> · _____ Bob apologized, Kathy is still angry with him.
> · _____ he studied hard, he didn't pass the test.
> · _____ it was very cold, she wasn't wearing a coat.

❶ Because ❷ While ❸ After
❹ If ❺ Although

2. 빈칸에 들어갈 말로 알맞은 것은?

> He can speak not only English _____ Spanish.

❶ and ❷ but ❸ so
❹ for ❺ or

3. 다음 빈칸에 공통으로 들어갈 말로 알맞은 것은?

> · Run to the station, _____ you won't see her.
> · Which do you like better, green tea _____ coffee?

❶ but ❷ so ❸ or
❹ and ❺ yet

4. 다음 밑줄 친 부분과 같은 의미가 되도록 빈칸에 알맞은 단어를 쓰시오.

> In some cases, you may like doing something, but you may not be good at it. So, consider your talents as well as your interests when you choose your job.

→ consider _____ _____ your interests
_____ _____ your talents

5. 다음 두 문장이 같은 의미가 되도록 빈칸에 들어갈 가장 적절한 말을 고르시오.

> Let's go to the movie tomorrow, unless you have other plans.
> = Let's go to the movie tomorrow, _____ _____.

❶ if you have other plans
❷ if you didn't have other plans
❸ if you don't have other plans
❹ as you have other plans
❺ as you don't have other plans

6. 밑줄 친 that의 쓰임이 나머지 넷과 다른 것은?

❶ That he won the first prize is hardly surprising.
❷ Remember that you should solve the problem.
❸ They fear that these climbers may try to climb the biggest and tallest trees if they learn their exact locations.
❹ The chart shows that exercise makes the body healthy.
❺ A computer is now a tool that everyone admits is a necessity for modern life.

7. 다음 두 문장이 같은 의미가 되도록 빈칸에 알맞은 말을 쓰시오.

> Whether it rains or not, take an umbrella with you.
> → _____ _____ _____ _____, take an umbrella with you.

오답 노트 만들기

★틀린 문제 : _____   ★다시 공부한 날 : _____

(1) 문제를 왜? 틀렸는지 곰곰이 생각하고 그 이유를 적어본다.

(2) 핵심 개념을 적는다.

(3) 자신이 몰랐던 단어와 숙어 표현이 있으면 정리한다.

(4) 해설집에서 필요한 부분을 골라 풀이 해법을 정리한다.

★틀린 문제 : _____   ★다시 공부한 날 : _____

(1) 문제를 왜? 틀렸는지 곰곰이 생각하고 그 이유를 적어본다.

(2) 핵심 개념을 적는다.

(3) 자신이 몰랐던 단어와 숙어 표현이 있으면 정리한다.

(4) 해설집에서 필요한 부분을 골라 풀이 해법을 정리한다.

★틀린 문제 : _____   ★다시 공부한 날 : _____

(1) 문제를 왜? 틀렸는지 곰곰이 생각하고 그 이유를 적어본다.

(2) 핵심 개념을 적는다.

(3) 자신이 몰랐던 단어와 숙어 표현이 있으면 정리한다.

(4) 해설집에서 필요한 부분을 골라 풀이 해법을 정리한다.

★틀린 문제 : _____   ★다시 공부한 날 : _____

(1) 문제를 왜? 틀렸는지 곰곰이 생각하고 그 이유를 적어본다.

(2) 핵심 개념을 적는다.

(3) 자신이 몰랐던 단어와 숙어 표현이 있으면 정리한다.

(4) 해설집에서 필요한 부분을 골라 풀이 해법을 정리한다.

1. 다음 밑줄 친 부분이 <u>잘못</u> 쓰인 것은?

❶ English has a few rivals, but no equals. Neither Spanish <u>nor</u> Arabic, both international languages, has the same influence in the world.

❷ Coins reflect both a country's history and its aspirations, <u>and</u> it is natural that collections based on place of origin should develop.

❸ Neither Patrick nor his parents <u>were</u> at home.

❹ The papers are either in my briefcase <u>or</u> under the books on my desk.

❺ Both coffee and tea <u>has</u> long and historic pasts.

오답노트

2. 다음 빈칸에 들어갈 말이 바르게 짝지어진 것은?

· I'll ask Nancy _____ she likes me or not.
· My idea is _____ we eat out this evening.

❶ that – whether
❷ if – that
❸ if – who
❹ whether – if
❺ whether – that

오답노트

[3-4] 다음 빈칸에 들어갈 말이 바르게 짝지어진 것은?

3.

· _____ all our careful plans, a lot of things went wrong.
· _____ we had planned everything carefully, a lot of things went wrong.

❶ Because of – If
❷ If – Due to
❸ Although – Despite
❹ In spite of – Although
❺ In spite of – Despite

4.

· Credit cards have become preferred method of payment _____ risks involved in handling cash.
· You won't pass the exam _____ you work a lot harder.

❶ because – in spite of
❷ since – unless
❸ because of – if
❹ because of – unless
❺ as – because

오답노트

5. 다음 두 문장이 같은 의미가 되도록 빈칸에 알맞은 표현을 쓰시오.

Kelly is popular not only for her beauty but also for her personality.
= Kelly is popular for her personality _____ for her beauty.

오답노트

6. 다음 빈칸에 들어갈 알맞은 접속사를 고르시오.

> _____ my son enters university, I'll have retired from my present job.

❶ Until ❷ By the time ❸ In case
❹ As long as ❺ Though

오답노트

7. 다음 빈칸에 알맞은 것은?

> As soon as you hear him speaking, you'll know he is a British.
> = _____ him speaking, you'll know he is a British.

❶ On hearing ❷ As soon as hearing
❸ Heard ❹ In hearing
❺ By hearing

오답노트

8. 다음 중 어법상 어색한 것은?

❶ We communicate not only with verbal language but also with body movements.

❷ Let's keep the heating on in case the temperature will drop below zero overnight.

❸ They'll make more money if we buy a new model as soon as the old one fails.

❹ I don't know if she will put out a new album again.

❺ Studies regarding our habits of eating out found that, when we eat out, we tend to underestimate the number of calories we consume by up to half.

오답노트

9. 다음 밑줄 친 단어의 쓰임이 나머지와 다른 하나는?

❶ I don't know when I'll see her again.
❷ She was twenty when she met him.
❸ When she heard the news, she was stunned.
❹ My dad always wears glasses when he reads the newspaper.
❺ What was your favorite television show when you were a child?

오답노트

10. 다음 빈칸에 들어갈 알맞은 말을 쓰시오.

> I'm not sure _____ Alice is home or not.
> (Alice가 집에 있는지 없는지는 확실하지 않다.)

→ _____

오답노트

11. 다음 중 밑줄 친 that의 쓰임이 다른 것은?

① I knew that he could accomplish his goals.
② It is certain that the company will recruit 100 employees.
③ Mrs. Pennies is so rich that she can purchase anything she wants.
④ It is obvious that she stole the secret document.
⑤ The problem is that I don't know how to swim.

오답노트

[12-14] 다음 우리말과 일치하도록 〈보기〉에서 알맞은 접속사를 골라 빈칸에 쓰시오.

보기			
	since	whether	until

12. 그의 이야기가 사실인지 아닌지 구별하기 어렵다.

→ _____ his story is true or not is hard to tell.

13. 그는 술을 너무 많이 마셨기 때문에, 자신의 집을 찾을 수 없었다.

→ _____ he drank too much, he couldn't find his home.

14. 내가 당신이 그렇게 하도록 허락할 때까지 움직이지 마시오!

→ Don't move _____ I allow you to do so.

오답노트

15. 다음 밑줄 친 부분과 쓰임이 같은 것은?

As I grew up, the city grew up, too.

① The girl is not as diligent as Wilson.
② As I am sick, I cannot go on a picnic.
③ As he gets older, he becomes smarter.
④ When in Rome, do as the Romans do.
⑤ As for me, I have nothing to tell you.

오답노트

16. 다음 밑줄 친 부분 중 생략할 수 없는 것은?

① You will find that the restroom is at the end of the hall.
② Did you notice that she lost a lot of weight recently?
③ I think that girl is smart.
④ Mac told me that he's had a hard time with his family recently.
⑤ You will find that Susan is the perfect woman for you.

오답노트

17. 다음 빈칸에 공통으로 들어갈 말로 알맞은 것은?

· I don't know ___ I'm going to need help. Thanks for asking. I'll let you know.
· ___ it rains tomorrow, we'll stay home.

① that　　② so　　③ even if
④ though　　⑤ if

오답노트

[18-19] 간접의문문을 활용하여 다음 문장을 완성하시오.

> **보기**
> How many people does your company employ?
> → Can you tell me *how many people your company employs*?

18. How many day's vacation do people get?
→ I wonder _____ .

19. How many people are you going to interview for this job?
→ Can you tell me _____
_____ ?

오답노트

20. **간접의문문을 이용하여 한 문장으로 쓰시오.**

Do you think? + Who is in the restroom?
→ _____

오답노트

21. **다음 빈칸에 알맞은 말을 쓰시오.**

> 매니저는 오늘 비번이라 오후에 전화를 받지도 전화를 다시 해주지도 않고 있다.
> = The manager is _____ receiving _____ returning calls this afternoon, as it's his day off.

오답노트

22. **다음 중 어법상 어색한 문장을 고르시오.**

❶ I like neither coffee nor tea.
❷ Not only fruit but vegetables are good for health.
❸ The company lounge is open to not only administrative staff and workers.
❹ Your salary can be either directly deposited or picked up at the payroll office.
❺ The weather on Sunday will be sunny as well as warm.

오답노트

23. **다음 중 문장 전환이 잘못된 것은?**

❶ Is it okay if I open the window?
→ Do you mind if I open the window?
❷ Although the traffic was heavy, we arrived on time.
→ The traffic was heavy, so we arrived on time.
❸ He was not only a champion on the field but also a champion of the heart.
→ He was a champion of the heart as well as a champion on the field.
❹ His sudden change surprised me.
→ I was surprised at his sudden change.
❺ I saw his father leaving by himself.
→ I saw his father leaving alone.

오답노트

A. 다음 밑줄 친 간접의문문은 직접의문문으로, 직접의문문은 간접의문문으로 바꿔 써 보시오.

1. A : _____

    B : I don't know <u>why Bob left</u>.

2. A : <u>What time will he return?</u>

    B : I don't know _____ .

3. A : _____

    B : I don't know <u>how far it is to his house</u>.

B. 다음 문장을 괄호 안의 접속사를 이용하여 한 문장으로 바꾸시오.

보기	He teaches Japanese. He also teaches Chinese. (not only ~ but also) → *He teaches not only Japanese but also Chinese.*

1. I couldn't sleep. I was tired. (despite)

   → _____

2. The street is slippery. It is covered with snow. (because)

   → _____

3. I'm going to major in sociology, or I'm going to major in economics. (either)

   → _____

4. Kevin is very famous. But he is not satisfied. (though)

   → _____

5. Some forms of radiation can be dangerous. They are handled properly. (unless)

   → _____

6. Alice didn't tell the truth. Janet didn't tell the truth, either. (neither)

   → _____

7. I know you're studying Korean. Are you studying Japanese, too? (not only ~ but also / ?)

   → _____

실전 서술형 평가문제

 출제의도 부사절과 함께 쓰이는 시제
평가내용 상황에 따라 알맞은 시제 사용하기

A. 다음 주어진 표현을 이용하여 알맞은 시제로 문장을 완성해 보시오. (단, 과거시제와 과거진행시제를 이용할 것)

[서술형 유형 : 8점 / 난이도 : 중]

| 보기 |  | when / I / arrive home / my mom / clean the room
→ *When I arrived home, my mom was cleaning the room.* |

1.

when / the e-mail / arrive / Karen / eat the hamburger

→ _____

_____

2.

everyone / dance / when / Janet / arrive / at the party

→ _____

_____

3.

while / Alice / drive / to the bank / her cell phone / ring

→ _____

_____

4.

we / have dinner / when / somebody / knock / on the door

→ _____

_____

실전 서술형 평가문제

B. 〈보기〉와 같이 다음 상황에 맞게 접속사 if와 unless를 이용하여 문장을 완성하시오.

[서술형 유형 : 6점 / 난이도 : 중하]

| 보기 |  | you / not eat / breakfast you / be hungry / all day
→ *If you don't eat breakfast, you'll be hungry all day.*
→ *Unless you eat breakfast, you'll be hungry all day.* |

1.

they / not come / in ten minutes I / leave

→ _____

→ _____

2.

he / not apologize I / not speak / to him again

→ _____

→ _____

3.

Karen / not like / her new dress she / can return it

→ _____

→ _____

출제의도 명사절을 이용하여 문장 완성하기

평가내용 명사절 접속사 that을 이용한 자신의 생각 표현하기

C. 다음 내용을 보고 자신의 생각을 괄호 안의 표현 중 하나를 이용하여 〈보기〉와 같이 서술하시오.

[서술형 유형 : 12점 / 난이도 : 중]

> | 보
기 | People can live without a cell phone. (believe / don't believe)
→ *I believe / don't believe that people can live without a cell phone.* |
> |---|---|

1. Smoking in public places should be prohibited. (feel / don't feel)

→ _____

2. There will be peace in the world soon. (doubt / don't doubt)

→ _____

3. Why does the world exist? (wonder / don't wonder)

→ _____

4. When will I die? (would like to know / wouldn't like to know)

→ _____

5. Someone may make unwise decisions about my future. (afraid / not afraid)

→ _____

6. What do I want to do with my life? (know / don't know)

→ _____

서술형 평가문제	채 점 기 준	배 점	나의 점수
A	표현이 올바르고 문법, 철자가 모두 정확한 경우	2점×4문항=8점	
B		2점×3문항=6점	
C		2점×6문항=12점	
D		2점×6문항=12점	
공통	문법, 철자가 1개씩 틀린 경우	각 문항당 1점씩 감점	
	내용과 전혀 일치하지 않거나 답을 기재하지 못한 경우	0점	

실전 서술형 평가문제

출제의도 의문사가 없는 간접의문문
평가내용 상대방에 대한 정보를 간접적으로 물어보기

D. Wilson과 Laura는 오늘 소개팅을 했다. 두 사람이 서로에 대해 궁금해 하는 질문을 보고 서로에게 했을
법한 말을 간접의문문으로 각각 세 문장씩 만드시오.
[서술형 유형 : 12점 / 난이도 : 중]

Wilson

1. Does she like classical music?
2. Did she have many boyfriends?
3. Does she like to watch soccer game?
4. Does she want me to call?
5. Is she thinking about me?
6. Has she lived in other countries?

Laura

1. Can he ski?
2. Does he like to go to the movies?
3. Has he done volunteer work?
4. Is he neat and tidy?
5. Should I call him?
6. Did he study Korean in school?

What Wilson would say....

보기	*I wonder if[whether] you like classical music.*

1. I don't know _____.

2. Please tell me _____.

3. I wonder _____.

What Laura would say...

4. I want to know _____.

5. Can I ask you _____?

6. I don't know _____.

Chapter 5

관계사 (Relatives)

형용사절

1-1 명사를 구체적으로 설명하는 형용사절

Jane bought an **interesting** book.
Jane은 재미있는 책을 한 권 샀다.
The book **that I bought** yesterday was very interesting.
내가 어제 산 그 책은 정말 재미있었다.

01 명사를 꾸며 주는 말은 형용사 외에도 여러 가지가 있다. 형용사는 명사의 상태를, '전치사+명사'는 명사의 위치나 장소를, 부정사와 분사는 명사의 동작이나 행위를 설명해 주는데 이중에서 관계사(형용사절)가 명사를 가장 구체적으로 설명해 준다. 이 모두 형용사와 똑같이 바로 앞의 명사를 수식한다.

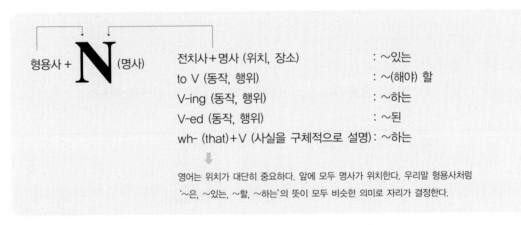

형용사 + **N** (명사)

전치사+명사 (위치, 장소) : ~있는
to V (동작, 행위) : ~(해야) 할
V-ing (동작, 행위) : ~하는
V-ed (동작, 행위) : ~된
wh- (that)+V (사실을 구체적으로 설명) : ~하는

영어는 위치가 대단히 중요하다. 앞에 모두 명사가 위치한다. 우리말 형용사처럼 '~은, ~있는, ~할, ~하는'의 뜻이 모두 비슷한 의미로 자리가 결정한다.

I met a **pretty** girl yesterday. 나는 어제 예쁜 소녀를 만났다. ▶ 형용사: 명사의 상태만 설명하며 동작은 표현 못함

The girls **in the shop** are ghosts. 가게 안에 있는 그 소녀들은 귀신이다.
▶ 전치사+명사: 위치나 장소를 설명하며 상태나 동작은 표현 못함

I have much assignment **to finish** by tomorrow.
나는 내일까지 끝내야 할 많은 과제가 있다. ▶ to부정사: 동작을 설명하며 상태는 표현 못함

The girl **playing tennis** over there is my sister.
저기에서 테니스를 치고 있는 소녀가 내 언니다. ▶ 현재분사: 동작을 설명하며 상태는 표현 못함

I bought a car **made in Japan**. 나는 일본에서 만들어진 차를 샀다. ▶ 과거분사: 동작을 설명하며 상태는 표현 못함

The man **who lives next door** is very friendly. 옆집에 사는 그 남자는 매우 친절하다.
▶ 형용사절: 사실을 구체적으로 설명

02 **명사 바로 뒤에 위치**하는 who, which, that, when, where, why 등을 **관계사**라고 한다. '누구', '어떤 것', '언제' 등과 같이 의문사로 해석하지 않고 '~하는, ~했던'의 의미로 명사를 수식한다.

It is the house [**which** she once lived in]. 그것은 그녀가 한때 살았던 집이다.

Tell me the reason [**why** you have done so]. 네가 그렇게 한 이유를 말해.

서술형 기초다지기

Challenge 1 다음 문장에서 명사를 꾸며 주는 부분을 대괄호[ ]로 묶고 그 부분만 해석해 보세요.

보기	The book [which you gave me] was interesting.	→	네가 나에게 준 책
	The novel [written by Hemingway] is interesting.	→	헤밍웨이에 의해 쓰여진/헤밍웨이가 쓴 소설

01. I can't remember the place where we met yesterday. → _____

02. I saw a girl who was playing tennis. → _____

03. The woman in the restaurant is my mother. → _____

04. I have some coffee to drink. → _____

05. Practice is the only way to learn a foreign language. → _____

06. There was a girl reading a newspaper. → _____

07. They were talking about something that I didn't know. → _____

08. Do you remember the day when we first met? → _____

09. What's the name of the restaurant where we had dinner last night? → _____

10. They have no children to take care of. → _____

11. Korea is the country which I want to live in. → _____

12. A kangaroo is an animal that lives in Australia. → _____

13. The car repaired by the man is mine. → _____

Unit 02 관계대명사

2-1 주격 관계대명사

I know **a woman**. + **The woman** wants to be a fashion model.

↓

who (주어를 대명사 처리=주격 관계대명사)

I know a woman **who** wants to be a fashion model.
나는 패션모델이 되고 싶어 하는 여자를 안다.

---

01 영어는 같은 말의 반복을 피하기 위해 대명사(she, he, it...)를 사용한다. 하지만 대명사는 대명사 역할만 할 뿐 문장과 문장을 연결할 수 없다. 따라서 **반복을 피하면서 문장도 연결할 수 있는 관계대명사 who, which, that이 탄생**하게 되었다.

I have **a friend**. + The friend lives in Mexico.

→ I have a friend **who** lives in Mexico. 나는 멕시코에 사는 친구가 있다.

▶ 똑같은 명사(a friend)가 반복된다. 둘 중 하나를 관계대명사 who로 쓰고 문장을 연결시켜 준다.

02 모든 명사나 대명사는 격(=자격)을 가지는데 주어 자리에 쓰면 주격이다. who는 사람을, which는 사물이나 동물을 대신하는 관계대명사이다. **주어 자리에 있는 명사를 대신하면 주격 관계대명사**라고 한다. 따라서 앞에 있는 선행사도 who일 때는 사람, which일 때는 사물이나 동물을 쓴다. who나 which 대신 that으로 바꾸어 쓸 수 있지만 who와 which를 더 자주 쓴다.

I met a boy. He had a special talent for the violin.

→ I met a boy **who** had a special talent for the violin. ▶ more common
나는 바이올린에 특별한 재능을 가진 소년을 만났다.

→ I met a boy **that** had a special talent for the violin.

The buildings will be torn down. They were built illegally.

→ The buildings **which** were built illegally will be torn down. ▶ more common
불법으로 지어진 건물들은 철거될 것이다.

→ The buildings **that** were built illegally will be torn down.

03 주격 관계대명사는 주어를 대명사 who/which/that으로 처리했으므로 이들 **관계대명사 바로 뒤에 동사부터 등장**한다. 동사의 단/복수는 바로 앞에 있는 선행사(명사)가 단수이면 단수 동사, 복수이면 복수 동사를 쓴다.

Do you know **the man** who **lives** next door? 옆집에 사는 남자를 아니?

I don't like **stories** which **have** unhappy endings. 나는 불행한 결말을 가진 이야기들을 좋아하지 않는다.

I know **the women** who **are** eating next to Tom. 나는 Tom 옆에서 식사를 하고 있는 여자들을 안다.

Give me **the book** which **is** on the desk. 책상 위에 있는 책을 주세요.

서술형 기초다지기

Challenge 1   다음 괄호 안의 관계대명사 중 알맞은 것을 고르세요.

01. A person (who / which) drinks a lot of water is healthy.

02. Anyone (who / which) is interested in the job must apply before next Friday.

03. The river (who / which) flows through London is the Thames.

Challenge 2   다음 두 문장을 관계대명사 who나 which를 사용하여 한 문장으로 쓰세요.

> **보기**
> I know a boy. He plays online games every night.
> → *I know a boy who plays online games every night.*

01. The girl is now in the hospital. She was injured in the accident.

→ _____

02. A building has now been rebuilt. It was destroyed in the fire.

→ _____

03. The bus runs every half hour. It goes to the airport.

→ _____

04. A passport is a special paper. It permits a citizen to travel to other countries.

→ _____

05. Ginny works for a company. The company makes washing machines.

→ _____

Challenge 3   다음 괄호 안의 표현 중 알맞은 것을 고르세요.

01. I can't find the book that (were / was) on the desk.

02. Food which (are / is) fresh is good for you.

03. Look at the house which (is / are) covered with snow.

04. I saw the people that (were / was) playing soccer at the park.

05. Where is the cheese which (were / was) in the refrigerator?

2-2 목적격 관계대명사

This is the car. Rita bought it last year.
→ This is the car **which** Rita bought last year.
→ This is the car **that** Rita bought last year.
→ This is the car Rita bought last year.
이것은 Rita가 작년에 구입한 자동차이다.

01 모든 명사나 대명사는 격(＝자격)을 가지는데 목적어 자리에 쓰면 목적격이다. 대명사(he, she, it..)는 목적어로 쓰인 명사를 대신할 뿐, 문장을 연결할 수 없다. 따라서 **반복을 피하면서 문장을 연결할 수 있는 목적격 관계대명사 whom, which, that이 탄생**하게 되었다.

Nancy is a student. + Everyone likes the student.

→ Nancy is a student **who(m)** everyone likes. Nancy는 모두가 좋아하는 학생이다.
  ▶ 똑같은 명사 2개 중 하나를 목적격 관계대명사 whom(＝the student)으로 바꿔서 문장을 연결한다.

02 목적격 관계대명사 whom은 목적어로 **사람**을, which는 목적어로 **사물이나 동물**을 대신한다. 따라서 앞에 있는 선행사도 whom은 사람, which는 사물이나 동물이 나온다. 둘 다 that으로 바꾸어 쓸 수 있다.

 The film was moving. I saw it last night. 그 영화는 감동적이었다. 나는 어젯밤 그것을 보았다.

→ The film **which**(＝**that**) I saw last night was moving. 어젯밤 내가 본 그 영화는 감동적이었다.

 The people were Korean. Tom visited them yesterday.
그 사람들은 한국인이었다. Tom은 어제 그들을 방문했다.

→ The people **who** Tom visited yesterday were Korean. Tom이 어제 방문한 사람들은 한국인이었다.

03 목적어를 대신한 **목적격 관계대명사는 항상 생략**이 가능하다. whom은 다소 형식을 갖춘 표현이기 때문에 일상 영어에서는 who를 더 많이 쓴다. 그러나 생략하는 것이 더 자연스럽다.

This orange (**which**) I bought in the market tastes good.
내가 시장에서 산 이 오렌지는 맛이 좋다.

The man (**whom**) we saw in the restaurant was a movie director.
우리가 식당에서 본 그 남자는 영화감독이었다.

※ 목적격 관계대명사는 목적어를 대명사 who/which/that으로 처리했으므로 who/which/that 바로 뒤에 '주어＋(타)동사'가 온다. 「명사＋명사＋동사~」로 이어지면 목적격 관계대명사가 생략된 것으로 보고 '~하는, ~했던'으로 해석하며 앞에 있는 명사를 꾸며 준다는 점을 염두에 두자.

서술형 기초다지기

Challenge 1 다음 두 문장을 관계대명사 who(m), which를 이용하여 한 문장으로 만드세요.

> **보기**
> The people were very friendly. We met them at the party.
> → *The people who(m) we met at the party were very friendly.*

01. That's the woman. I met her a few times last year.

    → _____

02. Albert Einstein is a name. Everybody knows the name.

    → _____

03. This is a new 3D game. I want to buy it.

    → _____

04. She is the author. The prosecutor accused her of a crime.

    → _____

05. The hard drive doesn't have a warranty. You bought it yesterday.

    → _____

Challenge 2 다음 중 생략할 수 있는 관계대명사를 괄호로 묶으세요.

01. The woman who lives next door is a dentist.

02. Have you found the keys which you lost?

03. The man who you saw was not the famous actor.

04. The movies that we watched this summer were all good.

05. Jane gave me a doll that was made of paper.

06. The tourists whom Wilson guided were from Germany.

07. We are looking for someone who is intelligent and dedicated.

08. She took the medicine that the doctor prescribed.

2-3 소유격 관계대명사

A mermaid is a legendary woman. **Her body** is like a fish from the waist down.
인어는 전설적인 여인이다. 그녀 몸의 하반신은 마치 물고기와 같다.

→ A mermaid is a legendary woman **whose body** is like a fish from the waist down.
인어는 하반신이 마치 물고기와 같은 전설적인 여인이다.

01

my book(나의 책)에서 소유격은 my이다. 이 **소유격을 대신할 수 있는 관계대명사가 whose**이다. 소유격은 뒤에 명사가 없으면 문장에서 아무런 역할도 할 수 없는 것과 마찬가지로 관계대명사 whose도 my, her, his 등과 같이 「~의+명사」와 같은 역할을 한다. whose가 my, her, his 등과 다른 것은 **문장과 문장을 연결**시켜 줄 수 있다는 점이다.

I know a girl.　**Her** father　is a movie star.
　　　　　　　　　　↓
　　　　　　　whose father

→ I know a girl **whose father** is a movie star. 나는 아빠가 영화배우인 소녀를 안다.

I know a man.　**His** house　is by the river.
　　　　　　　　　↓
　　　　　　whose house

→ I know a man **whose house** is by the river. 나는 강 옆에 자신의 집이 있는 사람을 알고 있다.

※ 소유격 관계대명사 whose는 선행사가 사람이든 사물이든 모두 사용하며 생략할 수 없다.

02

소유격 whose, of which는 주로 학술지 같은 문어체의 딱딱한 형식에서 자주 쓰이며 **일상 영어에서는 with를 사용하여 소유를 나타내는 간단한 문장으로** 쓴다.

I found a house **whose** walls were green. 나는 벽들이 초록색인 집을 발견했다. ▶ 문어체
I found a house **of which** walls were green. ▶ 문어체
I found a house **with** green walls. ▶ 자연스러운 표현

I need an iPad **whose** memory is vast. 나는 용량이 큰 아이패드가 필요하다. ▶ 문어체
I need an iPad **of which** memory is vast. ▶ 문어체
I need an iPad **with** a vast memory. ▶ 자연스러운 표현

03

관계대명사의 종류를 표로 정리해보면 다음과 같다.

선행사	주격	목적격	소유격
사람	who, that	who(m), that	whose
사물/동물	which, that	which, that	whose, of which

서술형 기초다지기

Challenge 1   다음 두 문장을 관계대명사 whose를 이용하여 한 문장으로 만드세요.

> 보기
> There are many words. + I don't know their meanings.
> → *There are many words whose meanings I don't know.*

01. I know a man. + His brother is a guitarist in a pop group.

→ _____

02. I met a pretty girl. + Her parents run a big bakery downtown.

→ _____

03. I know a man. + His daughter is a professional wrestler.

→ _____

04. We're going to buy a car. + Its color is very beautiful.

→ _____

05. The woman called the police. + Her purse was stolen.

→ _____

06. I apologized to the woman. + I spilled her coffee.

→ _____

Challenge 2   다음 빈칸에 who, which, whose 중 알맞은 것을 골라 쓰세요.

01. I hate the woman _____ I met at the party last night.

02. A widow is a woman _____ husband is dead.

03. I met somebody _____ mother writes detective stories.

04. What have you done with the money _____ I gave you?

05. Is this the book _____ you paid $30 for the other day?

06. We salute the wife _____ husband sacrificed himself for his country.

전치사와 관계대명사

Do you know the woman? Bob is talking <u>to</u> her.
너는 그 여자를 아니? Bob은 그녀와 이야기를 하고 있다.
→ Do you know the woman **who(m)** Bob is talking **to**?
→ Do you know the woman **that** Bob is talking **to**?
→ Do you know the woman **to whom** Bob is talking?
→ Do you know the woman Bob is talking **to**?
Bob이 이야기하고 있는 그 여자를 아니?

01 모든 명사는 격(=자격)을 가지는데 전치사는 뒤에 항상 명사 형태의 목적격을 가진다. (대)명사가 사람인 경우 whom으로 대명사 처리한다. 전치사는 뒤에 그대로 놔두고 who(m)만 쓸 수 있고, 전치사와 함께 '전치사+whom'으로 쓸 수도 있다. 하지만 전치사를 뒤로 보내고 관계대명사를 생략하는 것이 가장 자연스럽다.

She is the pretty model. I talked <u>about</u> **her.**
→ She's the pretty model **who(m)** I talked <u>about</u>. ▶ 전치사의 목적어인 her를 관계대명사 who(m)로 고침
→ She's the pretty model **that** I talked <u>about</u>. ▶ 전치사를 뒤로 보낼 때만 that 사용 가능
→ She's the pretty model <u>about</u> **whom** I talked. ▶ whom을 who로 쓰지 못함
→ She's the pretty model I talked <u>about</u>. ▶ 전치사를 뒤로 보내면 관계대명사 생략 가능
그녀는 내가 이야기했던 예쁜 모델이다.

02 전치사의 목적어인 (대)명사가 사람이 아닌 경우 which를 쓴다. 마찬가지로 전치사를 관계사절 뒤로 보내고 관계대명사 which를 생략하는 것이 가장 자연스럽다.

English is the subject. I'm interested <u>in</u> **it.**
→ English is the subject **which** I'm interested <u>in</u>. ▶ 전치사의 목적어인 it을 관계대명사 which로 고침
→ English is the subject **that** I'm interested <u>in</u>. ▶ 전치사를 뒤로 보낼 때만 that 사용 가능
→ English is the subject <u>in</u> **which** I'm interested. ▶ 「전치사+관계대명사」에서는 which를 that으로 바꿔 쓸 수 없음
→ English is the subject I'm interested <u>in</u>. ▶ 전치사를 뒤로 보낼 때만 관계대명사 생략 가능
영어는 내가 재미있어 하는 과목이다.

※ 「전치사+관계대명사(whom, which)」를 함께 쓸 경우에는 who 또는 that으로 바꿔 쓸 수 없고 관계대명사를 생략할 수도 없다. 목적격 관계대명사를 생략하기 위해서는 전치사를 형용사절 뒤로 보내야 한다.

This is the house in which I live. (O)
This is the house **in that** I live. (×)
This is the house I live in. (O)
This is the house **in** I live. (×)

서술형 기초다지기

정답 p. 18

Challenge 1   두 문장을 관계대명사를 이용하여 가능한 모든 형태의 한 문장으로 만들어 보세요.

보기	The music was good. We listened to the music. → *The music to which we listened was good.* → *The music which we listened to was good.* → *The music that we listened to was good.* → *The music we listened to was good.*

01. The woman left him after a few weeks. He fell in love with her.

→ _____

→ _____

→ _____

→ _____

02. This is the book. We talked about the book yesterday.

→ _____

→ _____

→ _____

→ _____

Challenge 2   다음 문장을 〈보기〉와 같이 바꿀 때 빈칸에 알맞은 말을 쓰세요.

보기	You were looking for some keys. → Are these the keys *you were looking for*?

01. You told me about a hotel.

→ What's the name of that hotel _____?

02. We were invited to a wedding.

→ Unfortunately, we couldn't go to the wedding _____.

2-5 관계대명사 what의 용법 / that만 사용하는 경우

The thing which(=that) made me upset was his attitude.
=what

→ **What** made me upset was his attitude.
나를 화나게 했던 것은 그의 태도였다.

01 what은 선행사인 the thing(s)과 관계대명사 which나 that을 대신하며 '~한 것'이란 뜻이다. 선행사를 포함하고 있으므로 what 앞에 선행사인 명사를 쓰지 않는다.

I don't want to remember **what** they did to me. 나는 그들이 내게 했던 것을 기억하고 싶지 않다.

=I don't want to remember **the things which(=that)** they did to me.

What happened last night was really shocking. 어젯밤 발생한 일은 정말 충격적이었다.

=**The thing that(=which)** happened last night was really shocking.

※ the thing(s) which/that처럼 선행사 뒤에 위치하는 관계대명사는 '~하는'으로 해석하지만 선행사가 없는 what은 문장에서 명사절이 되어 명사 자리인 주어, 목적어, 보어 자리에서 '~하는 (모든) 것'으로 해석된다.

02 관계대명사 what을 이용한 표현 중에는 단어나 구를 강조하는 표현이 있다.

I need a good dictionary.   →   **What I want** is a good dictionary.
나는 좋은 사전이 필요해.   내가 원하는 건 좋은 사전이야. ▶ good dictionary 강조

I want to sleep now.   →   **What I want to do now** is sleep.
나는 지금 자고 싶다.   내가 지금 하고 싶은 것은 잠자는 것이다. ▶ sleep 강조

03 다음의 경우에는 관계대명사 that만 쓴다.

① 선행사가 '사람+동물(사물)'일 때
　　Look at **the boy and his dog** that are running to the park. 공원으로 뛰어가고 있는 저 소년과 개를 봐라.

② all, any, every, no, -thing 등이 선행사에 사용된 경우
　　All that you read in this book will do you good. 이 책에서 읽는 것은 모두 네게 이익이 될 것이다.

③ 선행사가 부정대명사나 의문대명사인 경우

④ 최상급 형용사가 선행사를 수식하는 경우
　　This is **the longest novel** that I have ever read. 이것은 내가 지금까지 읽은 것 중에 가장 긴 소설이다.

⑤ 서수, the only, the same, the very 등이 선행사를 수식하는 경우
　　This is **the very book** that I have been looking for. 이것은 내가 찾고 있던 바로 그 책이다.

※ 현대 영어에서는 선행사 앞에 이러한 단어가 있더라도 선행사가 사람이면 that보다 who를 주로 쓰고, 사물이면 which보다 that을 주로 쓴다. 이는 구식 영어에 속하나, 현재 시험에 등장하고 있으므로 설명하였다. 사람과 사물이 함께 나오는 경우에는 that을 쓰지만 그런 예문은 극히 드물다.

서술형 기초다지기

Challenge 1 다음 두 문장을 what을 이용하여 한 문장으로 만드세요.

> **보기**
> I'm going to tell you the thing. It made me upset.
> → *I'm going to tell you what made me upset.*

01. I told you that at the meeting. That is really important.

→ _____

02. I can't believe that. She said that.

→ _____

03. Show me the thing. It is in your bag.

→ _____

04. Do you believe the thing? He said that last month?

→ _____

Challenge 2 다음 괄호 안의 표현 중에서 알맞은 것을 고르세요.

01. (What / That) I bought for you is good for your health.

02. (What / That) the atom is not a solid bit of matter became evident with the discovery of radioactivity.

03. The movie reminds me (that / what) honesty is important.

Challenge 3 다음 〈보기〉와 같이 빈칸에 알맞은 말을 쓰세요.

> **보기**
> What did he say? → *What he said* wasn't true.

01. What do you want?　　　　　　→ You may eat _____.

02. What did Kathy see in town?　→ I didn't know _____ in town.

관계대명사의 계속적 용법

I met Tom **who** gave me this ring.
나는 이 반지를 내게 준 Tom을 만났다.

I met Bob, **who** gave me this ring.
나는 Bob을 만났는데, 그가 이 반지를 내게 주었다.

01 계속적 용법은 관계대명사 앞에 comma(,)가 있어 선행사에 대해 **부가적인 설명을 덧붙이고자 할 때 사용**한다.

한정적 용법	계속적 용법
I saw a woman **who** was bleeding on her face. 나는 얼굴에 피를 흘리고 있던 여자를 봤다. ❶ 관계대명사 앞에 comma(,)가 없다. ❷ 형용사절의 수식을 받아 어떤 명사를 특정한 것으로 한정한다. (아무 여자가 아닌 피를 흘리는 여자로 한정) ❸ 선행사를 꾸며 주며 '~하는, ~하고 있는'으로 해석한다.	I saw Lisa, **who** was bleeding on her face. (=and she) 나는 Lisa를 보았는데, 그녀는 얼굴에 피를 흘리고 있었다. ❶ 관계대명사 앞에 comma(,)가 있다. ❷ 관계대명사절은 선행사가 어떤 명사인지를 이미 알고 있는 상황에서 선행사에 대한 부가적인 설명을 한다. ❸ 앞에서 뒤로 해석하며 who는 '그런데 그 사람은' 하고 쭉 읽어 내려가고, which는 '그런데 그것은' 하고 쭉 읽어 내려간다.
We stayed at the hotel **which** Jane recommended to us. 우리는 Jane이 추천했던 그 호텔에서 머물렀다. 형용사절의 수식을 받는 선행사(명사)를 아주 구체적으로 설명해 준다. '어떤 호텔인지'를 한정해 주는 구조이다.	We stayed at the Hyatt Hotel, **which** Jane recommended to us. 우리는 하얏트 호텔에서 머물렀는데, 그것은 Jane이 우리에게 추천했던 곳이다. '어떤 사람이나 사물인지'를 설명하지 않는다. 이미 어떤 사람(사물)인지를 알고 있어(the Hyatt Hotel), 부가적인 정보를 제공한다.

02 계속적 용법의 관계대명사는 「접속사+대명사」의 의미를 지닌다. 이때 접속사는 문맥에 맞게 and, but, for(=because) 등을 적절히 사용하면 된다. 계속적 용법으로 쓰이는 who(m)나 which는 that으로 바꾸어 쓸 수 없고 생략할 수도 없다.

Kevin married Alice, **whose** brother is a lawyer. Kevin은 Alice와 결혼했는데, 그녀의 오빠는 변호사이다.

→ Kevin married Alice, **and her** brother is a lawyer.

I like this show, **which** is very exciting. 나는 이 쇼를 좋아하는데, 그것은 흥미진진하다.

→ I like this show, **for it** is very exciting.

서술형 기초다지기

Challenge 1

다음 관계대명사의 계속적 용법과 의미가 같도록 빈칸을 「접속사(and, but, for)＋대명사」 형태로 써 보세요.

01. He likes her, who is very wealthy.

→ He likes her, _____ _____ is very wealthy.

02. I tried to move the sofa, which I found impossible.

→ I tried to move the sofa, _____ I found _____ impossible.

03. I met the man, who did not tell me the news.

→ I met the man, _____ _____ didn't tell me the news.

04. He passed the test, which surprised everyone.

→ He passed the test, _____ _____ surprised everyone.

Challenge 2

〈보기〉와 같이 주어진 표현을 이용하여 계속적 용법의 관계사 문장을 완성하세요.
(단, who, which 사용할 것)

보기	Kelly is a dentist. (She lives next door.) → *Kelly, who lives next door, is a dentist.* We went to the museum. (Bob recommended it to us.) → *We went to the museum, which Bob recommended to us.*

01. The new stadium will be opened next week. (It can hold 100,000 people.)

→ _____

02. My English teacher loves us. (She comes from Texas.)

→ _____

03. Wilson is one of my closest friends. (I have known him for a very long time.)

→ _____

04. I'll introduce our new program. (It will help you lose weight.)

→ _____

3-1 관계부사 when, where

That is **the library**. + We used to study **in that library**.
→ where(부사구 대신)
That is the library **where** we used to study.
That is **the library**. + We used to study in **that library**.
→ which(대명사 처리)
That is the library **which** we used to study **in**.
That is the library **in which** we used to study.
저것이 우리가 공부했던 도서관이다.

---

01 관계부사는 말 그대로 부사(구)를 대신하고 문장과 문장을 연결할 수 있는 말이다. 관계대명사와 마찬가지로 앞에 있는 명사(선행사)를 꾸며 주며 '~하는, ~했던, ~할+(앞에 있는) 명사'로 해석한다.

선행사의 종류	관계부사	전치사+관계대명사
장소(the place, the house 등)	where	at/on/in+which
시간(the time, the year 등)	when	at/on/in+which

02 관계부사 where는 장소를 나타내는 부사(구)를 대신한다. 부사구 「전치사+명사」에서 명사를 대신할 때는 당연히 which를 써야 한다. where 대신 which를 쓸 경우 **which가 생략되더라도 전치사는 생략할 수 없다.**

I remember **the house**. + I grew up **there(=in the house)**.
→ I remember the house **where(=that)** I grew up. 나는 내가 자랐던 집을 기억한다.
→ I remember the house **which(=that)** I grew up **in**.
→ I remember the house **in which** I grew up.
→ I remember the house I grew up **in**.

03 관계부사 when은 시간을 나타내는 부사(구)를 대신한다. 부사구 「전치사+명사」에서 명사를 대신할 때는 당연히 대명사인 which를 써야 한다. **when 또는 which가 생략될 경우 전치사를 쓰지 않는다.**

I can't forget **the year**. + We first met **then(=on that year)**.
→ I can't forget the year **when(=that)** we first met. 나는 우리가 처음 만났던 그 해를 잊을 수 없다.
→ I can't forget the year **which(=that)** we first met **on**.
→ I can't forget the year **on which** we first met.
→ I can't forget the year we first met. ▶ 전치사 on은 쓰지 않음

서술형 기초다지기

정답 p. 19

Challenge 1   다음 괄호 안의 관계사 중 알맞은 것을 고르세요.

01. Chicago is the city (when / where) Kevin lives.

02. Finally I arrived in Portugal (which / where) I always wanted to visit.

03. 1988 was the year (when / where) the Seoul Olympic Games were held.

Challenge 2   다음 두 문장을 가능한 모든 형태의 한 문장으로 만드세요.

01. The White House is the place. + The President of the United States lives in that place.

→ _____

→ _____

→ _____

→ _____

→ _____

02. 2002 was the year. + The World Cup was held in that year.

→ _____

→ _____

→ _____

→ _____

→ _____

Challenge 3   다음 두 문장을 관계부사 where 또는 when을 이용하여 한 문장으로 만드세요.

01. This is the building. The Japanese tortured out people in this building.

→ _____

02. 2007 was the year. They got married then.

→ _____

3-2 관계부사 why, how

My watch was broken. 내 손목시계가 고장 났다.
That is **the reason**. I missed the train **for that reason**.

— why (부사구 대신)

That's the reason **why** I missed the train.
그것이 내가 열차를 놓친 이유이다.

01 관계부사는 말 그대로 부사(구)를 대신하고, 문장과 문장을 연결할 수 있는 말이다. 관계대명사와 마찬가지로 앞에 있는 명사(선행사)를 꾸며 주며 '~하는, ~했던, ~할+(앞에 있는) 명사'로 해석한다.

선행사의 종류	관계부사	전치사+관계대명사
이유(the reason)	why	for+which
방법(the way)	how	in+which

02 관계부사 why는 이유(reason)를 나타내는 부사구를 대신한다. 부사구 「for+명사」에서 명사를 대명사 처리할 때는 당연히 which를 써서 'for which'로 쓴다. **why 또는 which를 생략할 경우 전치사를 쓰지 않는다.**

She didn't say **the reason**. + She was late **for the reason**.
→ She didn't say the reason **why**(=**that**) she was late. 그녀는 자신이 늦은 이유를 말하지 않았다.
→ She didn't say the reason **for which** she was late.
→ She didn't say the reason she was late.
→ She didn't say **why** she was late.

03 관계부사 how는 방법(way)을 나타내는 부사구를 대신한다. 부사구 「in+명사」에서 명사를 대명사 처리할 때는 당연히 which를 써서 'in which'로 쓴다. **how는 선행사 the way와 함께 쓰지 않고 the way 또는 how만 각각 따로 쓰거나 같이 쓸 경우에는 how 대신 that을 이용하여 the way that으로 써야 한다.**

Tell me the way. + She solved the problem in the way.
→ Tell me the way **in which** she solved the problem. 그녀가 그 문제를 푼 방법을 내게 말해줘.
→ Tell me **the way** she solved the problem. ▶ the way how 함께 쓰지 못함
→ Tell me **how** she solved the problem.
→ Tell me **the way that** she solved the problem.

※ 관계부사는 「선행사+관계부사」 둘 다 쓰기도 하고(the way how는 예외), 선행사를 생략할 수도 있으며, 선행사는 놔
　 두고 관계부사 자체만 생략해서 쓸 수도 있다.

서술형 기초다지기

정답 p. 19

Challenge 1 다음 괄호 안의 관계사 중 알맞은 것을 고르세요.

01. I don't know the reason (how / why) he resigned.

02. Can you tell me (the way how / how) you made it?

03. That's the way (how / that) the brain works under heavy pressure.

04. Tell me the reason (how / that) you came here.

05. That was the way (why / in which) Prince Charles got married.

06. That's the reason (how / for which) Kelly was absent from school yesterday.

Challenge 2 다음 두 문장을 관계부사 why 또는 how를 이용하여 한 문장으로 만드세요.

> **보기**
> I know the way. + He operated the machine in that way.
> → *I know how he operated the machine.*

01. Do you know the reason? + She moved to Chicago for the reason.

    → _____

02. Can you tell me the way? + You learned English in that way.

    → _____

Challenge 3 다음 우리말과 뜻이 같도록 빈칸에 알맞은 말을 쓰세요.

01. 나는 그녀가 숙제를 하지 않은 이유가 궁금하다.

    → I wonder _____ _____ _____ she didn't do her homework.

02. 그 공포영화가 내가 잠을 자지 못한 이유이다.

    → The horror film was _____ _____ _____ I couldn't sleep.

03. 우리는 북한이 핵 기술을 어떻게 가지게 됐는지 모른다.

    → We don't know _____ North Korea acquired their nuclear technology.

3-3 관계부사의 독특한 특징

Can you tell me **the reason why** she yelled at me?
그녀가 내게 소리를 지른 이유를 말해 줄 수 있니?
= Can you tell me **the reason** she yelled at me?
= Can you tell me **why** she yelled at me?

01 관계부사는 **선행사인 명사(시간, 이유, 방법, 장소)를 생략**해서 쓰기도 하고, **관계부사 자체를 생략**해서 쓰기도 한다. 특히, 관계부사가 생략되면 문장은 '명사＋명사'가 연이어 나와 목적격 관계대명사를 생략한 것과 혼동될 수 있다.

They still remember (**the time**) **when** people were dying of hunger in Seoul.
They still remember **the time** (**when**) people were dying of hunger in Seoul.
그들은 서울에서 사람들이 굶어 죽었던 때를 아직도 기억한다.

※ when은 일상 영어에서 빈번히 생략되지만 where와 why는 자주 생략하지 않는다.

02 목적격 관계대명사(whom, which)는 목적어를 대신하는 대명사이므로 관계절 안에 **타동사의 목적어 또는 전치사의 목적어가 반드시 빠져** 있다. 하지만 **관계부사**는 명사가 아닌 부사(구)를 대신하므로 관계부사절 문장은 '**주어＋타동사＋목적어 / 전치사＋목적어**'가 완벽하게 존재한다.

I'd like to visit **the house Jane** wants to buy. 나는 Jane이 사고 싶어 하는 그 집을 방문하고 싶다.
▶ buy의 목적어가 없으므로 목적격 관계대명사가 생략된 문장이다. 관계부사 where로 착각하면 안 된다.

I'd like to visit **the house Mozart** was born in. 나는 모차르트가 태어난 그 집을 방문하고 싶다.
▶ was born은 자동사로, 「주어＋동사」로 구성된 목적어가 필요 없는 완전한 문장이다. 따라서 관계부사 where가 생략된 문장이다.

03 **that은 모든 관계대명사와 관계부사를 대신**해서 사용할 수 있다. 단, 선행사가 있을 때에만 that을 쓰고, 관계부사와 함께 선행사를 생략할 경우에는 관계부사 대신 that을 쓸 수 없다.

I know **the reason that** she left you. 나는 그녀가 너를 떠난 이유를 알고 있다.
→ I know that she left you. (×) ▶ 선행사가 생략되었으므로 반드시 관계부사 why를 써야 한다.

Tell me **the way that** you fixed the broken computer. 고장 난 컴퓨터를 고친 방법을 내게 말해줘.
→ Tell me that you fixed the broken computer. (×) ▶ 선행사가 생략되었으므로 반드시 관계부사 how를 써야 한다.

서술형 기초다지기

Challenge 1
다음 문장에서 목적격 관계대명사나 관계부사가 생략된 부분에 V 표시하고 무엇이 생략되었는지 쓰세요.

| 보기 | I'll never forget the restaurant ⱽI met her. | → | _관계부사 생략_ |

01. This is the hotel Tom Cruise stayed.   → _____

02. The album he recorded in 2002 was a great success.   → _____

03. The documentary we saw last night was great.   → _____

04. I miss last summer vacation we first traveled to Europe.   → _____

05. Have you ever been in that shop Nancy bought her a beautiful dress? → _____

06. You have a sponsor you must submit a report to.   → _____

Challenge 2
다음 관계부사 문장을 〈보기〉와 같이 가능한 2~3가지 형태로 다시 써 보세요.

| 보기 | This is the city where we wanted to visit a long time ago.
 → _This is where we wanted to visit a long time ago._
 → _This is the city we wanted to visit a long time ago._
 → _This is the city that we wanted to visit a long time ago._ |

01. This is the reason why she became so excited.

→ _____

→ _____

→ _____

02. I remember the day when I took my first airplane ride.

→ _____

→ _____

→ _____

Unit 04 복합관계사

4-1 복합 관계대명사 / 복합 관계부사

The boss will hire **whoever** he likes.
= The boss will hire **anyone who** he likes.
사장은 자신이 마음에 들어 하는 사람은 누구든 고용할 것이다.

01 복합관계사는 모두 what처럼 선행사 없이 단독으로 절(wh-ever+주어+동사)을 구성한다.

복합 관계대명사	명사절	양보의 부사절
whoever	anyone who(~하는 사람은 누구나)	no matter who(누가 ~한다 할지라도)
whichever	anything that(~하는 것은 어느 것이나)	no matter which(어느 것이[을] ~한다 할지라도)
whatever	anything that(~하는 것은 무엇이나)	no matter what(무엇이[을] ~한다 할지라도)

복합 관계부사	부사절	양보의 부사절
whenever	at any time when(~하는 때는 언제나)	no matter when(언제 ~한다 할지라도)
wherever	at/to any place where(~하는 곳은 어디에나)	no matter where(어디서 ~한다 할지라도)
however		however+형용사/부사+S+V (아무리 ~한다 하더라도)
		no matter how(아무리 ~한다 하더라도)

Whoever finishes the race first will win the grand prize.
일등으로 경주를 마치는 사람은 누구든지 대상을 탈 것이다.
= **Anyone who** finishes the race first will win the grand prize.

Whoever you are, you shouldn't talk like that. 당신이 누구든지 그렇게 말하면 안 된다.
= **No matter who** you are, you shouldn't talk like that.

Whatever has a beginning has an end. 시작이 있는 것은 모두 끝이 있다.
= **Anything that** has a beginning has an end.

She was allowed to go **wherever** she liked. 그녀가 좋아하는 곳이면 어디든지 가도록 허락받았다.
= She was allowed to go **at any place where** she liked.

Wherever you may go, you can't succeed without perseverance.
네가 어디를 가더라도 인내 없이는 성공할 수 없다.
= **No matter where** you may go, you can't succeed without perseverance.

However far you may be, I will meet you someday. 당신이 아무리 멀리 있더라도 나는 언젠가 당신을 만날 것이다.
= **No matter how** far you may be, I will meet you someday.

서술형 기초다지기

Challenge 1 다음 괄호 안의 표현 중 어법상 올바른 것을 고르세요.

01. (Whoever / Whenever) I wash my car, it rains.

02. (Whoever / Whomever) broke the mirror will have to pay for it.

03. (Whoever / Whatever) visits this site is allowed access to all the information.

04. (However / Whichever) you buy, there is a one-year guarantee.

05. (Whatever / However) expensive it may be, I'll buy that cell phone.

Challenge 2 다음 복합관계사 문장을 no matter ~, anything, anyone, at any place[time] 중에서 알맞은 것을 이용하여 바꿔 쓰세요.

> **보기**
> Whatever she does, I'll always love her.
> → *No matter what she does, I'll always love her.*

01. Whoever comes to the office, don't bother our important meeting.

→ _____

02. However much you give them, it's never enough.

→ _____

03. There are times when you can't do whatever you like.

→ _____

04. Mother Teresa was welcomed wherever she went.

→ _____

05. Whoever arrives first will be the winner.

→ _____

06. You can talk to her whenever you want.

→ _____

01 출제 100 % - 선행사와 관계사는 관계사절 안에서 판단한다.

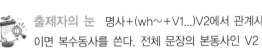 **출제자의 눈** 관계사의 선택은 선행사에 의해서 결정된다. 선행사가 사람, 사물, 장소, 시간일 때 알맞은 관계사를 고르는 문제가 기본으로 출제된다. 조심할 것은 선행사에 따라 관계부사를 써야 할 것 같지만 그렇지 않은 경우이다. 즉, 목적어가 빠져 있으면 아무리 장소/시간의 선행사가 오더라도 관계대명사를 써야 한다. 관계부사는 부사(구)를 대신하는 말이므로 관계부사절은 완벽한 문장을 이루게 된다.

Ex 1.

My father carried old furniture with my brother _____ had to be taken to the basement.

(a) who   (b) which   (c) where   (d) when

Ex 2.

The house _____ she wants to buy is very large.

(a) where   (b) who   (c) which   (d) at which

02 출제 100 % - 수의 일치는 선행사가 결정한다.

출제자의 눈 명사+(wh~+V1...)V2에서 관계사절 안의 동사 V1은 선행사가 단수이면 단수동사, 복수이면 복수동사를 쓴다. 전체 문장의 본동사인 V2 또한 선행사(주어)에 단, 복수를 일치시킨다. V1과 V2의 수를 틀리게 써넣는 경우가 많다. 학생들이 어려워하는 것 중 하나가 소유격 관계대명사를 구별하는 것인데, 소유격 관계대명사 바로 뒤에 명사 또는 명사+be동사가 있거나, 절 안에 타동사와 목적어가 완벽하게 있을 경우에 소유격을 쓴다. 관계부사 또한 소유격 관계대명사와 같이 관계사절 안의 문장성분이 완벽하게 존재하지만, 이때는 선행사로 이 둘을 구별하면 된다. 관계부사는 선행사를 사람으로 받을 수 없다는 것을 명심하면 된다.

Ex 3.

People who _____ chopsticks and spoons _____ mostly East Asians.

(a) uses – is   (b) use – is   (c) uses – are   (d) use – are

Ex 4.

I know a girl _____ brother is a movie star.

(a) who   (b) where   (c) whose   (d) which

03 **출제 100 % - 관계대명사를 이용한 영작문제는 반드시 출제된다.**

 출제자의 눈 관계대명사를 이용한 영작문제를 단답형 주관식 또는 서술형으로 반드시 출제한다. 두 개의 문장을 주고 관계사를 이용한 문장으로 쓰게 하거나 우리말이나 표현 몇 개를 주고 부분 영작하게 하는 문제도 출제 가능하다. 특히 선행사 없이 단독으로 절을 이끄는 what을 「선행사(the thing)＋관계대명사(which/that)」로 고쳐 쓰거나 이를 다시 what으로 고쳐 영작할 줄 아는지를 물어보기도 한다.

Ex 5.

다음 빈칸에 알맞은 말을 쓰시오.

The woman was away on vacation. ＋ I wanted to see her.

→ The woman ＿＿＿＿＿＿＿＿＿＿ was away on vacation.

Ex 6.

다음 두 문장의 의미가 같도록 빈칸에 알맞은 말을 쓰시오.

The thing that happened last night was really shocking.

＝＿＿＿＿ ＿＿＿＿ ＿＿＿＿ ＿＿＿＿ was really shocking.

04 **출제 100 % - 관계대명사 what과 접속사 that을 구별하라.**

 출제자의 눈 관계대명사 what과 명사절을 이끄는 접속사 that을 구별하는 문제가 출제될 수 있다. that절 뒤에는 완전한 문장이 오지만 what절에는 주어 또는 목적어가 빠져 있는 불완전한 문장이 온다. 관계대명사 what과 같은 의미의 문장을 찾는 문제나 접속사 that과 목적격 관계대명사 that을 섞어 놓고 구별하는 문제가 출제되기도 한다.

Ex 7.

＿＿＿＿ I said yesterday was not what I meant.

(a) That   (b) What   (c) Who   (d) Which

Ex 8.

밑줄 친 부분의 쓰임이 나머지와 다른 것은?

(a) What makes a diet good or bad is the way the foods fit together.

(b) What else do you want?

(c) She gave me what I want.

(d) What he asked for is this dictionary.

05 출제 100% - 관계부사절은 완전한 문장이 온다.

 출제자의 눈 관계부사는 장소, 방법, 시간, 이유 등의 부사(구)를 대신하며 관계부사절 안의 주어, 동사, 목적어 등 문장성분은 하나도 빠짐없이 완벽하게 존재한다. 이 내용을 기억한다면 관계대명사와 관계부사를 구별하는 문제는 쉽게 풀 수 있다. 한편, 관계대명사의 계속적 용법은 관계사 앞에 콤마(,)가 있으며 선행사를 수식하는 대신 문장을 이어나가면서 선행사를 부연 설명해 준다. 콤마(,)가 and 또는 but의 역할을 한다고 보면 된다. 계속적 용법으로 쓰인 관계사는 생략할 수 없으며, 콤마(,) 뒤에는 that을 쓰지 않는다. 계속적 용법의 관계대명사를 「접속사+대명사」로 바르게 고친 것을 고르는 문제가 출제된다.

Ex 9.

다음 빈칸에 알맞은 것은?

A boy entered a coffee shop _____ I worked as a waitress.

(a) which   (b) where   (c) when   (d) whose

Ex 10.

밑줄 친 부분과 바꿔 쓸 수 있는 것은?

He lent me a book, <u>which</u> I found very interesting.

(a) for it   (b) and he   (c) but he   (d) and it

06 출제 100% - 관계부사를 이용한 서술형 영작문제도 반드시 출제된다.

 출제자의 눈 두 문장을 주고 알맞은 관계부사를 이용하여 한 문장으로 만들게 하거나 부분 영작을 하라는 문제가 반드시 출제된다. 관계부사를 「전치사+관계대명사」로 바꿔 쓸 수 있는데, 관계부사 where와 when은 'in/at/on which'로, why는 'for which'로, how는 'in which'로 전환이 가능하다. 부사구 전체를 관계부사로 쓸 때는 전치사를 쓰지 않는다. 관계부사를 생략하면 전치사를 쓰지 않으나 where를 생략하는 경우에는 전치사를 빠뜨리지 않도록 주의하자.

Ex 11.

다음 두 문장을 관계부사 when을 이용하여 한 문장으로 쓰시오.

Valentine's Day was the day. + My boyfriend proposed to me on the day.

Valentine's Day was the day _____.

07 출제 100% - 관계대명사 that을 항상 쓸 수 있는 것은 아니다.

 출제자의 눈 관계부사 중에서 how는 유일하게 선행사(the way)와 함께 쓸 수 없어 둘 중 하나만 쓰거나 'the way that'으로 써야 한다. that은 관계대명사와 관계부사를 대신해서 쓸 수 있는 팔방미인이지만 관계부사와 함께 쓰인 선행사를 생략할 경우에는 that을 쓰지 못하고 관계부사(where, when, why, how)만 써야 한다.

Ex 12.
다음 중 어법상 어색한 것은?
(a) I tried to figure out the way how the machine works.
(b) Tomorrow is the last time that we will be able to see each other before you go.

Ex 13.
다음 중 어법상 어색한 것은?
(a) Can you explain that we need such big money?
(b) It was a time there was no freedom of speech.

08 출제 100% - 복합관계사의 의미와 어순을 조심하라!

 출제자의 눈 복합관계사와 같은 의미의 표현(no matter ~, anything that ~ 등)을 고르거나 영작하는 문제가 출제될 수 있다. 특히, 복합 관계부사 however에 유의하자. however는 양보의 의미만 있으며 no matter how로 바꿔 쓸 수 있다. 「however(=no matter how)+형용사/부사+주어+동사」의 어순에 유의하자.

Ex 14.
빈칸에 공통으로 들어갈 알맞은 단어를 쓰시오.
· _____ I am sad, I listen to music. (나는 슬플 때마다 음악을 들어.)
· _____ she sees me, she always smiles. (그녀는 나를 볼 때마다 항상 웃어.)

Ex 15.
괄호 안의 표현을 이용하여 우리말과 같은 의미가 되도록 빈칸을 채우시오.
_____, I'll buy that car. (그것이 아무리 비싸더라도)
(it, expensive, however, be, may)

1. 다음 밑줄 친 부분과 바꾸어 쓸 수 있는 것은?

> The place <u>where</u> they stole the bike was near the building.

① of which　② for which　③ in that
④ of whom　⑤ in which

[2-3] 다음 빈칸에 알맞은 것을 고르시오.

2.
> Over there is the man _____ daughter is in my English class.

① that　② which　③ of whose
④ who　⑤ whose

3.
> Do you know the woman _____ Bob is talking to?

① that　② which　③ of which
④ how　⑤ when

4. 다음 두 문장을 한 문장으로 만들 때 빈칸에 들어갈 알맞은 단어를 쓰시오.

> This is the house.
> I was born in the house.
> → This is the house _____ _____ I was born.

5. 다음 밑줄 친 부분 중 생략할 수 없는 것은?

① This is the bicycle <u>which</u> I bought yesterday.
② He is the man <u>whom</u> I met on the way home.
③ This is the picture <u>which</u> Seo-yoon painted.
④ They were sea merchants <u>that</u> sailed to many parts of the world.
⑤ I'll show you the digital camera <u>that</u> I bought yesterday.

6. 다음 빈칸에 들어갈 말이 바르게 짝지어진 것은?

> · The woman _____ he fell in love left him after a few weeks.
> · What have you done with the money _____ I gave you?

① which − whom　② with whom − that
③ to whom − who　④ with who − whose
⑤ who with − where

7. 다음 빈칸에 공통으로 들어갈 말을 쓰시오.

> A: What sports do you like best?
> B: _____ I like most is soccer.

> A: I think the baby may be hungry.
> B: _____ makes you think so?

8. 다음 괄호 안의 말을 알맞게 배열한 것은?

> (be, a desert, may, dry, however), it is not necessarily worthless.

① A desert may be dry however
② However may be a desert dry
③ However a desert may be dry
④ A desert may be however dry
⑤ However dry a desert may be

오답 노트 만들기

★틀린 문제 : _____   ★다시 공부한 날 : _____

(1) 문제를 왜? 틀렸는지 곰곰이 생각하고 그 이유를 적어본다.

(2) 핵심 개념을 적는다.

(3) 자신이 몰랐던 단어와 숙어 표현이 있으면 정리한다.

(4) 해설집에서 필요한 부분을 골라 풀이 해법을 정리한다.

★틀린 문제 : _____   ★다시 공부한 날 : _____

(1) 문제를 왜? 틀렸는지 곰곰이 생각하고 그 이유를 적어본다.

(2) 핵심 개념을 적는다.

(3) 자신이 몰랐던 단어와 숙어 표현이 있으면 정리한다.

(4) 해설집에서 필요한 부분을 골라 풀이 해법을 정리한다.

★틀린 문제 : _____   ★다시 공부한 날 : _____

(1) 문제를 왜? 틀렸는지 곰곰이 생각하고 그 이유를 적어본다.

(2) 핵심 개념을 적는다.

(3) 자신이 몰랐던 단어와 숙어 표현이 있으면 정리한다.

(4) 해설집에서 필요한 부분을 골라 풀이 해법을 정리한다.

★틀린 문제 : _____   ★다시 공부한 날 : _____

(1) 문제를 왜? 틀렸는지 곰곰이 생각하고 그 이유를 적어본다.

(2) 핵심 개념을 적는다.

(3) 자신이 몰랐던 단어와 숙어 표현이 있으면 정리한다.

(4) 해설집에서 필요한 부분을 골라 풀이 해법을 정리한다.

[1-2] 다음 글을 읽고 물음에 답하시오.

__(a)__ throws away empty cans by the roadside is as bad as the factory that pollutes the river. __(b)__ buys something made of the skins of animals that need protection is an accomplice of those __(c)__ killed the animals.

1. 빈칸 (a)와 (b)에 공통으로 들어갈 알맞은 말은?

❶ whatever   ❷ whenever   ❸ however

❹ whoever   ❺ whichever

2. 빈칸 (c)에 들어갈 말로 알맞은 것은?

❶ who   ❷ whose   ❸ that

❹ what   ❺ which

오답노트

[3-4] 다음 문장을 영작할 때 빈칸에 알맞은 표현은?

3.
한국 음식을 파는 곳이라면 어떤 식당에서라도 음식을 먹겠다.

=We'll eat at _____ restaurant serves Korean food.

❶ any   ❷ all   ❸ which

❹ whichever   ❺ whosever

4.
어느 팀이 이기든 나와는 상관없다.

=No matter _____ team wins, it doesn't matter to me.

❶ any   ❷ whatever   ❸ whichever

❹ how   ❺ which

오답노트

5. 다음 빈칸에 들어갈 관계부사가 바르게 짝지어진 것을 고르시오.

· I still don't know the reason _____ she cried.

· We need a place _____ we can stay for a few days.

· I don't like _____ he treats me.

· Do you know the time _____ he'll arrive?

❶ why – where – when – how

❷ how – where – why – when

❸ where – why – how – when

❹ why – where – how – when

❺ how – when – where – why

오답노트

6. 다음 문장의 밑줄 친 부분 중 생략할 수 있는 것은?

❶ Speech is the foundation on <u>which</u> all language is built.

❷ The car and the driver <u>that</u> fell into the river have not been found.

❸ Journalists are writers <u>who</u> work on a newspaper or a magazine gathering and presenting news.

❹ She talked on and on, <u>which</u> made everyone bored.

❺ The man <u>who</u> I was sitting next to on the plane talked all the time.

오답노트

7. 다음 밑줄 친 부분과 바꿔 쓸 수 있는 것을 바르게 나열한 것은?

> · John visited the town <u>in which</u> he was born.
> · I know the reason <u>for which</u> manhole covers are round.
> · I don't know the time <u>at which</u> he will fall asleep.

❶ where − why − when
❷ when − where − how
❸ how − where − why
❹ why − when − where
❺ where − how − when

오답노트

8. 다음 빈칸에 공통으로 들어갈 말은?

> According to a study, eating insects is popular in areas ____ there are not many large animals to eat, and ____ people can easily find a lot of large insects.

❶ why   ❷ when   ❸ how
❹ where   ❺ that

오답노트

9. 다음 빈칸에 들어갈 알맞은 말을 고르시오.

> By destroying our forests, we are destroying our home. No, we are destroying our body. The forests are the lungs of the planet _____.
> If the trees die, we will die, too.

❶ we are of a part
❷ of which we are a part
❸ of that we are a part
❹ which we are a part
❺ we are a part of which

오답노트

10. 밑줄 친 what의 쓰임이 〈보기〉와 같은 것은?

> **보기**   You can have <u>what</u> you like.

❶ <u>What</u> is his name?
❷ <u>What</u> she wants is your kind words.
❸ Tell me <u>what</u> kind of food you want.
❹ <u>What</u> do you think of it?
❺ <u>What</u> a wonderful garden it is!

오답노트

11. 다음 문장을 잘못 고친 것은?

> That's the woman. ＋ I was talking about the woman.

❶ That's the woman about whom I was talking.
❷ That's the woman who(m) I was talking about.
❸ That's the woman that I was talking about.
❹ That's the woman I was talking about.
❺ That's the woman about that I was talking.

오답노트

12. 다음 밑줄 친 부분을 잘못 바꾸어 쓴 것은?

❶ Peter met Jane, <u>who</u> told me the news.
   (=and she)

❷ <u>No matter who</u> comes, he will be
   welcomed. (=Whoever)

❸ This is the place <u>in which</u> they will build
   a hospital. (=where)

❹ <u>No matter how</u> far you may be, I will
   meet you someday. (=Whatever)

❺ There are times when you can't do
   <u>anything that</u> you like. (=whatever)

오답노트

13. 다음 밑줄 친 부분과 같은 뜻이 되도록 빈칸에 알
맞은 말을 쓰시오.

> <u>I like figure skating most.</u> Do Korean
> girls enjoy figure skating?

→ _____ I like most is figure skating.

오답노트

[14-16] 〈보기〉와 같이 두 문장이 같은 의미가 되도록
알맞은 관계사를 사용하여 빈칸을 완성하시오.

> **보**
> **기**
> A girl was injured in the accident. She
> is now in the hospital.
> → *The girl who was injured in the*
> *accident* is now in the hospital.

14. A waitress served us. She was very
impolite and impatient.
→ The waitress _____ was
   very impolite and impatient.

15. 2007 was the year. They got married
then.
→ 2007 was the year _____.

16. FMD spreads at varying speeds in
different areas. We still don't know the
reason for this.
→ We still don't know _____

_____.

＊FMD(food-and-mouth disease) 구제역

오답노트

17. 밑줄 친 부분의 쓰임이 나머지와 다른 것을 고르시오.

❶ I visited the village <u>where</u> they lived.

❷ I asked him <u>where</u> she lives.

❸ This is the house <u>where</u> she was born.

❹ There's the concert hall <u>where</u> Elton
   John first performed.

❺ That's the stadium <u>where</u> we saw our
   first soccer game.

오답노트

[18-20] 다음 문장에서 어색한 부분을 찾아 바르게 고치
시오.

18. I don't know the way how he invented
this funny toy.

_____ → _____

19. I remember the day where we entered the middle school.

_____ → _____

20. Can you tell me the reason what you were late for school?

_____ → _____

21. 다음 두 문장을 한 문장으로 만들 때 빈칸에 알맞은 말을 쓰시오.

> · I have a friend.
> · His sister is just like the girl in the story.
>   → I have a friend _____ sister is just like the girl in the story.

22. 다음 빈칸에 들어갈 알맞은 말을 고르시오.

> All _____ she had was a piece of soap and a little money.

❶ that　　❷ which　　❸ what
❹ whose　　❺ who

23. 다음 문장의 빈칸에 들어갈 계속적 용법의 관계사가 바르게 짝지어진 것은?

> · She graduated in 2010, but then Korea was experiencing an economic crisis.
>   → She graduated in 2010, _____ Korea was experiencing an economic crisis.
> · New York, and there my father is staying on business, is a much more dangerous city than Seoul.
>   → New York, _____ my father is staying on business, is a much more dangerous city than Seoul.

❶ when − where　　❷ which − whose
❸ when − which　　❹ which − when
❺ which − which

24. 다음 문장을 각각 관계대명사와 관계부사를 이용하여 한 문장으로 만드시오. (단, 전치사와 관계대명사는 붙여 쓸 것)

> I remember the day. I first rode my bike on that day.
> → I remember the day _____
>   _____ .
> → I remember the day _____
>   _____ .

A. 다음 문장을 no matter how~를 이용한 문장으로 고쳐 쓰시오.

1. However loud I shout, he wouldn't look over.

→ _____

2. However boring the class may be, you have to stay until it is over.

→ _____

3. However bad the weather may be, they will not postpone the game.

→ _____

B. 괄호 안의 단어를 이용하여 우리말에 맞는 문장을 완성하시오.

1. 나는 여러 사람 앞에서 처음 말했던 때를 잊지 못할 것이다.

(the time / speaking in public / never forget / for the first time)

→ _____

2. 지난 학기에 영어 수업을 들었던 강의실에서 만나자.

(in the lecture room / took / last semester / the English class)

→ _____

C. 다음 밑줄 친 부분을 괄호 안의 관계대명사로 고쳐 한 문장으로 쓰시오.

1. A building was destroyed in the fire. It is now being built. (which)

→ _____

2. I thanked the man. He helped me move the refrigerator. (who)

→ _____

3. The firefighters are very brave. Their department has won many awards. (whose)

→ _____

4. I watched a little girl. Her dog was chasing a ball in the park. (whose)

→ _____

실전 서술형 평가문제

정답 p. 22

 출제의도 관계대명사
평가내용 관계대명사를 활용하여 문장 완성하기

A. 〈보기〉와 같이 관계사가 있는 문장은 두 문장으로 나누고, 두 문장은 관계대명사를 이용하여 한 문장으로 고쳐 쓰시오.

[서술형 유형 : 12점 / 난이도 : 중하]

<table>
<tr><td rowspan="4">보
기</td><td>· The woman who answered the phone was polite.</td></tr>
<tr><td>→ The woman was polite.　+　She answered the phone.</td></tr>
<tr><td>· The girl is hurt. She fell down the stairs.</td></tr>
<tr><td>→ The girl who fell down the stairs is hurt.</td></tr>
</table>

1. A woman who was wearing a gray suit asked me for directions.

→ _____ + _____

2. The people were French. Kathy visited them yesterday.

→ _____

3. Two people I didn't know walked into the classroom.

→ _____ + _____

4. The girl apologized to Mrs. Cook. She broke the vase.

→ _____

5. I know a man whose daughter is a pilot.

→ _____ + _____

6. The reporter won an award. Her articles explained global warming.

→ _____

실전 서술형 평가문제

출제의도 관계대명사 which와 what
평가내용 관계대명사를 활용하여 문장 완성하기

B. 다음 두 문장을 관계대명사 which와 what을 이용하여 각각 한 문장으로 만드시오. [서술형 유형 : 8점 / 난이도 : 중]

The scarf is mom's birthday present. I bought it.
→ *The scarf which I bought is mom's birthday present.*
→ *What I bought is mom's birthday present.* It's the scarf.

1. The thing was shocking. We saw it.

→ _____

→ _____

2. The picture is very interesting. She drew it.

→ _____

→ _____ I mean the picture.

3. We are polluting the water and air. All life needs the water and air.

→ _____

→ _____ I mean the water and air.

4. That isn't the thing. We ordered it last night.

→ _____

→ _____

출제의도 관계대명사 whose

평가내용 소유격 관계대명사를 이용하여 묘사 또는 설명하기

C. 어제 생일파티에서 만난 사람들에 대해 친구에게 이야기해 주려고 한다. whose를 이용하여 내용에 맞도록 문장을 완성하시오.

[서술형 유형 : 8점 / 난이도 : 중하]

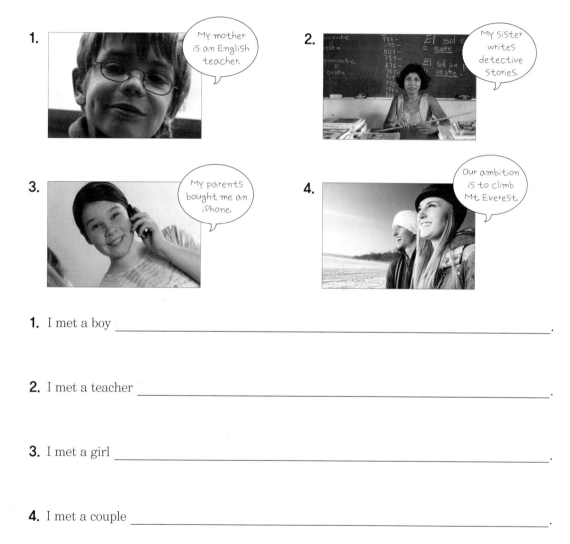

1. I met a boy _____ .

2. I met a teacher _____ .

3. I met a girl _____ .

4. I met a couple _____ .

실전 서술형 평가문제

출제의도 관계부사 where, when

평가내용 관계부사를 이용하여 문장 서술하기

D. 〈보기〉와 같이 관계부사 where 또는 when을 이용하여 'That is ~'로 시작하는 문장을 완성하시오.

[서술형 유형 : 14점 / 난이도 : 중상]

〈보기〉 We have class in that classroom.

1. We ate lunch at that cafeteria.

2. You spent your vacation on that island.

3. I was born in that year.

4. The space flight to Mars is scheduled to leave on that day.

5. The earthquake occurred in that country.

6. The examination will be given in that room.

7. You felt the happiest at that time.

보기	*That is the classroom where we have class.*

1. _____

2. _____

3. _____

4. _____

5. _____

6. _____

7. _____

서술형 평가문제	채 점 기 준	배 점	나의 점수
A	표현이 올바르고 문법, 철자가 모두 정확한 경우	2점×6문항=12점	
B		2점×4문항=8점	
C		2점×4문항=8점	
D		2점×7문항=14점	
공통	문법, 철자가 1개씩 틀린 경우	각 문항당 1점씩 감점	
	내용과 전혀 일치하지 않거나 답을 기재하지 못한 경우	0점	

Chapter 6

가정법 (Conditionals)

Unit 01 가정법

1-1 현재와 미래를 나타내는 1차 가정문

If we go to Seoul, we will see the 63 building.
우리가 서울에 가면, 우리는 63빌딩을 볼 수 있을 거야.
▶ 일어날 수 있는 현실로, 미래에 서울로 갈 가능성

---

01 if가 있다고 무조건 가정법은 아니다. **가정법과 조건절은 전적으로 말하는 사람의 태도나 확신의 정도, 가능성**에 달려 있다. 1차 가정문은 현재와 미래의 일을 가정한다.

If it **is** sunny tomorrow, we**'ll** go fishing.
내일 날이 맑으면 우린 낚시하러 갈 거야. ▶ 화자는 내일 날씨가 맑을 가능성이 있다고 보고 말하는 것(조건절)

If you **saw** a ghost breaking into your house, what **would** you **do**?
만약 귀신이 너의 집에 침입하는 걸 보면 넌 어떻게 할 거니? ▶ 화자는 가능성이 희박하지만 일단 한번 말해 보는 것(가정법)

02 미래에 일어날 가능성이 있는 일을 추측하거나 가정할 때 **if절 안에 현재시제를 쓰고, 주절에는 미래시제를** 쓴다(미래를 나타내는 조건의 부사절과 같다). 미래시제는 will뿐만 아니라 **미래를 나타내는 어떤 형태의 동사도 쓸 수 있다.**

If he **has** enough time, he **will** come to the party. 만약 그가 충분한 시간이 있다면, 그는 파티에 올 거야.

If I **finish** my homework soon, I **can** go to bed. 숙제를 곧 끝내면 나는 자러 갈 수 있어.

If Tom **visits** me, we**'re going to travel** around the country. Tom이 나를 방문하면 우린 국내를 여행할 계획이야.

03 **일반적인 사실, 일상적으로 일어나는 일 또는 정해진 상황을 가정할 때 if절과 주절에 현재시제를 쓴다.**

If you **mix** oil and water, the oil **stays** on top. 기름과 물을 섞으면 기름은 물 위에 뜰 거야. ▶ General Fact

If water **is** frozen, it **expends**. 물이 얼면 팽창한다. ▶ General Fact

If I **go** to work on foot, it **takes** thirty-five minutes. 내가 걸어서 일하러 가면 35분이 걸려. ▶ Everyday Thing

If you **have** a big lunch, it **makes** you sleepy. 네가 점심을 많이 먹으면 졸음이 올 거야. ▶ Definite Thing

※ 지금까지 우리나라 영문법에서는 가정법 현재라는 말로 현재나 미래에 대한 의심, 불확실 등을 나타내고, 조건절에 직설법 현재동사를 사용할 수 있다고 설명해왔기 때문에 가정법과 조건의 부사절을 이해하는 데 굉장한 어려움이 있었다. 현대 영어에서는 기본적으로 모두 다 조건의 부사절로 볼 수 있고 시제나 상황에 따라 가능성을 나타내는 것으로, 말하는 사람의 태도나 확신의 정도, 가능성에 전적으로 달려 있다.

기존의 영문법에서 가정법 현재의 if절에 will을 쓰지 않고 동사원형이나 현재형을 쓴다고 하는데, 현대 영어에서는 if절에 will이 생략되었다 하더라도 동사원형이 아닌 현재형을 쓴다.

If you **are** tired, you can go home.
→ If you **be** tired (×)

서술형 기초다지기

Challenge 1 〈보기〉와 같이 주어 we를 이용하여 1차 가정문을 만들어 보세요. (주절은 미래시제)

> **보기**
> Paris / the Eiffel Tower
> → *If we go to Paris, we will[can] see the Eiffel Tower.*

01. London / Buckingham Palace

→ _____

02. New York / the Statue of Liberty

→ _____

03. Sydney / the Sydney Opera House

→ _____

04. Rome / the Coliseum

→ _____

05. Tokyo / the Imperial Gardens

→ _____

Challenge 2 다음 괄호 안의 동사를 알맞은 형태로 바꾸어 빈칸을 완성하세요.

01. If people sneeze, they _____ (close) their eyes.

02. If I see Bob this afternoon, I _____ (tell) him to phone you.

03. If the temperature doesn't fall below 0℃, water _____. (not freeze)

04. If you _____ (exercise) a lot, you lose weight.

05. If you break nail, it _____ (grow) back again.

06. If an elephant has big ears, it _____ (come) from Africa.

07. If I have finished reading your book, I _____ (return) it.

Chapter 6 – 가정법 · 181

1-2 가능성이 거의 없는 2차 가정문 (1)

What **would** you do **if** you **saw** someone breaking into your house?
당신 집에 누군가 침입하는 것을 목격하면 어떻게 하실 겁니까?

01 그동안 우리나라 영문법에서 가정법 과거를 현재 사실과의 반대, 의심, 불확실이라고 설명해왔는데, 이는 일본 문법을 그대로 받아들인 구식 영어이다. 실제 **가정법 과거는 현재 사실에 대해 가능성(20% 미만)이 현저히 떨어지는 상황**을 나타낸다. 가능성이 희박하지만 일단 한번 말해 보는 것이다.

If절(if-clause)	주절(main clause)
If + 과거시제	Would(의도, 소망) Could(능력)　+　동사원형 might(가능성)

※ 현실에서 일어날 가능성이 희박하기 때문에 한 발짝 물러나서 말하는 과거시제와 과거 조동사를 쓰기로 약속했다.
　If절 안에 쓰이는 과거와 주절의 조동사를 과거시제로 보면 안 된다.

02 가정법 과거는 현재시점에서 **10%~20% 정도의 가능성을 염두에 두고 말하는 분위기**(mood)이다. 따라서 주절에도 조동사 과거형을 써서 현재 또는 미래의 결과를 상상하는 것이다.

If computers **were** cheap, I **would** buy ten of them for my home.
컴퓨터가 싸다면, 집에 놓을 컴퓨터 10대를 살 텐데.

If I **had** a car, I **would** drive you to the airport. 내가 차가 있다면 너를 공항까지 데려다 줄 텐데.

If I **didn't have** a friend like you, I **would** be very lonely. 너 같은 친구가 없다면 매우 외로울 텐데.

What **would** you do if you **became** the president? 만약 네가 대통령이 된다면 너는 무엇을 하겠니?

03 If조건절에 주어의 인칭과 수에 관계없이 be동사의 과거는 were를 쓴다. **주로 사람의 견해나 충고에 사용**하는데, 문법을 틀려가면서까지 **견해나 충고를 강조**하기 위해 사용한다. 일상 영어에서는 was를 쓰기도 하지만 If I were you(내가 만약 너라면)가 더 자연스러운 표현으로 굳어졌다. 마찬가지로 현재 또는 미래에 가능성이 매우 낮기 때문에 과거시제를 쓴다.

If I **were** a cheetah, I **could** run much faster. 만약 내가 치타라면 훨씬 더 빨리 달릴 수 있을 텐데.

If I **were** you, I **would** go and apologize to her. 내가 너라면 그녀에게 가서 사과할 텐데.

Lisa **would** answer the phone **if** she **were** in her office. Lisa가 사무실에 있다면 전화를 받을 텐데.

If I **were** you, I **would** call the restaurant to make sure it's open.
내가 너라면 식당에 전화를 해서 영업을 하는지 확인해 보겠다.

서술형 기초다지기

정답 p. 22

Challenge 1 | 다음 괄호 안의 단어를 알맞은 형태로 바꾸어 빈칸에 쓰세요.

> **보기** If I *were* (be) you, I would not go there alone.

01. If I _____ (win) the lottery, I would buy a car.

02. If it _____ (rain) tomorrow, what will you do?

03. If she _____ (study) harder, she could pass the bar exam.

04. If the weather is not fine tomorrow, we _____ (will cancel) the outdoor event.

05. If I _____ (be) a doctor, I could help sick children in Africa.

Challenge 2 | 괄호 안의 상황을 가정하여 'What would you do if ~?'를 이용한 문장을 만드세요.

> **보기** (Maybe one day your friend will be the president.)
> → *What would you do if you became the president?*

01. (Perhaps one day your friend will lose his/her cell phone.)

→ _____

02. (There has never been a fire in the building.)

→ _____

Challenge 3 | 다음 글을 읽고 괄호 안의 말을 알맞은 형태로 바꾸세요.

01. If my car *broke* (break) down at night, I *would lock* (lock) the doors. Then

I _____ (call) the emergency services on my mobile. If I _____ (not have) a

mobile, I _____ (walk) to the nearest phone box. If the phone box _____ (be) too

far away, I _____ (wait) in my car with my doors locked.

02. If I _____ (wake) up in the night and _____ (hear) something in my house,

I _____ (go) to the phone and call the police. If I _____ (be) alone, I _____

(lock) the door of the room and wait for the police to come.

1-3 가능성이 거의 없는 2차 가정문 (2)

If the weather **weren't** so bad, we **would** go to the park.
만약 날씨가 나쁘지 않았다면 우리는 공원에 갔을 텐데.
→ As the weather **is** bad, we **won't** go to the park.
날씨가 나쁘기 때문에 우리는 공원에 가지 않을 거다.

---

01 가정법 과거에서는 과거동사와 조동사 과거 형태를 과거시제로 보면 안 된다고 이미 언급하였다. 과거동사는 가능성이 현저히 낮은 현재를 나타내고 조동사는 현재나 미래에 대한 결과를 나타낸다. 가정법 과거를 **직설법으로 고치면 과거가 아닌 현재와 미래를 나타낸다는 것이 극명히 밝혀진다.**

〈가정법 과거의 직설법 문장 전환〉
시제: 과거 → 현재   동사: 긍정 → 부정, 부정 → 긍정

If I **were** rich, I **could** buy the house. 내가 부자라면 그 집을 살 수 있을 텐데.
→ Because I **am not** rich, I **can't** buy the house.

If she **didn't stay** up so late every night, she **wouldn't** be tired every day.
그녀가 매일 밤 늦게까지 잠을 안 자고 깨어 있지 않다면 매일 피곤하진 않을 텐데.
→ She **stays up** too late every night, so she **is** tired every day.

02 가정법 미래를 나타내는 should와 were to

① should : 실현 가능성은 있지만 일어날 것 같지 않다고 생각되는 경우에 쓴다. 주절에는 조동사의 현재형 또는 과거형을 모두 사용할 수 있다.

If he **should** lose his job, what **would** he do? 만일 그가 일자리를 잃는다면, 그는 무엇을 할까?
What **will** happen if the building **should** take fire? 만일 그 건물에 불이 난다면 어떻게 될까?

② were to : should보다 가능성이 더 적어서 불가능하다고 생각되는 경우에 쓴다. 주절에는 **조동사의 과거형만 쓸 수 있다.**

If the sun **were to** rise in the west, I **would** change my mind.
만일 해가 서쪽에서 뜬다면 나는 마음을 바꿀 것이다.
If I **were to** be born again, I **would** love you. 만일 내가 다시 태어나도 당신을 사랑할 겁니다.

※ 실제로 가정법 미래는 잘 사용하지 않는다. 현대 영어에서는 과거형 또는 현재형으로 가정법 미래의 내용을 명확히 전달할 수 있기 때문이다.

If it **should** rain tomorrow, she will be disappointed.
→ If it **rains** tomorrow, she will be disappointed.

서술형 기초다지기

Challenge 1 다음 문장을 가정법 과거 문장으로 바꾸세요.

> 보기
> As he is not clever, he does such a thing.
> → *If he were clever*, he wouldn't do such a thing.

01. As I don't have a job, I can't pay back the money.

→ _____, I could pay back the money.

02. She can't enjoy life because she works too much.

→ _____ less, she could enjoy life more.

03. As we don't have a car, we can't go on a vacation.

→ _____, we could go on a vacation.

04. As he doesn't study hard, he will get a bad grade.

→ _____, he wouldn't get a bad grade.

05. To hear her speak English, you would think her a native speaker.

→ _____, you would think her a native speaker.

06. Living in a rich country, he would be a great scientist.

→ _____, he would be a great scientist.

Challenge 2 직설법은 가정법으로, 가정법은 직설법으로 고쳐 보세요. (단, as, so, if를 이용할 것)

01. If she were not lazy, she could get a job.

→ _____

02. I don't know her address, so I can't write to her.

→ _____

03. If I knew her well, I could invite her to the party.

→ _____

04. As I don't have enough time, I can't take a long trip.

→ _____

1-4 가능성이 0%인 3차 가정문

It snowed yesterday.
If it **hadn't snowed**, we **might not have had** the accident.
→ It snowed, and we had the accident.
눈이 오지 않았더라면 우리는 사고가 나지 않았을 텐데.

01 우리나라 영문법에서는 흔히 가정법 과거완료라는 말로 과거사실에 대한 정반대, 가정, 소망을 나타낸다고 하는데 이는 일본 문법을 그대로 받아들인 잘못된 설명이다. 실제 가정법 과거완료는 **현재 시점에서 가능성이 전혀 없는(가능성 0%) 상황을 나타낸다.** 이미 **과거의 지난 상황을 말하므로 현재와는 아무런 관련이 없다.**

If절(if-clause)	주절(main clause)
If+had p.p.	Would(의도, 소망) Could(능력)　　+ have p.p. might(가능성)

※ 현재와 아무런 관련이 없다는 것을 나타내기 위해 특별한 시제를 쓴다.

If I **had studied** harder, I **would have passed** the test. 내가 더 열심히 공부했더라면 그 시험에 통과했을 텐데.
→ I didn't study harder, and I didn't pass the test.

If you **had paid** more attention, you **might not have burned** the food.
만약 네가 좀 더 주의를 기울였더라면 음식을 태우지 않았을 텐데.
→ I think it's possible that you wouldn't have burned it.

If you **had brought** your CDs, we **could have danced**.
만약 네가 CD를 가져왔더라면 우리는 춤을 출 수 있었을 텐데.
→ We would have been able to dance.

02 과거에 이미 끝나서 현재와는 아무런 관련이 없기 때문에 **현재나 미래에 단 1%의 가능성도 없다.** 이를 직설법으로 고치면 **과거시제를 써야 하는 것이 극명히 밝혀진다.**

If I **had known** her phone number, I **would have called** her.
내가 그녀의 전화번호를 알았다면 그녀에게 전화할 수 있었을 텐데.
→ I **didn't call** her because I **didn't know** her phone number.

If I **had been** your boss, I **would have fired** you. 내가 너의 상사였다면 너를 해고했을 텐데.
→ As I **was not** your boss, I **wouldn't fire** you.

If I **had had** enough free time, I **would have met** my girlfriend.
충분한 시간이 있었다면 나는 내 여자친구를 만났을 텐데.
→ As I **didn't have** enough free time, I **wouldn't meet** my girlfriend.

서술형 기초다지기

정답 p. 23

Challenge 1 다음 괄호 안의 표현 중 알맞은 것을 고르세요.

01. If Nicole had come, Jeff (might turn / might have turned) down the invitation.

02. She would have learned Korean if she (had / had had) the opportunity.

03. If I (had been / were) there, I would have done it.

04. If she had come, the party (would have been / would be) more delightful.

Challenge 2 다음 괄호 안의 단어를 이용하여 빈칸에 알맞은 말을 쓰세요.

> 보기 I'm sorry you had to take a cab to the airport. I didn't know you needed a ride. If you *had told* (tell) me, I *would have given* (give) you a ride gladly.

01. I didn't know you were in the hospital. If I _____ (know), I _____ (go) to see you.

02. I got wet because I didn't take my umbrella. However, I _____ (get, not) wet if I _____ (remember) to take my umbrella with me yesterday.

03. Many people were not satisfied with the leader after he took office. If they _____ (know) about his planned economic program, they _____ (vote, not) for him.

Challenge 3 다음 문장을 if 가정문으로 바꾸어 쓰세요.

> 보기 She wasn't hungry, so she didn't eat anything.
> → *If she had been hungry, she would have eaten something.*

01. I was able to buy the car only because Kevin lent me the money.

    → _____

02. I didn't know that Alex had to get up early, so I didn't wake him up.

    → _____

Unit 02 wish 가정법

2-1 현재의 소망을 나타내는 「wish+과거시제」

I wish I earned more money.
돈을 더 많이 벌었으면 좋을 텐데.
→ But I don't earn more money.

01 「wish+과거시제」를 써서 **현재나 미래에 대한 소망**을 나타내는데 이를 단순 과거로 보면 안 된다. 현재의 상황에 가능성이 현저히 떨어지기 때문에 **현실에서 한 발짝 물러선 과거동사**를 쓰는 것이다. 「wish (that) +주어+과거시제」에서 that은 주로 생략해서 쓴다.

Laura **wishes** (that) she **could go** to Italy for her vacation. Laura는 방학에 이탈리아로 가길 원한다.
I **wish** I **could speak** Chinese. 중국어를 말할 수 있으면 좋겠는데. (→ But I can't speak Chinese.)
I **wish** I **didn't** have to work on weekends. 주말마다 일할 필요가 없으면 좋겠다.
(→ But I have to work on weekends.)

02 2차 가정문(가정법 과거)과 똑같이 **주어의 인칭에 관계 없이 be동사는 were**를 쓴다. 일상 영어에서는 was를 쓰기도 한다.

I **wish** it **were** my wedding day. 이게 내 결혼식이면 얼마나 좋을까. (→ It is not my wedding day.)
I **wish** she **were** here with me. 그녀가 나와 함께 있으면 좋을 텐데. (→ I'm sorry that she isn't here with me.)

03 미래에 일어날 일에 대한 소망은 **will 대신 would**를, **be going to 대신 were/was going to**를 쓴다.

I **wish** she **were going to** wash her feet. (→ She isn't going to wash her feet.)
그녀가 발을 좀 씻었으면 좋겠다.
I **wish** she **would** come here. 그녀가 여기에 오면 좋을 텐데. (→ I want her to come here.)

04 'I wish I could ~'는 '내가 ~할 수 있으면 좋겠는데'라는 의미이고, 다른 사람이 미래에 해주길 바라는 소망은 'I wish you would/wouldn't ~'로 쓸 수 있다. 'I wish I would ~'라고 쓰지 않는다.

I **wish** I **could** speak Korean. 내가 한국어를 말할 수 있으면 좋겠는데.
I **wish** you **would** stop smoking so much. 난 네가 담배를 그렇게 많이 피우지 않았으면 좋겠어.

서술형 기초다지기

Challenge 1   〈보기〉와 같이 다음 문장을 wish를 이용한 가정문으로 바꾸어 쓰세요.

> 보 I can't speak Japanese.
> 기 → *I wish I could speak Japanese.*

01. I don't know Brian's phone number.

→ _____

02. I'm sorry I can't see her more often.

→ _____

03. I'm not allowed to go out after 8 o'clock.

→ _____

04. Nancy doesn't have a cell phone.

→ _____

05. Susan has to finish her assignment by tomorrow.

→ _____

Challenge 2   다음 문장을 I wish you would/wouldn't를 이용한 부탁의 표현으로 바꾸세요.

> 보 Clean up your room.
> 기 → *I wish you would clean up your room.*

01. Send me a copy of the document.

→ _____

02. Don't waste your time.

→ _____

03. Don't play the radio so loud.

→ _____

04. Be creative and think of a horse of another color.

→ _____

I **wish** I **had been** traveling with you.
내가 너랑 여행을 할 수 있으면 좋을 텐데.
→ I'm sorry that I **was not traveling** with you.

---

01 **과거의 상황에 대한 유감이나 과거의 사실과 다른 소망**은 wish 뒤에 과거완료(had+p.p.)를 쓴다. wish 뒤의 that은 주로 생략해서 쓴다.

I wish (that) I **had studied** for the test. 진작에 시험에 대비해 공부를 했었더라면 좋았을걸.
→ I'm sorry that I **didn't study** for the test.

I wish (that) we **had taken** a taxi last night. 지난밤에 택시를 탔더라면 좋았을 텐데.
→ I regret that we **didn't take** a taxi last night.

---

02 3차 가정문(가정법 과거완료)이 가능성이 전혀 없는(0%) 상황을 말하듯이, wish 뒤에 과거완료를 쓰는 이유도 과거에 이미 끝나 현재나 미래에 단 1%의 가능성이 없기 때문이다. 단지, 과거에 대해 후회하거나 소망한 일을 푸념하듯 말해 보는 것이다.

I told the secret to her. I **wish** I **hadn't told** the secret to her.
나는 그녀에게 비밀을 말했다. 그녀에게 비밀을 말하지 않았더라면 좋았을 걸. ▶ 현재 비밀을 말하지 않을 가능성 0%

※ 부정의 내용을 말하려면「had not+p.p.」로 쓴다.

---

03 우리나라 영문법에서 혼합 가정법을 주절과 종속절의 시제가 각각 다른 경우라고 하면서 복잡하게 설명하는데 이는 잘못된 설명이다. 혼합가정문은 if절 안에 가능성 0%인 'had+p.p.'를 쓰고, 주절에는 현재 사실에 대해 가능성이 낮은(20% 미만) '과거 조동사+동사원형'을 쓰는 것뿐이다.

If I **had slept** well last night, I **wouldn't be** very tired now.
내가 지난밤에 잘 잤다면(가능성 0%), 지금 매우 피곤하지 않을 텐데(가능성 20% 이하).
→ I **didn't sleep** well last night, so I **am** very tired now.

If the driver **had been** more careful, those people **would be** alive now.
그 운전자가 좀 더 주의를 기울였더라면(가능성 0%), 그 사람들은 지금 살아 있을 텐데(가능성 20% 이하).
→ The driver **was** not more careful, so those people **are** not alive now.

서술형 기초다지기

Challenge 1 다음 상황을 I wish로 시작하는 가정법 문장으로 만드세요.

> 보 I didn't buy the coat yesterday; now I'm sorry.
> 기 → *I wish I had bought the coat.*

01. I'm sorry that I didn't study harder when I was a student.

→ _____

02. I'm sorry that I told the secret to him.

→ _____

03. Kevin has eaten too much and now he feels sick.

→ _____ so much.

04. I regret that I didn't read many good books in my school days.

→ _____

Challenge 2 다음 직설법을 혼합가정법을 이용하여 다시 쓰세요.

> 보 The room is full of flies because you left the door open.
> 기 → *If you hadn't left the door open, the room wouldn't be full of files.*

01. I didn't finish my report yesterday, so I can't begin a new project today.

→ _____

02. I'm hungry now because I didn't eat lunch.

→ _____

03. I received a good job offer from the oil company, so I won't seriously consider taking the job with the electronics firm.

→ _____

Unit 03 기타 가정법

3-1 as if[though]+가정법 / It's time+가정법 과거

She acts **as if** she **were** a movie star.
그녀는 마치 영화배우인 것처럼 행동한다.

It's time you **went** to bed. It's so late.
자야 할 시간이야. 너무 늦었어.

01 as if 또는 as though는 '(사실은 그렇지 않지만) 마치 ~인 것처럼'이란 뜻이다. **말하는 시점과 같을 때는 as if[though]절 안의 동사를 '과거'로 쓰고, 말하는 시점보다 더 이전의 일을 가정하고 있으면 과거완료 (had+p.p.)를 쓴다.**

He **acts as if** he **were** a movie star. 지금 현재 영화배우인 것처럼 행동한다. (현재=현재)

He **acted as if** he **were** a movie star. 과거 당시에 마치 영화배우인 것처럼 행동했다. (과거=과거)

He **acts as if** he **had been** a movie star. 전에 영화배우였던 것처럼 현재 행동한다. (더 과거)

He **acted as if** he **had been** a movie star. 그 이전에 마치 영화배우였던 것처럼 행동했다. (과거보다 더 과거)

※ She says as if she is[were] a violinist. 여기서 were를 쓰면 '바이올린을 못 켜면서 켜는 척하는 느낌'을 주지만 is와 같은 현재시제를 쓰면 글자 그대로 현실에 가까운 느낌을 주어서 '정말 바이올린 연주자일 가능성이 있다'는 것이다. 따라서 as if에는 현재시제나 will 또는 be going to도 쓸 수 있다.

He looks **as if** he **is** cold. 그는 마치 추운 것처럼 보인다.

→ He looks cold, but I don't know if he really is cold.

It looks **as if** it**'s going to** snow. 곧 눈이 올 거 같다.

→ The weather looks like it might snow, but I don't know if it really will snow.

02 「It's time+주어+(가정법) 과거시제」는 **'이제 ~해야 할 시간이다' 또는 '진작 그렇게 했어야 했는데 지금 하고 있지 않다'는 의미이다.** 과거시제를 단순히 과거로 보아서는 안 된다. **주로 나무라거나 불평할 때 쓰는데** 좀 더 강조해서 'It's about[high] time ~'으로 쓰기도 한다.

It's high time you **took** care of your brother. 동생을 돌볼 때가 왔다. (→ 그런데 왜 아직 동생을 돌보지 않고 있니?)

It's time you **went** to bed. 너는 잤어야 할 시간이야. (→ 그런데 왜 아직까지 안자고 있니?)

※ 앞서 It's time 뒤에 가정법 과거가 아닌 to부정사가 오는 경우를 배웠는데, 이때는 현재 사실과 반대인 유감을 나타내는 어감은 없고, 단순히 '~할 때이다'라는 의미만 있다.

It's time to go to school. Are you ready? 학교 갈 시간이다. 준비됐니?

It's time to do your homework. 숙제를 할 시간이다.

서술형 기초다지기

정답 p. 23

Challenge 1 〈보기〉와 같이 as if[though]를 이용한 가정법 문장으로 만드세요.

보 기	In fact, she is not a famous painter.
	→ She talks *as if[though] she were a famous painter.*

01. In fact, she doesn't know everything about the accident.

　→ She talks _____ .

02. In fact, he is not rich.

　→ He speaks to others _____ .

03. In fact, she was not a famous painter.

　→ She talks _____ .

04. In fact, she didn't know everything about the accident.

　→ She talks _____ .

05. In fact, he was not rich.

　→ He speaks to others _____ .

06. In fact, he hadn't seen a ghost.

　→ Jason talked _____ .

07. In fact, I'm not her younger brother.

　→ She treats me _____ .

Challenge 2 다음 괄호 안의 동사를 알맞은 형태로 바꾸세요.

01. It's time we _____ (return) their invitation.

02. It's time you _____ (start) on your homework.

03. Kelly, it's time _____ (get up) for school.

04. It's time he _____ (be) taking strong action against them.

05. It's time _____ (have) some fun. The weather is fantastic!

3-2 if를 사용하지 않는 가정법

Had we **known** it would rain so much, we would have stayed home.

= If we had known it would rain so much, we would have stayed home.

비가 이렇게 많이 올 줄 알았다면 우리는 집에 있었을 텐데.

01 If절의 **동사가 were, had, should인 경우 if를 생략**할 수 있다. 이때 **주어와 (조)동사의 위치가 서로 바뀐다.**

Were I you, I would forgive him. 내가 너라면, 그를 용서해줄 텐데.

=If I were you

Should a war break out, we will fight to defend our country.

=If a war should break out,

만약 전쟁이 일어난다면, 우리는 나라를 지키기 위해 싸울 것이다.

Had I known you were coming, I would have prepared some food.

=If I had known you were coming

네가 오는 걸 알았다면 음식을 준비했을 텐데.

02 '~이 없다면'의 뜻을 지닌 가정법 표현들

	If절(if-clause)	주절(main clause)
가능성 20% 이하	If it were not for =Were it not for =But for / Without	would could + 동사원형 might
가능성 0%	If it had not been for =Had it not been for =But for / Without	would could + have+p.p. might

※ If절이 과거면 주절도 조동사 과거로, 과거완료(had+p.p.)이면 「조동사+have+p.p.」로 일치시킨다.

Without water and air, we **could** not survive. 물과 공기가 없다면 우리는 생존할 수 없을 거야.

=**But for** water and air, we **could** not survive.

=**If it were not for** water and air, we **could** not survive.

=**Were it not for** water and air, we **could** not survive. ▶ If 생략

But for your advice, I **would have lost** all my money. 네 충고가 아니었더라면 나는 내 모든 돈을 잃었을 거야.

=**Without** your advice, I **would have lost** all my money.

=**If it had not been for** your advice, I **would have lost** all my money.

=**Had it not been for** your advice, I **would have lost** all my money. ▶ If 생략

서술형 기초다지기

정답 p. 24

Challenge 1   다음 문장을 if를 생략한 문장으로 다시 쓰세요.

> **보기**
> If she were my girlfriend, I would be happy.
> → *Were she my girlfriend, I would be happy.*

01. If I hadn't realized you need help, I couldn't have helped you.

→ _____

02. If I should see her, I'll give her the message.

→ _____

03. If I were you, I wouldn't go.

→ _____

04. If I had known the mixer was broken, I would never have bought it.

→ _____

Challenge 2   〈보기〉와 같이 두 문장이 같은 뜻이 되도록 빈칸을 채우세요.

> **보기**
> Without your help, I couldn't have finished the project on time.
> → *If it had not been for your help,* I couldn't have finished the project on time.

01. But for this horrible weather, we could go fishing in the ocean.

→ _____, we could go fishing in the ocean.

02. Without her help, I might have failed in the business.

→ _____, I might have failed in the business.

03. Without protection, such industries might be weakened by foreign competition.

→ _____, such industries might be weakened by foreign competition.

04. But for your wise advice, I might never have gone to university.

→ _____, I might never have gone to university.

01 출제 100% - 반드시 함께 쓰이는 단짝들이 있다.

출제자의 눈 가정법 과거는 if절 안에 과거형 또는 were를 쓰고, 주절에도 과거형인 「could (would, might)+동사원형」을 쓴다. be동사는 인칭에 상관없이 were를 쓴다는 것을 반드시 명심하자. 과거면 과거 조동사로 일치시켜야 하는데 이를 서로 틀리게 해놓는 문제가 출제된다.

Ex 1.

If Rain were in Korea now, I bet his fans _____ going nuts.

(a) will be   (b) would be   (c) are   (d) would have been

Ex 2.

_____, I would travel all around the world.

(a) If I was   (b) If I am   (c) Am I rich   (d) If I were rich

02 출제 100% - 가정법을 직설법으로 고치는 주관식 문제는 반드시 출제된다.

출제자의 눈 가정법 과거와 과거완료를 주고 직설법으로 고치는 부분 영작문제는 매번 출제된다. 또는 바르게 고친 것을 고르거나 틀린 것을 고르는 문제로도 출제 가능하다. 가정법 과거완료는 If절 안에 「had+p.p.」를 쓰고 주절에는 「조동사 과거+have+p.p.」를 써야 한다. 이를 틀리게 하거나 맞는 표현을 고르는 문제도 출제된다. 주절에 등장하는 조동사 could와 would의 의미 차이를 묻는 문제는 시험에 거의 나오지 않으니 걱정하지 않아도 된다.

Ex 3.

If I _____ that the movie would be so lousy, I would've suggested seeing another one.

(a) will known   (b) had known   (c) knew   (d) should know

Ex 4.

다음 문장과 의미가 같도록 할때 빈칸에 들어갈 알맞은 말은?

As I don't know about it, I cannot tell you.

=If I _____ about it, I _____ tell you.

(a) know - can   (b) don't know - cannot

(c) didn't know - could not   (d) knew - could

03 출제 100 % - 직설법을 가정법으로 고치는 주관식 문제는 반드시 출제된다.

 출제자의 눈 I wish 가정법에서 현재의 소망은 '과거시제', 과거의 소망은 '과거완료'를 쓴다. 시험에서 과거 대신 현재를 써 놓고 함정에 빠뜨리거나, 문맥을 통해 '과거시제'와 '과거완료'를 구별할 수 있는지를 묻는 문제가 가장 많이 출제된다. 문장 속에 과거를 써야 할지 과거완료를 써야 할지에 대한 시간의 정보는 반드시 존재하기 때문에 서두르지 않도록 한다. as if(=as though)도 같은 맥락으로 뒤에 올 알맞은 시제를 고르는 문제가 출제된다. 이 둘을 직설법 문장으로 보여 주고 가정법으로 고쳐 쓰게 하는 주관식 문제도 출제 가능하다.

Ex 5.

I wish my father _____ here with me to see me graduate next week.

(a) were   (b) had been   (c) is   (d) has been

Ex 6.

다음 문장을 as if를 이용한 문장으로 다시 쓰시오.

In fact, he was not a famous soccer player.

=He talks _____.

04 출제 100 % - if가 생략된 가정법을 알아둬라.

 출제자의 눈 if가 생략되면 주어와 동사의 자리가 바뀌는 도치 현상이 일어난다. 이 어순을 바르게 쓸 줄 아는지를 묻거나 틀린 어순을 바로 잡는 어법 문제가 출제될 수 있다. if가 생략되어 도치되었다 하더라도 주절에는 가정법 과거면 '과거 조동사', 가정법 과거완료면 「조동사 과거+have+p.p.」를 써야 한다. 이를 역으로 물어보는 문제도 가능하다. '~가 없다면'의 가정법 If it were not for에서 if를 생략한 Were it not for, If it had not been for에서 if를 생략한 Had it not been for의 어순도 반드시 기억해 두자. 같은 의미의 but for와 without은 가정법 과거와 과거완료에 모두 쓸 수 있다.

Ex 7.

_____ my teacher was going to cancel the test, I wouldn't have stayed up all night.

(a) Had I known   (b) I had known   (c) If I knew   (d) Knew I

1. 두 문장의 의미가 같도록 빈칸에 알맞은 말을 쓰시오.

> I'm sorry I didn't have enough time to read the novel.
> =I wish I _____
> the novel.

2. 다음 우리말을 영어로 바르게 옮긴 것은?

> 내가 너라면 더 일찍 일어날 텐데.

❶ If I am you, I will get up earlier.
❷ If I am you, I would get up earlier.
❸ If I was you, I wouldn't get up earlier.
❹ If I were you, I would get up earlier.
❺ If I were you, I won't get up earlier.

3. 다음 두 문장의 의미가 같도록 빈칸에 알맞은 단어를 고르시오.

> Leave now, or you'll be late for school.
> =If you _____ now, you'll be late for school.

❶ don't leave   ❷ won't leave
❸ leave   ❹ left
❺ didn't leave

4. 다음 빈칸에 들어갈 말이 바르게 짝지어진 것은?

> A : I will go to the dance club alone tonight.
> B : Well, but if I _____ you, I _____ go there alone.

❶ am – will not   ❷ was – can't
❸ were – would not ❹ was – will not
❺ were – can't

[5-6] 다음 빈칸에 알맞은 말을 쓰시오.

5.

> They didn't work harder, so they didn't pass the exam.
> → If they _____ _____ harder, they would have passed the exam.

6.

> I don't have enough money, so I can't buy a new computer.
> → If I _____ enough money, I _____ _____ a new computer.

7. 다음 중 어법상 어색한 문장을 고르시오.

❶ If all of your friends wore purple jeans, you would wear them, too.
❷ If she got the job, how much would she earn?
❸ If your best friend had cool sneakers, you want to buy them.
❹ If I were you, I would not tell a lie.
❺ What would you do if your friend got married at the age of 17?

8. 다음 문장을 as if 가정법으로 완성하시오.

> In fact, she is not Canadian.
> → She talked _____.

9. 우리말과 의미가 같도록 할 때 빈칸에 알맞은 표현은?

> 그녀의 충고가 없었다면, 나는 담배를 끊지 못했을 텐데.
> → _____ her advice, I couldn't have stopped smoking.

❶ Had it not been for   ❷ Were it not for
❸ Without for   ❹ But it's
❺ If it were not for

오답 노트 만들기

★틀린 문제 : _____ ★다시 공부한 날 : _____

(1) 문제를 왜? 틀렸는지 곰곰이 생각하고 그 이유를 적어본다.

(2) 핵심 개념을 적는다.

(3) 자신이 몰랐던 단어와 숙어 표현이 있으면 정리한다.

(4) 해설집에서 필요한 부분을 골라 풀이 해법을 정리한다.

★틀린 문제 : _____ ★다시 공부한 날 : _____

(1) 문제를 왜? 틀렸는지 곰곰이 생각하고 그 이유를 적어본다.

(2) 핵심 개념을 적는다.

(3) 자신이 몰랐던 단어와 숙어 표현이 있으면 정리한다.

(4) 해설집에서 필요한 부분을 골라 풀이 해법을 정리한다.

★틀린 문제 : _____ ★다시 공부한 날 : _____

(1) 문제를 왜? 틀렸는지 곰곰이 생각하고 그 이유를 적어본다.

(2) 핵심 개념을 적는다.

(3) 자신이 몰랐던 단어와 숙어 표현이 있으면 정리한다.

(4) 해설집에서 필요한 부분을 골라 풀이 해법을 정리한다.

★틀린 문제 : _____ ★다시 공부한 날 : _____

(1) 문제를 왜? 틀렸는지 곰곰이 생각하고 그 이유를 적어본다.

(2) 핵심 개념을 적는다.

(3) 자신이 몰랐던 단어와 숙어 표현이 있으면 정리한다.

(4) 해설집에서 필요한 부분을 골라 풀이 해법을 정리한다.

1. 다음 빈칸에 들어갈 말로 알맞은 것은?

> In fact, she doesn't do housework.
> But she talks as if she _____ housework.

❶ does ❷ were done ❸ did
❹ would do ❺ has done

오답노트

2. 〈보기〉의 문장과 의미가 같은 것은?

> | 보 기 | If I hadn't been busy, I could have talked with you. |

❶ As I am busy, I can't talk with you.
❷ As I am busy, I could talk with you.
❸ As I was busy, I could talk with you.
❹ As I was busy, I couldn't talk with you.
❺ As I had been busy, I couldn't talk with you.

오답노트

3. 빈칸에 들어갈 말이 바르게 짝지어진 것은?

> I'm sorry, but I didn't see you at that time.
> → If I _____ you there, I _____ hi to you.

❶ saw − said
❷ saw − would say
❸ had seen − would say
❹ saw − would have said
❺ had seen − would have said

오답노트

4. 다음 빈칸에 들어갈 알맞은 말을 쓰시오.

> 나에게 차가 한 대 있다면 좋을 텐데.
> = I wish I _____ a car.

오답노트

5. 다음 밑줄 친 동사를 알맞은 형태로 바꾸시오.

> 당신이 제 입장이라면 어떻게 하시겠습니까?
> = What would you do if you (be) in my position?

_____

오답노트

6. 〈보기〉의 문장과 의미가 같은 것을 고르시오.

> | 보 기 | If I had enough money, I could buy all the items in this store. |

❶ Because I didn't have enough money, I couldn't buy all the items in this store.
❷ Although I don't have enough money, I can buy all the items in this store.
❸ Because I don't have enough money, I can't buy all the items in this store.
❹ As I have enough money, I can buy all the items in this store.
❺ Though I have enough money, I can't buy all the items in this store.

오답노트

7. 다음 가정법 문장을 직설법으로 고치시오.

> If he had not helped me, I could not
> have finished it.
> = _____ he _____ me, I could
>   finish it.

오답노트

[8-10] 다음 문장을 「I wish+가정법」 문장으로 고치시오.

8. I'm sorry that I have so much assignment.
→ I wish _____.

9. I'm sorry that Mom found out about my
bad behavior at school.
→ I wish _____
_____.

10. I'm sorry that you broke up with him.
→ I wish _____.

오답노트

[11-12] 다음 문장을 if로 시작하는 문장으로 바꿔 쓰시오.

11. Without oxygen, all animals would
disappear.
→ _____

12. But for his skill, the bridge would have
never been built.
→ _____
_____

13. 다음 문장을 가정법으로 바꿀 때 옳은 것은?

> It snowed yesterday, so we didn't climb
> the mountain.

❶ If it snowed yesterday, we could not
climb the mountain.
❷ If it have snowed yesterday, we could
not climb the mountain.
❸ If it didn't snow yesterday, we could
have climb the mountain.
❹ If it had snowed yesterday, we could
climb the mountain.
❺ If it had not snowed yesterday, we could
have climbed the mountain.

오답노트

14. 다음 밑줄 친 부분과 바꿔 쓸 수 있는 것을 모두
고르면?

> <u>Without</u> my advice, he might have lost
> the chance.

❶ But for
❷ If it were for
❸ If it had been for
❹ If it were not for
❺ If it had not been for

오답노트

15. 다음 빈칸에 들어갈 말로 알맞게 짝지어진 것을 고르시오.

> A: What would you like to be if you
> _____ a man, Susan?
> B: I think I _____ like to be a soccer
> player.

❶ would be – might　　❷ are – were to
❸ were – would　　❹ have been – will
❺ are – should

오답노트

[16-17] 다음 빈칸에 알맞은 것을 고르시오.

16.

> My teacher is going to give an exam
> tomorrow. I wish he _____ us an
> exam tomorrow.

❶ give　　❷ is not going to give
❸ gave　　❹ were not going to give
❺ didn't give

오답노트

17.

> She is not American. But she talks
> as if she _____ American.

❶ is　　❷ be　　❸ has been
❹ hadn't been　　❺ were

오답노트

18. 다음 밑줄 친 부분 중 그 쓰임이 바르지 <u>못한</u> 것은?

❶ I am not an astronaut. If I <u>were</u> an astronaut, I would take my camera with me on the rocket ship next month.
❷ I'm sorry you had to take a cab to the airport. I didn't know you needed a ride. If you had told me, I <u>would have given</u> you a ride gladly.
❸ If he had not been killed in the war, he <u>would have been</u> thirty years old now.
❹ If we go to New York, we <u>will see</u> the Statue of Liberty.
❺ If he <u>hadn't gone</u> to the Vietnam War, he should be 60 by now.

오답노트

[19-20] 다음 글을 읽고 물음에 답하시오.

> Look at the unusual building in the picture.
> It looked ⓐ _____ it ⓑ (be) made out of
> precious jewels. But it was made out of old
> bottles. Look at this tower standing in the
> middle of the Expo site.

19. ⓐ에 들어갈 알맞은 접속사는?

_____

20. ⓑ의 괄호 안의 동사를 알맞은 형태로 고쳐 쓰시오.

_____

오답노트

[21-22] 다음 빈칸에 들어갈 알맞은 말을 쓰시오.

21. As he doesn't know what kind of books she likes, he cannot choose easily.
  → If he _____ what kind of books she likes, he _____ choose easily.

오답노트

22. I'd like to ask her, but she doesn't answer the phone.
  → If she _____ the phone, I _____ ask her.

오답노트

24. **빈칸 (A), (B)에 들어갈 말이 바르게 짝지어진 것은?**

> If we (A) _____ television about thirty years ago, we (B) _____ so much time talking with our family. And we wouldn't have enjoyed running and playing outdoors together, and fishing in the river together with our friends.

	(A)	(B)
❶	would have	would not spend
❷	had had	wouldn't have spent
❸	have not	won't have spent
❹	have	won't have spent
❺	could have	could spend

오답노트

23. **다음 빈칸에 들어갈 말이 바르게 짝지어진 것은?**

> · It's high time we _____ something to drink.
> · _____ your kindness, I would be very lonely.

❶ have – Without
❷ had – If it hadn't been for
❸ were – But for
❹ can have – If it were not for
❺ had – Without

오답노트

25. **다음 〈보기〉의 문장과 의미가 같은 것은?**

> **보기** Hadn't you helped me, I would have failed.

❶ As you help me, I don't fail.
❷ As you help me, I will not fail.
❸ As you helped me, I didn't fail.
❹ As you helped me, I failed.
❺ As you hadn't helped me, I didn't fail.

오답노트

A. 〈보기〉와 같이 다음 문장을 가정법으로 바꿀 때 빈칸에 알맞은 표현을 써 넣으시오.

보기	It is raining, so we won't finish the game. → If it *weren't raining*, we *would finish* the game.

1. I didn't eat lunch, and now I'm hungry.

→ If I _____ lunch, I _____ hungry now.

2. The sun was shining, so we went to the beach yesterday.

→ If the sun _____, we _____ to the beach yesterday.

3. The library is closing now, so Wilson will have to leave before finishing his research.

→ If the library _____ now, Wilson _____ before finishing his research.

B. 〈보기〉와 같이 다음 문장에서 if를 생략하여 다시 쓰시오.

보기	If you should need my help, please call. → *Should you need* my help, please call.

1. If I were you, I wouldn't go there.

→ _____, I wouldn't go there.

2. If I had been offered a job at the law office, I would have gladly accepted.

→ _____ a job at the law office, I would have gladly accepted.

C. 다음 문장을 가정법 과거완료나 혼합가정법을 이용하여 고치시오. (단, 조동사 would를 사용할 것)

1. Jane didn't come with us, so she didn't see the wonderful concert.

→ If Jane _____.

2. I skipped breakfast in the morning, so I am hungry now.

→ If I _____.

3. Scott didn't have the opportunity, so he never learned Korean.

→ If Scott _____.

실전 서술형 평가문제

출제의도 wish+가정법
평가내용 자신의 소망 표현하기

A. Nancy는 유명한 영화배우이다. 그녀는 현재의 삶을 좋아하지 않아 다른 삶을 살고 싶어 한다. Nancy의 소망을 〈보기〉와 같이 서술하시오.

[서술형 유형 : 14점 / 난이도 : 중]

Nancy

> **보기**
> Reporters follow me everywhere.
> → *I wish reporters didn't follow me everywhere.*

1. Newspapers write untrue stories about me.

→ _____

2. Moviegoers touch me and pull my clothes.

→ _____

3. I have to sign autographs all the time.

→ _____

4. I have to smile all the time.

→ _____

5. I can't wear anything I want.

→ _____

6. I can't go to the restaurant to get food.

→ _____

7. I haven't got privacy.

→ _____

실전 서술형 평가문제

🔍 출제의도 가정법 과거와 과거완료

평가내용 2차, 3차 가정문을 이용하여 상황 묘사하기

B. 〈보기〉와 같이 주어진 상황을 읽고 가정법 과거 또는 과거완료를 이용하여 문장을 다시 쓰시오.

[서술형 유형 : 9점 / 난이도 : 중상]

보기

If she hadn't spent all her money on CDs last Sunday, she could have bought the jeans she liked.

1.

> I didn't go to the coffee shop yesterday, so I didn't see my friends.

_____

_____

2.

> I don't know Peter's phone number. I can't call him

_____

_____

3.

> I caught a bad cold because I walked in the rain yesterday.

_____

_____

서술형 평가문제	채 점 기 준	배 점	나의 점수
A	표현이 올바르고 문법, 철자가 모두 정확한 경우	2점 × 7문항 = 14점	
B		3점 × 3문항 = 9점	
C		3점 × 5문항 = 15점	
D		3점 × 3문항 = 9점	
E		2점 × 2문항 = 4점	
공통	문법, 철자가 1개씩 틀린 경우	각 문항당 1점씩 감점	
	내용과 전혀 일치하지 않거나 답을 기재하지 못한 경우	0점	

출제의도 가정법 과거
평가내용 실생활에서 가정법 과거 표현하기

C. 〈보기〉와 같이 상대방에게 자신이 해줄 수 있는 충고를 자유롭게 쓰시오.   [서술형 유형 : 15점 / 난이도 : 상]

보기

I have put on five kilos since last year.

If I were you, I would start exercising. / If I were you, I would go on a diet.

1.

Susan lent me her digital camera last week and I think I've lost it.

_____

_____

2.

I was very rude to Kevin this morning.

_____

_____

3.

What color should I paint my bedroom?

_____

_____

4.

Where can I buy a birthday present for my mom?

_____

_____

5.

I always miss the school bus.

_____

_____

실전 서술형 평가문제

 출제의도 가정법 과거 / I wish + 가정법
평가내용 실생활에서 가정법 표현하기

D. 다음 상황이 벌어지면 당신은 어떻게 할 것인가? 가정법을 이용하여 자신의 생각을 자유롭게 기술하시오.

[서술형 유형 : 9점 / 난이도 : 상]

보기	If someone called you in the middle of the night ~ → *If someone called me in the middle of the night, I would get out of bed and answer the phone.*

1. If all the lights suddenly went out ~

→ _____

2. If you saw a strange person breaking into your neighbor's house ~

→ _____

3. If you smelled smoke in your house ~

→ _____

E. Kelly와 Bob은 어제 파티에서 만난 뒤 각자 돌아와서 다음과 같이 생각한다. 〈보기〉와 같이 「I wish + 가정법」을 이용하여 두 사람의 생각을 써 보시오.

[서술형 유형 : 4점 / 난이도 : 중하]

보기	I didn't give her my phone number. → *I wish I had given her my phone number.*

1. Bob says to himself : I didn't ask her to dance with me.

→ _____ .

2. Kelly says to herself : I told him I was tired.

→ _____ .

Chapter 7

일치와 화법
(Agreement & Narration)

Unit 01 수의 일치

1-1 주어와 동사의 일치 (1)

All the students in the photo **have** graduated.
사진 속에 있는 모든 학생들은 졸업을 했다.
Everyone is happy.
모든 사람들은 행복하다.

01   주어의 수에 따라 동사의 형태를 일치시키는 것을 수의 일치라고 한다. 단수형 주어는 단수형 동사를, 복수형 주어는 복수형 동사를 쓰는 것이 원칙이나, 경우에 따라서는 예외가 존재하므로 이에 주의해야 한다.
먼저, **관계사, 관계사 생략, 동격어구, to부정사, 전치사구 그리고 분사가 주어 뒤에 있는 경우** 동사가 멀리 떨어져 **수의 일치를 방해**한다.

The people who live in the desert **move** about a great deal. 사막에 사는 사람들은 많이 이동한다.
The woman we met at the party **was** very friendly. 우리가 파티에서 만났던 그 여자는 매우 친절했다.
Boys wearing hairstyles like movie stars **are**n't rare anymore.
영화배우와 비슷한 머리 모양을 한 소년들은 더 이상 낯설지 않다.
Mr. Brown, an English teacher, **lives** in the next door. Brown 씨는 영어선생님인데 옆집에 산다.

02   주격 관계대명사 즉, 형용사절 안의 동사는 **선행사에 수를 일치**시킨다.

We know the man who **speaks** English well. 우리는 영어를 잘하는 남자를 안다.
English spellings have considerable differences which **make** it difficult to read words.
영어 철자법에는 단어를 읽기 어렵게 하는 상당한 차이점이 있다.

03   **부정사, 동명사, 명사절이 주어가 되면 동사는 단수 취급**한다.

Providing medical care for people **is** very important in society.
사람들에게 의료보험을 제공하는 것은 사회적으로 매우 중요한 일이다.
Whether she has a degree **is** very important. 그녀가 학위를 소유했는지가 매우 중요하다.
To analyze the data **is** the most important mission. 데이터를 분석하는 것이 가장 중요한 임무이다.
That human beings can think **is** another matter. 인간이 생각할 수 있다는 것은 또 다른 문제이다.

04   **「all+주어」는 복수 동사로, each, every, -thing, -one, -body 등은 단수 동사로** 일치시킨다.

Each of the subjects in a sentence **has** to agree with its verb.
각각의 문장 주어는 그것의 동사와 일치시켜야 한다.
Every person at this meeting **looks** exhausted. 이 회의에 참석한 모든 사람은 지쳐 보인다.
Every doctor and nurse in this hospital **is** going to take a vacation.
이 병원에 있는 모든 의사와 간호사는 휴가를 갈 예정이다.

Challenge 1 다음 괄호 안의 표현 중 알맞은 것을 고르세요.

01. All the students (eats / eat) lunch at noon.

02. Reading a book (makes / make) me want to fall asleep.

03. What I remember about her (are / is) a willingness to negotiate.

04. The statement drawn up by Werner Accountants (provide / provides) a benchmark for evaluation.

05. Every boy and girl in this class (is / are) good at math.

06. The rules that people keep in their own country (varies / vary) from culture to culture.

07. Brad Pitt, the hero in the movies, (becomes / become) popular.

Challenge 2 다음 괄호 안의 단어를 알맞은 형태로 쓰세요.

01. Exercising daily and not skipping breakfast _____ (be) important.

02. The woman sitting in front of me at the movie _____ (be) snoring.

03. The window broken in the storm last night _____ (have) now been repaired.

04. The company needs some people who _____ (have) the vision of their future.

05. A group of bees, called a colony, _____ (use) smell to protect itself from other bees.

06. Elephants have an essential and unique trunk that _____ (serve) many purposes.

07. Part A in the last section divided into two parts _____ (consist) of identifying sentence error.

08. Every man, woman, and child _____ (need) love.

1-2 주어와 동사의 일치 (2)

Three hundred dollars is all the money I have.
300달러가 내가 가지고 있는 전부이다.

01 시간, 돈, 거리, 무게 그리고 양을 나타내는 명사는 복수형이라 하더라도 하나의 단위로 생각하기 때문에 **단수 취급**한다.

Thirty dollars a week **is** not a small sum for a student. 일주일에 30달러는 학생에게 적은 금액이 아니다.
Two hours **is** enough for me to read a newspaper. 2시간이면 신문을 읽는 데 충분하다.
Three weeks **is** a long time to wait for the results of the test. 3주면 시험의 결과를 기다리는 데 오랜 시간이다.

02 「The number of+복수 명사」는 '그 수'라는 뜻으로 **the number가 주어가 되어 단수 취급**하고 「A number of+복수 명사」는 **many**의 뜻으로 a number of가 뒤에 나오는 복수 명사를 수식해 주는 형용사 역할을 한다. 따라서 주어가 복수 명사이므로 동사도 **복수 동사**를 쓴다.

The number of students in our class **is** twenty. 우리 학급의 학생 수는 20명이다.
A number of citizens **are** gathering in front of the city hall. 많은 사람들이 시청 앞에 모여들고 있다.

03 부분을 나타내는 most of / some of / the rest of / half of / 분수 of / percent of / all of 등은 of 뒤의 **명사의 수에 동사의 수를 일치**시킨다.

Some of the fruit **is** still fresh. 과일 몇 개는 아직 신선하다.
Some of the oranges **are** still fresh. 오렌지 몇 개는 아직 신선하다.
Most of the residents **are** Christian. 주민들의 대부분은 기독교인이다.
Most of the river **has** dried up. 그 강의 대부분이 말라버렸다.
40 percent of the book **was** written by students. 그 책의 40%는 학생들에 의해 쓰여졌다.
Two thirds of the area **was** flooded when the sewers backed up. 하수도가 막히자 그 지역의 2/3가 침수됐다.

04 one of ~는 단수 취급하여 **단수 동사**를 쓴다. 「many+복수 명사」는 복수 동사, 「many a+단수 명사」는 **단수 동사**를 쓴다. a lot of, lots of, plenty of도 뒤따라 오는 명사에 동사의 수를 일치시킨다.

One of my friends **is** here. 내 친구 중에 한 명이 여기에 있다.
Plenty of seats **are** reserved. 충분한 좌석이 예약되어 있다.
Lots of money **was** stolen from the safe. 금고에서 많은 돈이 도난당했다.
Many young men **have** tried and failed. 많은 젊은이들이 시도했지만 실패했다.
=Many a young man **has** tried and failed.

서술형 기초다지기

정답 p. 27

Challenge 1 다음 괄호 안의 표현 중 알맞은 것을 고르세요.

01. Most of the apples in the basket (is / are) green.

02. Twenty minutes (is / are) not enough time for an essay.

03. Some of the fruit in this bowl (is / are) rotten.

04. Some of the apples in that bowl (is / are) rotten.

05. Half of the students in the class (is / are) from Arabic-speaking countries.

06. A lot of clothing in those stores (is / are) on sale this week.

07. A number of students (is / are) absent today.

08. The number of employees in my company (is / are) approximately ten thousand.

09. One of the chief materials in bones and teeth (is / are) calcium.

10. 20 percent of the onion (was / were) used for appetizer.

11. No one knows the number of the population that (has / have) been remarkably increasing.

12. About three-fifths of the houses (is / are) reconstructed.

13. Three-fourths of the pizza (has / have) already been eaten.

14. One of the houses (was / were) destroyed by fire.

15. The number of desks in that classroom (is / are) thirty-five.

16. A number of stores (is / are) closed today because of the holiday.

1-3 주어와 동사의 일치 (3)

The United States **consists** of diverse ethnic groups.
미국은 다양한 인종 집단으로 구성되어 있다.
English **is** spoken in many countries.
영어는 많은 나라에서 사용된다.

01 economics(경제학), mathematics(수학), physics(물리학), linguistics(언어학), ethics(윤리학), fine arts(미술)와 같은 **학문의 분야는 복수 명사처럼 보이지만 단수 취급**하여 **단수 동사**를 쓴다.

Economics **is** my favorite subject. 경제학은 내가 좋아하는 과목이다.

02 **국가명**과 같은 고유명사에 -s가 붙어 **복수처럼 보이는 명사** 역시 **단수 취급**하여 단수 동사를 쓴다. 대명사로 대신할 때도 they 대신 it을 쓴다.

> the United States 미국   the Philippines 필리핀   the Netherlands 네덜란드
> the United Nations 유엔   the Maldives 몰디브

The Philippines **consists** of more than 7,000 islands. 필리핀은 7천 개 이상의 섬으로 구성되어 있다.

03 diabetes(당뇨병), measles(홍역), rabies(광견병), rickets(구루병)과 같이 **질병을 나타내는 단어도** -s로 끝나지만 **단수 취급**하여 단수 동사를 쓴다. **news(뉴스, 소식)도 항상 단수 취급**한다.

Diabetes **is** an illness. 당뇨병은 질병이다.
Rabies **is** a preventable viral disease. 광견병은 예방 가능한 바이러스 질병이다.

04 the people, the police, the jury(배심원), the nobility(귀족), the crew(승무원), cattle(소)은 **-s로 끝나지 않지만 복수 취급**하여 동사도 복수형을 쓴다.

The police **are** on the track of the murderer. 경찰이 그 살인자를 추적하고 있다.
Cattle **are** domestic animals. 소는 가축이다. / No news **is** good news. 무소식이 희소식이다.

05 English, Spanish, Chinese, Japanese, French, Portuguese, Vietnamese 등이 그 나라의 **언어를 나타낼 때는 단수 취급**하고 'the'와 함께 쓰여 '**국민 전체 또는 그 나라 사람들**'을 의미할 때는 **복수 취급**한다. 「**the+형용사**」는 '~인 사람들'이란 뜻의 **복수 명사**이므로 동사도 복수형을 쓴다.

Chinese **is** his native language. 중국어는 그의 모국어이다.
The Chinese **have** an interesting history. 중국인들은 재미있는 역사를 가지고 있다.
The rich **are** not always happy. 부자들이 항상 행복한 것은 아니다.

서술형 기초다지기

Challenge 1 다음 괄호 안의 표현 중 알맞은 것을 고르세요.

01. The United States (is / are) a big country.

02. The news about Mr. Hogan (is / are) surprising.

03. The police (is / are) prepared in case there is a riot.

04. The English (is / are) proud, independent people.

05. English (is / are) not my native language.

06. Portuguese (is / are) somewhat similar to Spanish.

07. The poor (is / are) helped by government programs.

08. Economics (is / are) an important area of study.

09. Rabies (is / are) a disease you can get from being bitten by an infected animal.

10. A lot of Brazilians (speaks and understands / speak and understand) Spanish.

11. Why (is / are) the police standing over there?

12. The news on the radio and TV stations (confirms / confirm) that a serious storm is approaching our city.

13. Mathematics and geography (is / are) my favorite subjects.

14. The elderly in my country (is / are) given free medical care.

15. Physics (seeks / seek) to understand the mysteries of the physical world.

16. The United States (has / have) a population of around 250 million.

주어와 동사의 일치 (4)

Both my boyfriend and I **are** pretty quiet.
내 남자친구와 나는 둘 다 아주 내성적이다.
Not only my boyfriend but also I **am** pretty quiet.
내 남자 친구뿐만 아니라 나도 아주 내성적이다.

01 명사가 and로 연결되거나 Both A and B로 연결되어 주어 역할을 할 때는 **복수 취급**하여 복수 동사를 쓴다.

He and I **are** responsible for it. 그와 내가 그것에 대해 책임이 있다.
Both he and I **are** to be blamed for this result. 그와 나 둘 다 그 결과에 대해 비난받아야 한다.
Swimming and Biking **are** my favorite sports. 수영과 자전거 타기는 내가 좋아하는 스포츠이다.

※ and로 연결되더라도 하나의 사람 또는 사물을 나타낼 때는 단수 동사를 쓴다.

The poet and statesman **is** present. 시인이자 정치가인 그 사람이 참석하고 있다. (한 명)
The poet and the statesman **are** present. 그 시인과 그 정치가가 참석하고 있다. (두 명)
Bread and butter **is** nutritious. 버터 바른 빵은 영양이 풍부하다.

02 다음 (상관) 접속사 표현들은 **동사와 가까운 것(B)에 동사의 수를 일치**시킨다.

A or **B**	not only A but (also) **B**	**B** as well as A
either A or **B**	neither A nor **B**	not A but **B**

Chopsticks or <u>spoon</u> **is** used to eat food on the table. 젓가락이나 숟가락은 식탁에서 음식을 먹는 데 사용된다.
Not only the mice but also <u>the cat</u> **wants** to live peacefully. 쥐들뿐 아니라 고양이도 평화롭게 살기를 원한다.
= <u>The cat</u> as well as the mice **wants** to live peacefully.
Neither Kelly nor <u>her sisters</u> **are** going to take the test. Kelly도 그녀의 자매들도 시험을 보지 않을 것이다.
Either milk or <u>dairy products</u> **contain** a lot of calcium. 우유나 유제품들은 칼슘을 많이 함유하고 있다.
Not Steve but <u>you</u> **are** the one who should be responsible for the result.
Steve가 아니라 네가 그 결과에 책임을 져야 할 사람이다.

서술형 기초다지기

정답 p. 27

Challenge 1 다음 괄호 안의 표현 중 알맞은 것을 고르세요.

01. Either you or he (is / are) responsible for the accident.

02. Not Annie but her two sisters (wants / want) to go to the festival.

03. His students as well as he (was / were) very helpful yesterday.

04. Both Tom and Jerry (has / have) the plan to go camping.

05. Steve and his friend (is / are) coming to dinner.

06. Either Mr. Anderson or Ms. Wiggins (is / are) going to teach our class today.

07. Neither she nor you (is / are) able to do the work.

08. Not only Jane but also I (are / am) bored with this class.

09. Either of my sisters (is / are) going to stay at home.

10. Neither of the teams (want / wants) to start first.

11. Neither of those books (is / are) available in the library.

12. A white and black dog (is / are) barking at me.

13. A white and a black dog (is / are) barking at me.

14. Bread and butter (is / are) what he eats for breakfast.

15. Neither you nor he (is / are) able to play the violin.

16. The coach as well as the players (was / were) late for the game.

1-5 시제의 일치

I **think** (that) she **is** rich.
나는 그녀가 부자라고 생각한다.
I **thought** (that) she **was** rich.
나는 그녀가 부자였다고 생각했다.

01 주절의 동사와 종속절의 동사의 시제에 관한 일치를 시제의 일치라고 한다. 여기에는 원칙과 예외가 있다.

	주절의 시제		종속절의 시제
①	현재, 현재완료, 미래	→	모든 시제가 다 올 수 있음
②	과거, 과거완료	→	과거, 과거완료

I **know** that she **lives** in Singapore. 나는 그녀가 싱가포르에 살고 있다는 것을 알고 있다.
I **have known** that she **will go** to Singapore. 나는 그녀가 싱가포르에 갈 거라는 것을 알게 되었다.
John **will know** that she **lived** in Singapore. John은 그녀가 싱가포르에 살았다는 것을 알게 될 것이다.
I **know** that she **has gone** to Singapore. 나는 그녀가 싱가포르에 갔다는 것을 알고 있다.

02 주절의 시제가 과거인 경우 종속절의 시제는 과거나 과거완료가 되어야 한다. 종속절의 현재시제는 과거로, will과 must는 각각 would와 had to로, 현재완료는 과거완료로, 과거도 과거완료로 시제를 일치시킨다.

I think that he **is** busy. → I **thought** that he **was** busy. 나는 그가 바빴다고 생각했다.
I think that he **will be** busy. → I **thought** that he **would be** busy. 나는 그가 바쁠 거라고 생각했다.
I think that he **has been** busy. → I **thought** that he **had been** busy. 나는 그가 바빴었다고 생각했다.
I think that he **was** busy. → I **thought** that he **had been** busy. 나는 그가 바빴었다고 생각했다.
I think that you **must** take charge of the project.
→ I **thought** that you **had to** take charge of the project.
나는 네가 그 프로젝트에 책임을 져야 한다고 생각했다.

03 불변의 진리나 격언, 현재의 습관, 지속적인 사실은 항상 현재시제로, 역사적인 사실은 항상 과거시제로 쓴다. 시간상의 내용이 비교되는 **비교 구문**은 시제를 일치시킬 수 없다.

The teacher **told** us that the earth **moves** round the sun. 선생님은 지구가 태양 주위를 돈다고 말씀하셨다.
She **said** that she **takes** a walk every morning. 그녀는 매일 아침 산책을 한다고 말했다.
The book **said** that Columbus **discovered** America in 1492.
콜럼버스가 1492년에 아메리카대륙을 발견했다고 그 책에 쓰여 있었다.
It **is** warmer this winter than it **was** last year. 이번 겨울이 작년보다 더 따뜻하다.
It **was** not so cold yesterday as it **is** today. 어제는 오늘만큼 춥지 않았다.

서술형 기초다지기

정답 p. 27

Challenge 1 다음 문장을 과거시제로 바꿀 때 빈칸에 알맞은 형태의 시제를 써 넣으세요.

01. He says that he will study abroad.

→ He said that he _____ abroad.

02. She says that her mother has been ill for a month.

→ She said that her mother _____ ill for a month.

03. They know that she went to Japan.

→ They knew that she _____ to Japan.

04. I think that he must win the game.

→ I thought that he _____ the game.

Challenge 2 다음 괄호 안의 단어를 알맞은 시제로 고쳐 쓰세요.

01. Kevin said that he _____ (go) to the gym every morning.

02. They knew that the temperature _____ (rise) at first and then falls at some point.

03. The teacher said to us that the earth _____ (rotate) in one direction on its axis.

04. She was wiser then than she _____ (be) now.

05. She always repeated that money _____ (make) the world go round.

06. My teacher told us that Thomas Edison _____ (invent) the light bulb.

Challenge 3 다음 괄호 안의 단어를 이용하여 빈칸을 완성하세요.

01. 매일 아침 6시에 일어난다고 그녀는 어제 말했다. (get up / every morning / at 6)

→ She said yesterday that she _____.

02. 그는 물이 100℃에서 끓는다는 것을 알고 있었다. (at 100℃ / boil)

→ He knew that _____.

03. 우리는 미국의 남북전쟁이 1865년에 끝났다고 배웠다. (in 1865, be over)

→ We learned that the American Civil War _____.

Unit 02 화법

2-1 평서문의 화법 전환

She **said**, "**I am** busy." 그녀는 "난 바빠"하고 말했다.

She **said** that **she was** busy. 그녀는 바쁘다고 말했다.

01 어떤 사람이 한 말이나 생각을 다른 사람에게 전하는 방법을 '화법'이라고 한다.

① **직접화법** : 다른 사람이 한 말을 그대로 전달하는 방법

She said, "I am tired." 그녀는 "나는 피곤해."라고 말했다.
　　　전달동사　　　피전달문

② **간접화법** : 다른 사람이 한 말을 전달하는 사람의 말로 고쳐서 전달하는 방법

She said that she was tired. 그녀는 피곤하다고 말했다.
　　　전달동사　　　피전달문

02 직접화법을 간접화법으로 전환하는 방법

① 전달동사를 바꾼다.

say → say　　　said → said　　　say to → say to 또는 tell　　　said to → said to 또는 told

② 쉼표와 인용 부호(" ")를 없애고, **접속사 that으로 연결**한다.

③ 인칭대명사는 전달자의 입장에서, **적당한 인칭으로** 바꾼다.

④ 전달동사의 시제가 **과거**일 때는 인용 부호 안의 시제를 **현재 → 과거로, 과거 → 과거완료로** 바꾼다.

⑤ 형용사나 부사도 전달하는 시점과 입장에 맞게 고친다.

now → then	this → that	here → there
ago → before	tonight → that night	these → those
today → that day	next week → the next week	next year → the next year

yesterday → the day before 또는 the previous day
tomorrow → the next day 또는 the following day
last night → the night before 또는 the previous night
last month → the month before 또는 the previous month

She **said**, "I always **drink** coffee in the morning."

→ She **said** that **she** always **drinks** coffee in the morning. 그녀는 아침마다 늘 커피를 마신다고 말했다.

He **said** to me, "I **met** a strange woman **yesterday**."

→ He **said** to(=**told**) me (that) **he had met** a strange woman **the day before**.
그는 어제 이상한 여자를 만났다고 내게 말했다.

03 주절의 (전달동사의) 시제가 **현재**이면 **인용문의 시제와 조동사는 변하지 않고 대명사와 부사만 바뀐다.**

He **says to** me, "I **am studying** Japanese."

→ He **tells** me that he **is studying** Japanese. 그는 내게 일본어를 공부하고 있다고 말한다.

04 주절의 (전달동사의) 시제가 **과거**이면 **인용문의 시제와 조동사도 바뀐다**. 단, should/ought to, might는 과거형으로 바뀌지 않는다.

현재 → 과거	She said, "I **study** Korean."	→	She said that she **studied** Korean. 그녀는 한국어를 공부한다고 말했다.
현재진행 → 과거진행	She said, "I **am studying** Korean."	→	She said that she **was studying** Korean. 그녀는 한국어를 공부하고 있다고 말했다.
과거 → 과거완료	She said, "I **studied** Korean."	→	She said that she **had studied** Korean. 그녀는 한국어를 공부했다고 말했다.
과거진행 → 과거완료진행	She said, "I **was studying** Korean."	→	She said that she **had been studying** Korean. 그녀는 한국어를 공부해왔었다고 했다.
현재완료 → 과거완료	She said, "I **have studied** Korean."	→	She said that she **had studied** Korean. 그녀는 한국어를 공부했었다고 했다.
will → would	She said, "I **will** study Korean."	→	She said that she **would** study Korean. 그녀는 한국어를 공부할 거라고 했다.
be going to → was/were going to	She said, "I'**m going to** study Korean."	→	She said that she **was going to** study Korean. 그녀는 한국어를 공부할 거라고 했다.
can → could	She said, "I **can** study Korean."	→	She said that she **could** study Korean. 그녀는 한국어를 공부할 수 있을 거라고 했다.
must, have to → had to	She said, "I **must** study Korean."	→	She said that she **had to** study Korean. 그녀는 한국어를 공부해야 한다고 했다.
might/should → 변화 없음	She said, "I **might** study Korean."	→	She said that she **might** study Korean. 그녀는 한국어를 공부할지도 모른다고 했다.

05 시제 일치와 마찬가지로 **인용문의 내용이 일반적인 사실이거나 현재의 습관인 경우에는 주절의 시제가 과거라도 현재시제를 쓴다.** 또는 **역사적 사실**인 경우에도 전달동사의 시제와 관계없이 **피전달문은 항상 과거시제를 쓴다.**

She said, "I always take a walk every morning."

→ She said (that) she always **takes a walk** every morning.
그녀는 항상 아침 산책을 한다고 말했다. ▶ 현재의 습관

He said, "the American Civil War was over in 1865."

→ He said (that) the American Civil War **was over** in 1865.
그는 남북전쟁이 1865년에 끝났다고 말했다. ▶ 역사적 사실

보기	She said, "I really like this house." → *She said that she really liked that house.*

01. She said, "I can walk to the shops from the house."

→ _____

02. Steve says, "I love swimming."

→ _____

03. They said, "We have looked for a long time."

→ _____

04. Kelly says, "I can't swim, but I can ride a bicycle."

→ _____

05. He said to me, "It will rain tomorrow."

→ _____

06. He says to me, "I am studying hard to pass the bar exam."

→ _____

07. He said to me, "I met this boy three years ago."

→ _____

08. He said, "I am going to do the work."

→ _____

09. Tony said, "I went to the gym yesterday."

→ _____

10. Paul said, "I have been to the gym this week."

→ _____

Challenge 2 다음 우리말을 참고하여 직접화법과 간접화법 문장을 완성하세요.

> **보기**
> 선생님은 내게 "너는 열심히 공부해야 한다"라고 말했다. (study hard, have to)
> → The teacher said to me, *"You have to study hard."* (직접화법)
> → The teacher told *me that I had to study hard.* (간접화법)

01. 그는 "비가 많이 오고 있었다. 하지만 나는 거기에 갔다."라고 말했다. (rain hard, go there)

    → He said, "_____." (직접화법)

    → He said that _____. (간접화법)

02. 그는 나에게, "나는 2년 전에 이 소녀를 만났다."라고 말했다. (this girl, two years ago, meet)

    → He said to me, "_____." (직접화법)

    → He told _____. (간접화법)

03. 그는 나에게 "나는 이 만화책을 너에게 내일 돌려줄게"라고 말했다. (will return, to you, this comic book)

    → He said to me, "_____." (직접화법)

    → He told _____. (간접화법)

Challenge 3 다음 일기예보 내용을 직접화법으로 가장 정확히 표현한 것에 **V** 표 하세요.

> **보기**
> She said it was going to be a terrible storm.
> → "It was a terrible storm." (   )
> → "It's going to be a terrible storm." (∨)

01. She said the winds might reach 170 miles per hour.

    → "The winds may reach 170 miles per hour." (   )

    → "The winds would reach 170 miles per hour." (   )

02. She said there would be more rain the next day.

    → "There will be more rain the next day." (   )

    → "There will be more rain tomorrow." (   )

2-2 의문사가 있는 의문문의 화법 전환

Jane **said to** me, "**Where did you buy** the cell phone?"

Jane **asked** me **where I had bought** the cell phone.
Jane이 "너는 그 휴대전화를 어디서 샀니?"하고 내게 말했다.
Jane은 내가 어디서 그것을 샀는지를 물었다.

---

01 의문사가 있는 의문문의 간접화법은 **say, say to를 ask로 바꾸고**, 「**의문사＋주어＋동사**」의 어순으로 쓴다. 시제, 대명사와 부사(구) 등은 평서문의 화법 전환과 동일하게 바꾼다.

She **said to** him, "What are you eating?"
→ She **asked** him **what he was eating.** 그녀는 그에게 무엇을 먹는지를 물었다.

She **asked** me, "Where do you live?"
→ She **asked** me **where I lived.** 그녀는 내가 어디에 사는지를 물었다.
→ She **wondered where I lived.** 그녀는 내가 어디에 사는지 궁금해 했다.
→ She **wanted to know where I lived.** 그녀는 내가 어디에 사는지 알고 싶어 했다.

※ ask, wonder, want to know 등을 전달동사로 쓸 수 있지만, say 또는 tell은 쓰지 않는다.

02 접속사 that을 쓰지 않고 주어진 의문사를 그대로 사용하며 「**의문사＋주어＋동사**」의 어순으로 쓴다.
Ted **said to** Peter, "Where did you buy this shirt?"
→ Ted **asked** Peter **where he had bought** that shirt. Ted는 Peter에게 어디서 그 셔츠를 샀는지 물었다.

03 의문사가 있는 직접의문문에 쓰인 do(does, did)를 없애고 **주어에 따라 동사의 수를 결정하고 시제도 일치**시킨다.
She **said to** me, "What **is** your hobby?"
→ She **asked** me what my hobby **was.** 그녀는 나에게 내 취미가 뭐냐고 물었다.

He **said to** me, "Where **did** you **live** ten years ago?"
→ He **asked** me where I **had lived** ten years before. 그는 내가 10년 전에 어디에 살았었는지를 물었다.

04 **의문사 자체가 주어인 경우에는 「의문사＋동사」의 어순으로 쓴다.**
The teacher **said,** "Who can speak Chinese?"
→ The teacher **asked who could speak** Chinese. 선생님은 누가 중국어를 할 수 있는지 물었다.

She **said to** me, "What makes you think so?"
→ She **asked** me **what made me think so.** 그녀는 어째서 내가 그렇게 생각하는지를 물었다.

서술형 기초다지기

Challenge 1 다음 의문사가 있는 의문문을 간접화법으로 고쳐 쓰세요.

> | 보
기 | Kathy asked her, "How long have you lived here?"
→ Kathy asked her *how long she had lived there*. |
> |---|---|

01. Tom said to Judy, "Why are you practicing it?"

    → Tom asked Judy _____.

02. Tom said, "Where are you going?"

    → Tom asked _____.

03. The teacher said to me, "Why is your brother late for school?"

    → The teacher asked me _____.

04. I said to Peter "Where is your office?"

    → I asked Peter _____.

Challenge 2 다음 직접화법을 간접화법으로 고치세요.

> | 보
기 | He said to me, "When can we meet again?"
→ *He asked me when we could meet again.* |
> |---|---|

01. She said to me, "Where are you from?"

    → _____

02. My mom said to Jina, "Where were you?"

    → _____

03. The reporter said to me, "When will the train arrive?"

    → _____

04. He said to me, "How long does it take to get there?"

    → _____

2-3 의문사가 없는 의문문의 화법 전환

She **said to** me, "**Will it rain** this afternoon?"

She **asked** me **if it would rain** that afternoon.

그녀는 내게 말했다, "오후에 비가 올 것 같니?"
그녀는 오후에 비가 올지를 내게 물었다.

01

의문사가 없는 의문문의 간접화법은 say, say to를 ask로 바꾸고, 「if(whether)+주어+동사」의 어순으로 쓴다. 인용문에 의문사가 없는 Yes/No 의문문은 if나 whether 둘 다 쓸 수 있지만 일상 영어에서는 if가 더 자주 쓰인다.

I **said to** her, "**Are you** a violinist?"

→ I **asked her if she was** a violinist. 나는 그녀가 바이올린 연주자인지 아닌지를 물었다.

02

반드시 「의문사(if, whether)+주어+동사」의 어순으로 쓰고 시제, 대명사와 부사(구) 등은 평서문의 화법전환과 동일하게 바꾼다. 이때 if와 whether는 명사절 접속사로 '~인지 아닌지'의 뜻이다.

He **said to** me, "Do you speak English?"

→ He **asked** me **if** I **spoke** English. 그는 내게 영어를 할 줄 아는지를 물었다.

I **said to** him, "Can you do me a favor?"

→ I **asked** him **whether** he could do me a favor. 나는 그에게 내 부탁을 좀 들어줄 수 있는지 없는지를 물었다.

The boss **said to** her, "Did you finish the work?"

→ The boss **asked** her **if**(=**whether**) she **had finished** the work (**or not**).

그 사장은 그녀가 그 일을 끝냈는지 아닌지를 물었다.

※ if, whether 뒤에 or not을 쓰기도 한다.

03

의문사가 없는 Yes/No 의문문일 경우 전달동사 ask, wonder, want to know, inquire 등 다양하게 쓸 수 있지만, say 또는 tell은 쓰지 않는다.

She said, "Are you happy?" 그녀는 "너 행복하니"라고 말했다.

→ She **asked** if I was happy. 그녀는 내가 행복한지 아닌지를 물었다.

→ She **wondered** if I was happy. 그녀는 내가 행복한지 아닌지 궁금해 했다.

→ She **wanted to know** whether I was happy. 그녀는 내가 행복한지 아닌지 알고 싶어 했다.

→ She **inquired** whether I was happy (or not). 그녀는 내가 행복한지 아닌지를 물었다.

서술형 기초다지기

정답 p. 28

Challenge 1 다음 의문사가 없는 의문문을 간접화법으로 바꿔 쓰세요.

> 보기
> She said to me, "Is this yours?"
> → She asked me *if[whether] that was mine*.

01. Brian said, "Have you met Cindy before?"

→ Brian asked _____.

02. She said to me, "Are you happy now?"

→ She asked me _____.

03. He said, "Do you like to play basketball?"

→ He wanted to know _____.

04. Bob says, "Can we go to the moon someday for a field trip?"

→ Bob wants to know _____.

Challenge 2 다음 직접화법을 간접화법으로 고치세요.

> 보기
> She said to me, "Have you ever been abroad?"
> → *She asked me if[whether] I had ever been abroad.*

01. He said to me, "Did you go to the park last night?"

→ _____

02. I said to her, "Are you angry now?"

→ _____

03. He said to me, "Did you go to the meeting last night?"

→ _____

04. Wilson said to us, "Did you have a chance to talk to Johnson?"

→ _____

2-4 요청과 명령의 화법 전환

The police officer **said**, "**Stop**."

→ The police officer **ordered** me **to stop**.

그 경찰관은 "멈춰."하고 말했다.
그 경찰관은 나에게 멈추라고 명령했다.

01 명령이나 요청, 충고 등의 간접화법은 to부정사를 사용한다. 전달동사는 내용에 따라 명령이나 충고를 나타내는 advise, order, ask, tell, invite, permit, remind, encourage, warn 등을 다양하게 쓸 수 있다. 이때 간접화법은 「동사＋목적어＋to부정사」의 어순으로 5형식 문장을 이룬다.

The teacher **said to** me, "**Tell** me the truth."

→ The teacher **told** me **to tell** the truth. 선생님은 나에게 진실을 말하라고 말했다.

She **said to** me, "**Wait** outside!"

→ She **ordered[told]** me **to wait** outside. 그녀는 나에게 밖에서 기다리라고 했다.

The teacher **said to** the children, "**Be** quiet!"

→ The teacher **warned** the children **to be** quiet. 그 선생님은 아이들에게 조용히 하라고 경고했다.

02 '~하지 마라'라는 **부정 명령문의 간접화법은 to부정사 앞에 'not'을 붙여 부정사를 부정한다.

My dad **said to** me, "**Don't go** near the fire."

→ My dad **advised** me **not to go** near the fire. 아빠는 나에게 불 가까이 가지 말라고 충고했다.

She **said to** me, "**Don't call** me tomorrow."

→ She **told** me **not to call** her the next day. 그녀는 나에게 다음 날 전화하지 말라고 말했다.

Jane **said to** them, "**Don't bother** me with questions."

→ Jane **ordered** them **not to bother** her with questions.

Jane은 그들에게 질문들로 그녀를 귀찮게 하지 말라고 명령했다.

서술형 기초다지기

정답 p. 28

Challenge 1   괄호 안의 동사를 이용하여 명령문의 직접화법을 간접화법으로 바꾸세요.

> **보기**
> The doctor said to me, "Stay in bed for a few days." (tell)
> → *The doctor told me to stay in bed for a few days.*

01. She said to him, "Please lend me some money. (ask)

→ _____

02. The doctor said to him, "Stop drinking." (advise)

→ _____

03. My mom said to me, "Do your homework at once." (order)

→ _____

04. My father said to me, "Clean the car tomorrow." (tell)

→ _____

Challenge 2   〈보기〉와 같이 아래의 지시사항을 간접화법 문장으로 바꾸세요.

> **보기**
> Listen carefully. (tell)
> → *She told us to listen carefully.*

01. Please put all your books and papers away. (ask)

→ _____

02. Please do not try to copy your classmates' work. (ask)

→ _____

03. Don't talk. (tell)

→ _____

04. Check the answers carefully before handing in your papers. (advise)

→ _____

"출제자가 노리는 급소" 이것이 시험에 출제되는 영문법이다!

01 출제 100% - 주어와 동사를 멀리 떨어뜨려 놓고 수의 일치를 묻는다.

🔍 출제자의 눈

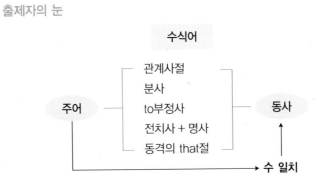

Ex 1.

다음 괄호 안의 표현 중 어법상 알맞은 것을 고르시오.
Many people who live in this part of the world (is / are) likely to be worried again with the beginning of the cold weather.

02 출제 100% - 수능, 토익, 텝스에서도 자주 물어보는 수의 일치 유형

🔍 출제자의 눈

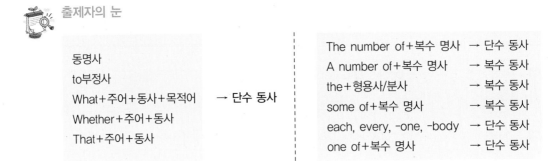

Ex 2.

다음 괄호 안의 표현 중 어법상 알맞은 것을 고르시오.
· Some of the most important books for my report (is / are) not available in the school library.
· Each of these mobile phones (is / are) exported to oversea markets.

03 출제 100% - 부분을 나타내는 표현과 (상관) 접속사의 수 일치

 출제자의 눈

some of most of the rest of half of 분수 of percent of all of	+	복수 명사 → 복수 동사 단수 명사 → 단수 동사

A or B 「A 또는 B」
not A but B 「A가 아니라 B」
either A or B 「A나 B 둘 중 하나」
neither A nor B 「A와 B 둘다 아닌」
not only A but also B
(=B as well as A) 「A뿐만 아니라 B도」

→ B에 일치

Ex 3.

다음 괄호 안의 표현 중 어법상 알맞은 것을 고르시오.
· Not only does the 'leaf fish' look like a leaf, but it also (imitates / imitate) the movement of a drifting leaf underwater.
· Nearly 40 percent of the people in our town never (votes / vote) in local elections.

04 출제 100% - 시제 일치는 예외를 조심하고, 화법은 영작문제에 대비하라.

 출제자의 눈 주절의 시제가 현재(현재완료, 미래)일 경우 종속절에는 모든 시제가 올 수 있다. 주절의 시제가 과거(완료)일 때는 종속절의 시제도 과거 또는 과거완료로 일치시킨다. 하지만 불변의 진리, 현재의 습관, 지속적인 사실은 주절의 시제와 관계 없이 현재시제를 쓰고, 역사적인 사실은 항상 과거시제를 쓴다. 이를 묻는 문제가 출제 가능하다. 화법은 직접화법을 간접화법으로 전환하는 부분 영작 또는 서술형 문제로 출제된다. 특히 의문사가 없는 의문문의 화법 전환에서는 접속사 if 또는 whether를 고르는 문제가 나올 가능성이 높고 명령문의 화법 전환에서는 to부정사를 쓸 줄 아는지를 물어볼 수 있다.

Ex 4.

다음 문장을 간접화법으로 바꿀 때 빈칸에 알맞은 말을 쓰시오.
Mom said to me, "Don't be late for school."
= Mom told _____ .

[1-2] 다음 빈칸에 들어갈 말로 알맞은 것은?

1.

> Mary said, "Do the work, Peter."
> → Mary ordered me _____ the work.

① does ② did ③ has done
④ doing ⑤ to do

2.

> Tom said, "I was shopping with her."
> → Tom said that he _____ shopping with her.

① is ② was ③ has been
④ had been ⑤ have been

3. 다음 중 어법상 어색한 것은?

① We learned that the earth is round.
② He said that he takes a walk every morning.
③ I met Mr. Smith yesterday and recognized him at once because I had met him before.
④ He told me that he got up at six every morning.
⑤ The teacher said that Columbus discovered America in 1492.

4. 다음 문장을 간접화법으로 고쳐 쓰시오.

> I asked Bob, "What do you like to do?"
> → I asked Bob _____.

5. 다음 밑줄 친 부분을 간접화법으로 바르게 바꾼 것은?

> When the day of our final game came, my top players were all ready. Then suddenly Billy said to me, "Can I be a starter?" He said in a strong voice, "Coach, I'm ready to do everything to help the team win."

① Billy asked me that he can be a starter.
② Billy asked me that he could be a starter.
③ Billy asked me if I can be a starter.
④ Billy asked me if he could be a starter.
⑤ Billy asked me if he can be a starter.

6. 다음 우리말과 같은 뜻이 되도록 빈칸에 알맞은 말을 넣으면?

> 학생들과 선생님도 그 답을 모른다.
> → Neither the students nor the teacher _____ the answer.
> → Neither the teacher nor the students _____ the answer.

① know – know ② knows – know
③ know – knows ④ known – known
⑤ knows – knows

7. 다음 문장을 간접화법으로 고쳐 쓰시오.

> Nancy says, "I can't swim, but I can ride a bicycle."
> → Nancy says that _____
> _____.

8. 다음 중 수의 일치가 바르지 않은 것은?

① My parents as well as my sister are here.
② The elderly in my country are given free medical care.
③ The number of students who knew the answer to the last question on the exam was very low.
④ Three-fourths of the pizza has already been eaten.
⑤ Mathematics and geography is my favorite subjects.

오답 노트 만들기

★틀린 문제 : _____   ★다시 공부한 날 : _____

(1) 문제를 왜? 틀렸는지 곰곰이 생각하고 그 이유를 적어본다.

(2) 핵심 개념을 적는다.

(3) 자신이 몰랐던 단어와 숙어 표현이 있으면 정리한다.

(4) 해설집에서 필요한 부분을 골라 풀이 해법을 정리한다.

★틀린 문제 : _____   ★다시 공부한 날 : _____

(1) 문제를 왜? 틀렸는지 곰곰이 생각하고 그 이유를 적어본다.

(2) 핵심 개념을 적는다.

(3) 자신이 몰랐던 단어와 숙어 표현이 있으면 정리한다.

(4) 해설집에서 필요한 부분을 골라 풀이 해법을 정리한다.

★틀린 문제 : _____   ★다시 공부한 날 : _____

(1) 문제를 왜? 틀렸는지 곰곰이 생각하고 그 이유를 적어본다.

(2) 핵심 개념을 적는다.

(3) 자신이 몰랐던 단어와 숙어 표현이 있으면 정리한다.

(4) 해설집에서 필요한 부분을 골라 풀이 해법을 정리한다.

★틀린 문제 : _____   ★다시 공부한 날 : _____

(1) 문제를 왜? 틀렸는지 곰곰이 생각하고 그 이유를 적어본다.

(2) 핵심 개념을 적는다.

(3) 자신이 몰랐던 단어와 숙어 표현이 있으면 정리한다.

(4) 해설집에서 필요한 부분을 골라 풀이 해법을 정리한다.

1. 다음 문장을 간접화법으로 바꿀 때 빈칸에 들어갈 말이 바르게 짝지어진 것은?

> Mom, I have some good news. Mr. Brown said to me, "Do you want to get a scholarship?"
> → Mom, I have some good news. Mr. Brown asked me _____ I _____ to get a scholarship.

❶ if – had wanted
❷ how – wanted
❸ whether – wants
❹ if – wanted
❺ whenever – wanted

오답노트

2. 다음 빈칸에 들어갈 말로 알맞은 것은?

> Economics _____ the most difficult subject among all others.

❶ are
❷ is
❸ be
❹ has
❺ have

오답노트

3. 다음 중 화법 전환이 바르지 <u>않은</u> 것은?

❶ She said to me, "Don't make a noise."
  → She told me not to make a noise.
❷ I said to her, "What food do you like best?"
  → I asked her what food she liked best.
❸ She said to me, "What are you doing?"
  → She asked me what she was doing.
❹ He said to her, "My favorite subject is English."
  → He told her that his favorite subject was English.
❺ He said to me, "Marry me."
  → He proposed me to marry him.

오답노트

4. 다음 빈칸에 들어갈 말이 바르게 짝지어진 것은?

> · A number of students _____ studying in the library.
> · The number of students who want to go to the park _____ increasing.

❶ is – are
❷ are – is
❸ are – are
❹ were – are
❺ was – is

오답노트

5. 다음 중 빈칸에 is가 들어갈 수 <u>없는</u> 것은?

❶ Three hundred dollars _____ enough.
❷ Three weeks _____ a long time to wait for the result of the test.
❸ Every one of the students _____ on time for the exam.
❹ Thursday or Friday _____ the best day to go.
❺ Both Tom and Jason _____ fond of soccer.

오답노트

6. 다음 문장에서 잘못된 부분을 찾아 바르게 고쳐 쓰시오.

> Neither she nor I is going to the festival.

_____ → _____

오답노트

7. 다음 빈칸에 들어갈 알맞은 말은?

> He said to me, "Where do you live?"
> → He asked me where I _____.

❶ had lived ❷ lives ❸ live
❹ lived ❺ don't live

오답노트

8. 다음 문장을 간접화법으로 바꿀 때 빈칸에 알맞은 말은?

> The doctor said to the patient, "Do not smoke anymore."
> ＝The doctor _____.

❶ asked the patient that to not smoke anymore
❷ told the patient not to smoking anymore
❸ advised the patient not to smoking anymore
❹ warned the patient not to smoke anymore
❺ advised the patient to not smoke anymore

오답노트

9. 다음 중 우리말을 영어로 잘못 옮긴 것은?

❶ 우리들은 각자 해야 할 일이 있다.
　→ Each of us has a job to do.
❷ 너도 너의 아내도 고기를 먹지 않는다.
　→ Neither you nor your wife eats meat.
❸ Kate와 Jane 둘 다 커피를 마신다.
　→ Both Kate and Jane drink coffee.
❹ 엄마 또는 아빠가 나를 학교에 태워 주신다.
　→ Either my mother or my father drives me to school.
❺ 선생님도 학생들도 여기에 없다.
　→ Neither the teacher nor the students is here.

오답노트

10. 다음 빈칸에 들어갈 말로 알맞은 것은?

> He said that he _____ jogging every morning.

❶ go ❷ goes ❸ went
❹ is going ❺ has gone

11.

> The teacher said that the United States _____ one of the most powerful countries in the world.

❶ is ❷ was ❸ will be
❹ would be ❺ has

오답노트

12. 다음 중 어법에 맞지 <u>않는</u> 문장은?

① The shows on TV tonight are interesting.
② The story about kings and queens are fascinating.
③ Walking alone at night is very dangerous.
④ The news on the radio and TV stations confirms that a serious storm is approaching our city.
⑤ Being a good flight attendant is making your passengers feel relaxed and comfortable throughout trip.

오답노트

13. 다음 문장을 직접화법으로 바르게 바꾼 것은?

He once said that his son was the biggest joy in his life.

① He once told, "His son is the biggest joy in my life."
② He once said, "His son is the biggest joy in his life."
③ He once said, "My son is the biggest joy in my life."
④ He once said, "My son was the biggest joy in my life."
⑤ He once told me, "My son was the biggest joy in my life."

오답노트

[14-15] 다음 문장을 간접화법으로 바르게 고친 것은?

14.

I said to her, "Do you have a puppy?"

① I told her to have a puppy.
② I asked her to have a puppy.
③ I told her when she has a puppy.
④ I asked her if she has a puppy.
⑤ I asked her whether she had a puppy.

오답노트

15.

She said to us, "Water boils at 100℃."

① She said us that water boils at 100℃.
② She said us that water boiled at 100℃.
③ She told us that water boiled at 100℃.
④ She told us that water boils at 100℃.
⑤ She advised us that water boils at 100℃.

오답노트

16. 다음 문장을 간접화법으로 바꿀 때 빈칸에 알맞은 말을 쓰시오.

He said to me, "Open the door, please."
→ He _____ _____ _____ _____
_____ _____.
(그는 나에게 문을 열어달라고 부탁했다.)

오답노트

17. 다음 문장에서 어법상 <u>잘못된</u> 부분을 찾아 <u>모두</u> 고치시오.

> Cindy told me that she had got her leg broken three days before.
> =Cindy said to me, "I have got my leg broken three days before."

_____

오답노트

18. 다음 중 어법상 <u>틀린</u> 것은?

❶ Seven hundred miles is a long drive.
❷ Everybody wants to get the promotion.
❸ Measles is not common in Canada.
❹ To be the best in any field takes dedication and determination.
❺ One of the difficult problems were overcoming poverty.

오답노트

19. 다음 문장을 간접화법으로 바꿀 때 빈칸에 알맞은 말을 쓰시오.

> He said to me, "Do you like that music?"
> → He _____ me _____ _____ _____ that music.

오답노트

20. 다음 두 문장을 〈보기〉와 같이 한 문장으로 다시 쓰시오.

보기	Tom said to me, "I will help you." → Tom told me (that) he would help me.

> She said, "I have to go down to the main office for a meeting."
> → She said that _____ _____ to go down to the main office for a meeting.

오답노트

21. 다음 빈칸에 들어갈 단어가 바르게 짝지어진 것은?

> 그녀는 매일 아침 우유만 마시고 출근한다고 말했다.
> → She told me that she only _____ milk before _____ to work every day.

❶ drinks – goes
❷ drank – going
❸ drank – had gone
❹ drinks – went
❺ drinks – going

오답노트

A. 다음 직접화법을 간접화법으로 바꾸어 쓰시오.

보 기	He said to me, "I am taller than you." → *He told me that he was taller than I[me].*

1. Seo-yoon said, "I like listening to music."

→ _____

2. She said to me, "What time is it now?"

→ _____

3. My teacher said to us, "Be quiet."

→ _____

4. Tom said to me, "Who wrote this book?"

→ _____

5. She said to me, "Don't open the door."

→ _____

B. 다음 문장을 직접화법으로 바꾸어 쓰시오.

보 기	He told me to work hard every day. → *He said to me, "Work hard every day."*

1. She asked him where he lived.

→ _____

2. I asked the woman if she knew Mr. Smith.

→ _____

3. I asked her where she had been the night before.

→ _____

C. 〈보기〉와 같이 괄호 안의 접속사를 이용하여 문장을 연결하시오.

보기	Kate drinks coffee. Jane drinks coffee, too. → _Both Kate and Jane drink coffee._	(both ~ and)

1. David will help you. Otherwise, Kim will help you.　　(either ~ or)

→ _____

2. My mother drives me to school. If she can't, my father drives me　　(either ~ or)
to school.

→ _____

3. John hasn't been to Spain. Fiona hasn't been to Spain, either.　　(neither ~ nor)

→ _____

4. Tom is learning Korean this year. I am learning Korean this year, too.　　(both ~ and)

→ _____

5. Emma didn't win the race. Kathy didn't win the race, either.　　(neither ~ nor)

→ _____

D. 다음 괄호 안의 표현 중 알맞은 것을 고르시오.

1. About two-thirds of my books (is / are) novels.

2. The number of cars (has / have) been remarkably increasing.

3. There (was / were) lots of people suffering from tuberculosis.

4. Mary is one of those women who (believe / believes) that the success of any marriage
depends entirely on the husband.

5. The English (is / are) often said to be a practical people.

6. A needle and thread (was / were) needed to sew the button.

7. He said that Europe (is / was) separated from America by the Atlantic Ocean.

8. I agree that physics (is / are) badly taught in our schools.

실전 서술형 평가문제

출제의도 주어와 동사의 수 일치
평가내용 주어에 따른 수 일치 구별하기

A. 다음 사진을 보고 빈칸을 채운 후 괄호 안에서 알맞은 것을 고르시오. [서술형 유형 : 8점 / 난이도 : 중하]

a number of	none of the	the number of	one of the	each of the

보기

The number of women playing cards (ⓘs / are) three.

1. _____ (is / are) sitting down at a table and playing cards.

2. _____ (is / are) not wearing glasses.

3. _____ is not eating cookies at the moment.

4. _____ (is / are) wearing glasses.

B. 〈보기〉와 같이 적절한 상관접속사를 이용한 문장으로 만드시오. [서술형 유형 : 6점 / 난이도 : 중]

보기
Fruits have vitamin C. Vegetables have vitamin C, too.
→ *Both fruits and vegetables have vitamin C.*

1. Peter usually takes the dog out for a walk. If he can't do it, his sister does.

   → _____

2. They say vitamin C prevents heart disease. They say vitamin C prevents colds.

   → _____

3. Lisa didn't tell the truth. James didn't tell the truth, either.

   → _____

출제의도 평서문의 간접화법
평가내용 다른 사람의 말을 간접화법으로 전달하기

C. 말풍선에 들어 있는 말을 알맞은 간접화법으로 옮겨 쓰시오. [서술형 유형 : 8점 / 난이도 : 중]

1. _My granddaughter plays the piano beautifully._

   → The woman said that _____

   _____.

2. _My husband and I enjoyed the movie last night_

   → Mrs. Allen said that _____

   _____.

3. _I'm going to buy a new cell phone next month_

   → David said that _____

   _____.

4. _Dad, I have been washing the car all morning!_

   → Frank told his dad that _____

   _____.

실전 서술형 평가문제

 출제의도 의문사가 있는 의문문과 의문사가 없는 의문문의 간접화법 전환

평가내용 다른 사람의 말을 간접화법으로 전달하기

D. 두 사람의 대화를 읽고 〈보기〉와 같이 간접화법 문장으로 만드시오.　　　　　[서술형 유형 : 12점 / 난이도 : 중상]

> **보기**
>
> Tom : What are you doing?
> Wilson : I'm tidying my desk.
> → Tom *asked Wilson what he was doing.*
> → Wilson *told Tom that he was tidying his desk.*

1. Bob : Will you go to the soccer game on Saturday?

　　Peter : No, I won't because I'm going camping at the weekend.

　　→ Bob _____ .

　　→ Peter _____ .

2. Cindy : Why didn't you buy the blue dress?

　　Kathy : I liked the pink one better.

　　→ Cindy _____ .

　　→ Kathy _____ .

3. Tina : Have you bought any new CDs, boys?

　　Billy and Harry : Yes, we have, but we haven't listened to them all yet.

　　→ Tina _____ .

　　→ Billy and Harry _____ .

4. Susan : Did you watch the movie last night?

　　Philip : No, I didn't, because I was reading a very interesting book.

　　→ Susan _____ .

　　→ Philip _____ .

출제의도 요청이나 명령 문장의 화법 전환
평가내용 다른 사람의 말을 간접화법으로 전달하기

E. 〈보기〉와 같이 주어진 질문에 알맞은 대답을 쓰시오. [서술형 유형 : 9점 / 난이도 : 중상]

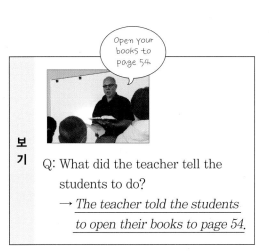

보기

Open your books to page 54

Q: What did the teacher tell the students to do?
→ *The teacher told the students to open their books to page 54.*

1.

Stop eating!

Q: What did Tom tell his wife to do?
→ _____
_____

2.

Don't drive so fast, Karen!

Q: What did Karen's husband tell her?
→ _____
_____

3.

Lend me five dollars, please.

Q: What did Lucy ask her brother to do?
→ _____
_____

서술형 평가문제	채 점 기 준	배 점	나의 점수
A		2점×4문항=8점	
B		2점×3문항=6점	
C	표현이 올바르고 문법, 철자가 모두 정확한 경우	2점×4문항=8점	
D		3점×4문항=12점	
E		3점×3문항=9점	
F		2점×6문항=12점	
공통	문법, 철자가 1개씩 틀린 경우	각 문항당 1점씩 감점	
	내용과 전혀 일치하지 않거나 답을 기재하지 못한 경우	0점	

출제의도 **평서문의 간접화법**
평가내용 **다른 사람의 말을 간접화법으로 전달하기**

F. 〈보기〉와 같이 두 사람의 대화를 모두 간접화법으로 서술하시오.　　　[서술형 유형 : 12점 / 난이도 : 중상]

Tiffany : My sister went to the new French restaurant around the corner yesterday.

Emily　: Really? My husband and I are planning to go there tomorrow evening.

Tiffany : I've heard that it's quite expensive.

Emily　: I know that, but it's my birthday tomorrow and I want to do something special.

Tiffany : In that case, it's the right place to go to. You know, the chef is from Paris and the service is excellent. I'm sure you'll have a delicious meal.

보 기	Tiffany said that *her sister had gone to the new French restaurant around the corner the day before*.

1. Emily told Tiffany that _____.

2. Tiffany said that _____.

3. Emily answered that _____.

4. Tiffany told her that in that case, _____.

5. She explained that _____.

6. She also told Emily that _____.

Chapter 8

특수 구문
(Emphasis, Inversion, Ellipsis)

Unit 01 강조

1-1 도치가 일어나지 않는 강조 (1)

Cindy saw a ghost at the park.
Cindy는 공원에서 귀신을 봤다.
→ It was **Cindy** that[who] saw a ghost at the park.
공원에서 귀신을 본 사람은 바로 Cindy였다.

01 「It is/was ~ that」 구문을 사용하여 주어, 목적어, 수식어구 등을 강조할 수 있다. '~인 것은 바로 ~이다(였다)'로 해석한다. 단, 동사는 강조할 수 없다.

> I went fishing with my friends last Sunday. 나는 지난 일요일에 친구들과 낚시를 갔다.

① 주어 강조
   It was **I** that went fishing with my friends last Sunday.
   지난 일요일에 친구들과 함께 낚시를 간 것은 바로 나였다.

② 시간을 나타내는 부사구 강조
   It was **last Sunday** that I went fishing with my friends.
   내가 친구들과 낚시하러 간 것은 바로 지난 일요일이었다.

02 강조하는 대상에 따라 that 대신에 who, which, when, where 등을 쓸 수 있다.

It was **a new cell phone** which I wanted to buy. 내가 사고 싶었던 것은 바로 새 휴대전화였다.
It was **last Friday** when they visited the museum. 그들이 박물관을 방문한 것은 바로 지난 금요일이었다.
Do you know it was **Napoleon** who invented canned food?
통조림을 발명한 사람이 바로 나폴레옹이란 것을 너는 아니?

※ 강조 구문은 강조하기 위해 없는 내용(it is/was ~ that)을 만들어 넣었으므로 모두 제거해도 문장에 아무런 영향을 끼치지 않는다. 하지만 비슷한 형태의 가주어, 진주어 구문(It ~ that ~)에서는 It과 that을 제거하면 틀린 문장이 된다.

~~It is~~ obvious ~~that~~ he doesn't understand English. 그가 영어를 이해하지 못한다는 것은 분명하다.
→ He doesn't understand English obvious. (×)

03 **동사를 강조**할 때에는 주어의 인칭과 수, 시제에 맞는 **조동사 do를 이용**하여, 'do/does/did+동사원형'으로 쓴다. '정말로 ~하다, 참으로 ~하다' 등으로 해석한다.

Nancy **does** like math and science. Nancy는 정말로 수학과 과학을 좋아한다.
I **did** send the e-mail to you yesterday. 나는 정말 어제 너에게 이메일을 보냈어.
I **do** hate her. 나는 그녀가 정말 싫다.

서술형 기초다지기

Challenge 1 다음 문장의 밑줄 친 부분을 강조하는 「It was ~ that ~」 구문을 만들어 보세요.

> **보기**
> I met Susan in London last month.
> → *It was I that met Susan in London last month.*

01. I met Susan in London last month.

→ _____

02. Tom returned the money last night.

→ _____

03. She saw the man break into the house last night.

→ _____

04. Bob picked up a coin on the road yesterday.

→ _____

Challenge 2 밑줄 친 부분을 강조하는 문장으로 만들 때 빈칸에 알맞은 말을 쓰세요.

01. My brother likes the rock band.

→ My brother _____ _____ the rock band.

02. My mom forgave me, but she never forgot my error.

→ My mom _____ _____ me, but she never forgot my error.

03. I remember her name and address.

→ I _____ _____ her name and address.

04. We ate chicken for breakfast this morning.

→ We _____ _____ chicken for breakfast this morning.

05. She finished all her winter vacation assignment before school started.

→ She _____ _____ all her winter vacation assignment before school started.

Chapter 8 – 특수 구문 · 247

1-2 도치가 일어나지 않는 강조 (2)

Why **on earth** are you weeping?
도대체 왜 울고 있니?

This is **the very** book I have been looking for.
이것이 바로 내가 찾고 있던 책이다.

---

01 **명사 강조**: 형용사로 쓰인 very가 「the/this/that/one's+very+명사」의 형태로 쓰이면 '바로'의 의미로 명사를 **강조**한다.

He died in **this very** room. 그는 바로 이 방에서 죽었다.

This is **the very** dictionary (that) I need. 이것이 바로 내가 필요한 사전이다.

02 **의문문 강조**: 의문사 바로 뒤에 ever, in the world, on earth를 붙여 의문문을 **강조**한다. '도대체'라는 의미로 쓰인다.

What **on earth** do you mean by it? 도대체 그것은 무슨 뜻이니?

Where **in the world** did you find the lost purse? 도대체 어디서 잃어버린 지갑을 찾았니?

03 **부정문 강조**: 부정문을 **강조**하기 위해 not이나 no 다음에 at all, in the least, by any means, a bit, on any way 등을 쓴다. '조금도, 아무것도'의 뜻이다.

I am not hungry **at all**. 나는 전혀 배고프지 않다.

A foreign language isn't **by any means** easy to master. 외국어를 습득하는 것은 결코 쉽지 않다.

04 **동일어구 반복에 의한 강조**: 동일어구를 and로 연결하여 의미를 **강조**한다.

It rained for hours **and** hours. 몇 시간이고 계속해서 비가 내렸다.

05 **의문사 강조**: 의문사를 강조하기 위해 「의문사+is/was+it that ~?」의 형태로 쓴다.

Who invented the telephone? 누가 전화기를 발명했니?

→ **Who was it that** invented the telephone? 전화기를 발명한 사람이 누구니?

Where did you see Peter an hour ago? 한 시간 전에 Peter를 어디서 봤니?

→ **Where was it that** you saw Peter an hour ago? 한 시간 전에 Peter를 본 곳이 어디였니?

서술형 기초다지기

정답 p. 31

Challenge 1 다음 괄호 안의 표현 중 알맞은 것을 고르세요.

01. She is (a very / the very) woman he has wanted to marry.

02. I don't understand (in the least / at the last) what you mean.

03. They didn't see the accident (themselves / at all).

04. We ran (or / and) ran, till we reached our destination.

05. I thought about the matter over (and / or) over again.

06. Whom (in the least / on earth) did you meet yesterday?

07. What (the very / in the world) are you talking about?

08. We had no choice (at once / at all).

Challenge 2 다음 문장을 의문사를 강조하는 문장으로 바꾸고, 강조된 문장은 원래대로 고치세요.

> **보기**
> Who broke the window yesterday?
> → *Who was it that broke the window yesterday?*

01. When was it that you saw Kelly in front of the bank?

→ _____

02. What did you buy at the store?

→ _____

03. When does the winter vacation begin?

→ _____

04. When was it that you had the happiest moment of your life?

→ _____

05. What saw Kelly in front of the bank an hour ago?

→ _____

Unit 02 도치

2-1 도치를 통한 강조 (1)

Between Korea and Japan **is the East Sea**.
= The East Sea is between Korean and Japan.
한국과 일본 사이에 동해가 있다.

So great **was their astonishment** that they were speechless.
= Their astonishment was so great that they were speechless.
그들은 너무 놀라서 입을 열 수가 없었다.

01 영어 어순은 「주어+동사」지만, 문법적 이유에서 또는 어떤 어구를 강조하기 위해서 「동사+주어」의 어순이 되는 것을 '도치'라고 한다.

① 장소나 방향의 부사(구)를 문장 앞으로 도치시켜 강조할 경우 「장소/방향 부사(구)+동사+주어」로 어순이 도치된다.

On the platform **stood a strange woman**. 이상한 여자가 승강장에 서 있었다.

Under the table **sat a little puppy**. 탁자 아래에 작은 강아지가 앉아 있었다.

In the newspaper **found the man** his name. 신문에서 그 남자는 자기 이름을 발견했다.

Out **came the sun** through a break in the clouds. 구름들 사이의 틈으로 해가 나왔다.

※ 주어가 대명사인 경우에는 도치되지 않는다.

Down the street **she walked**. 그녀는 길거리를 따라서 걸었다.

Happy **I was** when I was a child. 어린 시절에 난 행복했다.

② **보어를 강조할 때** 보어를 문장 맨 앞으로 보낸다. 이때 **어순은** 「보어+동사+주어」가 된다.

Very happy **was Tom** who know the pleasure of doing good.
좋은 일을 하는 즐거움을 아는 Tom은 행복했다.

Lovely **is her smile**. 그녀의 미소는 사랑스럽다.

③ **목적어를 강조할 때** 목적어를 문장 맨 앞으로 보낸다. 하지만 이 경우엔 **주어와 동사는 도치되지 않아** 「목적어+주어+동사」의 어순이 된다.

That **I can't say**. 그것은 말할 수 없다.

That promise **she broke** within a week. 그 약속을 그녀는 일주일도 안돼서 어겼다.

※ 목적어가 대명사일 경우에는 대명사를 문두에 보내어 도치시키지 않는다.

He built it. → It he built. (×)

서술형 기초다지기

Challenge 1 다음 문장을 주어진 단어로 시작하여 다시 쓸 때 빈칸에 알맞은 말을 쓰세요.

01. Her mother stood in the doorway.

→ In the doorway _____ _____ _____.

02. She is great.

→ Great _____ _____.

03. The girl fell down.

→ Down _____ _____ _____.

04. An old woman stood on the platform.

→ On the platform _____ _____ _____ _____.

05. He walked down the street with the children.

→ Down the street _____ _____ with the children.

06. He was so shocked that he didn't know what to do.

→ So shocked _____ _____ that he didn't know what to do.

Challenge 2 다음 밑줄 친 부분을 문두에 놓고 문장을 다시 써 보세요.

보기	An old woman sat <u>on the chair</u>. → *On the chair sat an old woman.*

01. The joy of Columbus was <u>great</u>.

→ _____

02. The performance was <u>great</u> yesterday.

→ _____

03. Thomason is <u>in New York</u> now.

→ _____

04. I will remember <u>the trip to Australia with my family</u> forever.

→ _____

2-2 도치를 통한 강조 (2)

Little did **I think** that he would fail.
나는 그가 실패하리라고 거의 생각하지 못했다.

A: I'm feeling tired. 나는 피곤해.
B: **So am I**. 나도 그래.

01 부정어 never, little, hardly, seldom, only, scarcely, nowhere, not until, not only 등이 **의미가 강조되어 문장 맨 앞에 오면 「부정어＋조동사＋주어＋동사」의 어순**이 된다. 이때 동사는 원형으로 쓴다.

I never saw her again.
→ Never **did I see** her again. 다시는 그녀를 만나지 않았다.

I little dreamed that I should meet her again.
→ Little **did I dream** that I should meet her again. 그녀를 다시 만날 거라고 전혀 꿈도 꾸지 못했다.

02 「No sooner A ~ than B」와 「Hardly A ~ when B」는 'A하자마자 B하다'의 뜻으로, 주어와 동사는 도치된다. A의 동사는 과거완료(had＋p.p.), B의 동사는 과거형을 쓴다. 이 두 구문은 as soon as 구문으로 바꾸어 쓸 수 있다.

No sooner **had she seen** the police than she ran away. 경찰을 보자마자 그녀는 도망쳤다.
＝She had no sooner seen the police than she ran away.
＝As soon as she saw the police, she ran away.

Hardly **had he left** home when it began to rain. 그가 집을 떠나자마자 비가 오기 시작했다.
＝He had hardly left home when it began to rain.

03 상대방 의견에 동의할 때 「So＋동사(do동사/be동사/조동사)＋주어」는 '~도 또한 그렇다'라는 의미이고, 「Neither＋동사(do동사/be동사/조동사)＋주어」는 '~도 또한 아니다'라는 의미이다.

1 앞 문장이 긍정일 때
A: I like this music.　　B: **So do I**.(＝I do, too. / I like it, too.)
A: I am a student.　　B: **So am I**.(＝I am, too. / I am a student, too.)

2 앞 문장이 부정일 때
A: I'm not hungry.　　B: **Neither am I**.(＝I'm not, either. / I'm not hungry, either.)
A: They won't go.　　B: **Neither will we**.(＝We won't, either. / We won't go, either.)

서술형 기초다지기

정답 p. 32

Challenge 1 — 다음 밑줄 친 부분이 강조되도록 도치 문장을 만드세요.

01. I have never seen such a beautiful girl.

→ _____

02. I had no sooner gone to bed than I got a phone call.

→ _____

03. I can hardly believe what she said.

→ _____

04. She had no sooner heard the word than she turned pale.

→ _____

05. They had hardly started watching the movie when the power went out.

→ _____

06. I had never seen so many people in one room.

→ _____

Challenge 2 — so와 neither를 이용하여 상대방의 의견에 동의하는 문장을 완성하세요.

보기	A: I love this kind of music.	B: _____ *So do I.* _____

01. A: I am not good at making conversation.　　　B: _____

02. A: I love to read.　　　B: _____

03. A: I haven't got many friends.　　　B: _____

04. A: I would like to make new friends.　　　B: _____

05. A: I am very shy.　　　B: _____

06. A: Diane liked the movie.　　　B: _____

Unit 03 기타 용법

3-1 생략

Some children can speak English, and others (can speak) French.
어떤 아이들은 영어를 할 줄 알고, 다른 아이들은 불어를 할 줄 안다.

They were good friends when (they were) in school.
그들은 학창시절에 친한 친구였다.

01 접속사로 연결되어 반복되는 어구는 생략한다. 또한 생략해도 문장의 의미에 오해가 생기지 않을 경우, **동일 어구를 생략하여 문장을 간결**하게 한다.

My mom has washed the dishes and (she) will dry them. 엄마는 접시들을 씻었고 그것들을 건조시킬 것이다.

Some people believe that the development of technology leads to happiness, and others don't (believe that the development of technology leads to happiness).
어떤 사람들은 기술의 발전이 행복을 이끈다고 생각하고 다른 사람들은 그렇게 생각하지 않는다.

Some people go to the mountain. Others (go) to the seaside.
어떤 사람들은 산으로 가고 다른 사람들은 바다로 간다.

02 부사절의 **주어가 주절의 주어와 같을 때에는 종종 「주어＋be동사」를 생략**해서 쓴다.

Though (he was) tired, he went on working. 비록 지쳤지만 그는 일을 계속했다.

When (you are) in Rome, do as the Romans do. 로마에 있을 때는 로마법을 따라라. (속담)

03 비교 구문의 **than이나 as 뒤의 말이 중복되면 생략**할 수 있다. 또, to부정사의 내용이 **반복되면 to만 쓰고 나머지는 생략**한다.

He is taller than she (is tall). 그는 그녀보다 키가 더 크다.

He asked me to go to the movies, but I don't want to (go to the movies).
그는 내게 영화를 보러 가자고 했지만, 나는 가고 싶지 않다.

04 질문에 대한 응답에서 **동사가 반복될 때에는 조동사만 쓰고 나머지는 생략**한다. 주격 관계대명사에서는 문법과 내용에 큰 영향을 끼치지 않는 「주격 관계대명사＋be동사」를 생략해서 쓴다.

A: Can you speak Japanese? 일본어를 할 줄 아니?

B: Yes, I can (speak Japanese). 응, 할 수 있어.

Do you know the woman (who is) sitting on the bench? 벤치에 앉아 있는 저 여자를 아니?

The man (who was) arrested by the police last week died in jail.
지난주 경찰에 의해 체포된 그 남자는 감옥에서 죽었다.

서술형 기초다지기

정답 p. 32

Challenge 1 다음 문장에서 생략할 수 있는 부분을 괄호로 묶으세요.

01. They were good friends when they were in school.

02. This is the book which was given by my teacher.

03. When I was young, I used to like rock bands.

04. I came here because I just wanted to come.

05. He speaks English as fluently as you speak English.

06. Though she was sick, she went to work as usual.

07. To some studying is pleasure, others studying is suffering.

08. Will you come to the party? – I'll be glad to come to the party.

09. He should not be late for school, but sometimes he is late for school.

Challenge 2 다음 문장에서 생략된 내용을 찾아 다시 쓰세요.

보기	You may come if you want to.
	→ *You may come if you want to come.*

01. She pretended to be pleased, but she wasn't.

   → _____

02. He was very healthy when young.

   → _____

03. He is far better than yesterday.

   → _____

04. The first commercial film made in California was completed in 1907.

   → _____

3-2 삽입, 동격, 무생물 주어

This is the suit which **I think** will become you.
이것이 네게 어울리는 옷이라고 생각한다.

This path will lead you to the house.
이 작은 길을 따라 가면 그 집에 도착할 것이다.

01 삽입은 주로 설명을 덧붙이거나 의미를 보충하기 위해 쓴다. 문장이나 절 전체를 목적어로 취하는 **I think, I suppose, I am sure, I suggest, I hear 등이 삽입**되는데 삽입 구문 전후에는 보통 쉼표를 넣어서 구분한다.

Mr. Smith, **it seems**, has little to do with the matter. 스미스 씨는 그 일과 거의 관계가 없는 것 같다.
The boy who **I thought** was honest deceived me. 정직하다고 생각했던 그 소년이 나를 속였다.

02 as, if, though, whether 등이 이끄는 **부사절 또는 구(phrase)가 문장 중간에 삽입**되는 경우가 있다.

She, **as far as I know**, is a reliable woman. 그녀는 내가 아는 한 믿을 수 있는 사람이다.
The newspaper is, **so to speak**, the eyes and ears of society. 신문은 말하자면 사회의 눈과 귀이다.

※ if ever: '설령 ~한다고 해도'(동사가 따라옴), if any: '설령 ~가 있다 해도'(명사가 따라옴)

He seldom, **if ever**, goes there. 그는 거기에 가는 일이 있다 해도 별로 없다.
There are few, **if any**, mistakes in your composition. 너의 작문에는 실수가 있다 해도 별로 없다.

03 동격 구문: **명사, 대명사의 의미를 보충하거나 다른 말로 표현**하기 위해 또 다른 명사 상당어구 또는 동격의 of를 두는 경우이다.

Mr. James, **our new teacher**, is from New York. 우리의 새로운 선생님인 제임스 씨는 뉴욕 출신이다.
No one can deny the fact **that the earth is round**. 지구가 둥글다는 사실은 누구도 부정할 수 없다. ▶ 동격의 명사절
She committed a crime **of murder**. 그녀는 살인죄를 저질렀다.

※ 동격의 명사절을 관계사절로 보면 안 된다. 동격의 명사절은 완전한 문장이지만 관계대명사절은 불완전한 문장이다.

This is the idea that she has in mind. ▶ that 이하는 목적어가 빠져 있는 관계대명사절이다.

04 영어 문장에서 사물이 주어인 경우를 무생물 주어(물주구문)라고 한다. 사물 주어를 '이유, 때, 조건, 양보, 결과' 등의 부사구로 바꾸어서 해석해야 자연스럽다.

His wealth enables him to go abroad. 그는 부자이기 때문에 외국에 갈 수 있다.
Ten minutes' walk took him to the station. 그는 10분 걸은 후에 역에 도착했다.
The heavy snow prevented him from going there. 폭설 때문에 그는 거기에 갈 수가 없었다.

서술형 기초다지기

정답 p. 32

Challenge 1 다음 문장에서 삽입 구문에 밑줄을 그으세요.

01. Scott has, surprisingly, passed the bar exam.

02. He is, so to speak, a walking dictionary.

03. Competition, we have learned, is neither good nor evil in itself.

04. I hired the man who I thought was capable and honest.

05. She seldom, if ever, goes shopping.

Challenge 2 다음 문장에서 동격을 이루고 있는 곳에 밑줄을 그으세요.

보기	Mother Teresa worked in a school in *Calcutta*, *a very poor city in India*.

01. I had no idea that he would fail in the exam.

02. The news of her death was a great shock to me.

03. Graham Bell, an American scientist, invented the telephone.

04. We heard the news that he had entered Harvard.

Challenge 3 다음 우리말과 같은 뜻이 되도록 괄호 안의 단어를 재배열하세요.

01. 그의 아버지가 갑자기 돌아가셔서 그는 할 수 없이 학교를 그만두어야 했다. (death, sudden, his father's)

→ _____ forced him to give up school.

02. 몇 분을 걸어서 나는 그 농장에 도착했다. (walk, few minutes', a)

→ _____ brought me to the farmhouse.

03. 거리의 소음 때문에 나는 밤새 잠을 이루지 못했다. (the street, the noise, in)

→ _____ kept me awake all night.

04. 20분을 걸은 후에 그녀는 버스 정류장에 도착했다. (walk, twenty, minutes')

→ _____ brought her to the bus stop.

01 출제 100% - It ~ that 강조 구문은 부분 영작 문제로 출제된다.

출제자의 눈 It ~ that 강조 구문은 부분 영작 문제로 출제된다. 강조할 부분에 밑줄을 그어 놓고 그 부분을 강조하는 문장으로 고쳐 쓰라는 문제가 나온다. 여기서 주의할 것은 원래 문장의 시제에 따라 It is ~ that 또는 It was ~ that처럼 is와 was의 시제에 조심해야 한다. 조동사 do/does/did도 종종 출제된다. 동사를 강조할 때와 조동사로 쓰이는 do/does/did를 구별하라는 문제가 출제되기도 한다.

Ex 1.

밑줄 친 부분을 강조하는 문장으로 다시 쓰시오.
An <u>adventurous spirit</u> makes people invent things.
→ _____

Ex 2.

밑줄 친 부분을 강조할 때 빈칸에 들어갈 알맞은 말은?
The couple <u>seemed</u> very happy.
→ The couple _____ very happy.
(a) do seemed   (b) did seemed   (c) does seem   (d) did seem

02 출제 100% - 강조, 생략, 동격을 조심하라.

출제자의 눈 의문사를 강조하는 「의문사＋is/was＋it that ~」의 형태를 쓰라는 문제가 출제된다. 공통되는 어구나 내용을 생략하여 같은 의미가 되도록 고쳐 쓰는 문제도 출제 가능하다. 또는 생략할 수 있는 부분을 고르게 할 수도 있다. 동격 구문에서는 계속적 용법의 관계사절을 동격 구문으로 고치게 하거나, 관계대명사절과 동격으로 쓰인 절을 구별하는 문제도 가능하다. 관계대명사절은 불완전한 문장이고 동격절은 완전한 문장으로 구성되어 있다.

Ex 3.

다음 의문문을 의문사를 강조하는 문장으로 바꿀 때 빈칸에 들어갈 말은?
Who broke the window yesterday?
→ Who _____ broke the window yesterday?
(a) it was that   (b) it that was   (c) was it that   (d) was that it

출제 100 % – 도치할 때는 어순에 주의해야 한다.

 출제자의 눈 도치의 기본은 강조하고자 하는 말을 앞으로 끌어내는 것이다. 「보어＋동사＋주어」, 「전치사구/부사＋동사＋주어」, 「부정어구＋조동사＋주어＋동사」의 어순에 익숙해져야 한다. 어법상 틀린 것을 고르거나 올바른 도치문을 고르라는 문제가 출제된다.

부정어 not, never, seldom, hardly, barely, only, scarcely, little, few	＋	조동사(do/may/can) be 동사	＋	주어＋동사(have＋p.p.의 경우 have가 조동사 역할을 하여 주어 앞에 위치한다.)

Ex 4.

> 두 문장이 같은 뜻이 되도록 빈칸에 알맞은 말을 쓰시오.
> He had hardly gone out when it began to snow.
> ＝Hardly _____ when it began to snow.

Ex 5.

> 다음 문장의 밑줄 친 부분 중 어법상 잘못된 곳은?
> (a) Near my house (b) a tiny dry-cleaning shop is (c) run by (d) two chatty old ladies.

출제 100 % – So와 Neither를 이용한 동의의 표현은 어순에 주의하라.

 출제자의 눈 so와 neither를 구별하는 기본적인 문제에서 출발하여, 동의의 표현인 「So[Neither]＋동사＋주어」에서 동사 자리에 들어가는 알맞은 조동사나 be동사 또는 do동사를 고르는 문제가 출제된다. 동의하는 표현을 써 넣는 부분 영작 문제가 가장 많이 출제된다.

Ex 6.

> · Sunny likes dancing, and so _____ Nancy.
> (Sunny는 춤추는 것을 좋아한다. Nancy도 그렇다.)
> (a) do   (b) does   (c) did   (d) is

1. 다음 중 밑줄 친 부분의 쓰임이 잘못된 것은?
   ❶ <u>Do</u> go and talk to him.
   ❷ I <u>do</u> like pizza very much.
   ❸ She <u>did</u> put them in the refrigerator.
   ❹ He <u>does</u> play the piano well.
   ❺ Mr. Kim <u>did</u> taught Korean two years ago.

2. 다음 우리말에 해당하는 문장을 고르시오.

   > A : I will try out for the baseball team.
   > B : 나도 그럴 거야.

   ❶ So am I.
   ❷ So do I.
   ❸ So will I.
   ❹ Neither am I.
   ❺ Neither will I.

3. 밑줄 친 부분과 바꾸어 쓸 수 있는 것은?

   > Olivia has been interested in K-pop, and <u>Kelly has been interested in it, too.</u>

   ❶ so is Kelly
   ❷ so has Kelly
   ❸ neither is Kelly
   ❹ neither has Kelly
   ❺ so does Kelly

4. 다음 문장을 It ~ that 강조 구문으로 바꾸시오.

   I met Wilson at his birthday party last month. (목적어 강조)
   → _____
   _____

5. 다음 문장을 never를 강조하는 문장으로 바꾸시오.

   > I never do things I don't like to do.
   > → _____

6. 밑줄 친 부분을 강조할 때, 빈칸에 알맞은 단어를 쓰시오.

   > A : Who broke the window?
   > B : <u>Tom</u> broke the window.
   > → It _____ _____ _____ broke the window.

7. 다음 의문사를 강조할 때 빈칸에 알맞은 말은?

   > When did you see Nancy in front of the bank?
   > → When _____ you saw Nancy in front of the bank?

   ❶ it was that
   ❷ it that was
   ❸ was that it
   ❹ was it that
   ❺ that it was

8. 다음 중 〈보기〉와 다른 의미로 쓰인 것은?

   > 보기　I <u>do</u> worry about his hearing with all that loud music.

   ❶ You <u>did</u> have the game CD with me.
   ❷ I <u>do</u> like dogs.
   ❸ He <u>did</u> go there.
   ❹ I'll <u>do</u> my homework tomorrow.
   ❺ He <u>does</u> talk a lot.

9. 다음 문장에서 "I was"가 생략된 곳을 고르시오.

   > ❶ While ❷ staying ❸ in Korea, I visited ❹ Gyeongbok Palace ❺ twice.

오답 노트 만들기

★틀린 문제 : _____   ★다시 공부한 날 : _____

(1) 문제를 왜? 틀렸는지 곰곰이 생각하고 그 이유를 적어본다.

(2) 핵심 개념을 적는다.

(3) 자신이 몰랐던 단어와 숙어 표현이 있으면 정리한다.

(4) 해설집에서 필요한 부분을 골라 풀이 해법을 정리한다.

★틀린 문제 : _____   ★다시 공부한 날 : _____

(1) 문제를 왜? 틀렸는지 곰곰이 생각하고 그 이유를 적어본다.

(2) 핵심 개념을 적는다.

(3) 자신이 몰랐던 단어와 숙어 표현이 있으면 정리한다.

(4) 해설집에서 필요한 부분을 골라 풀이 해법을 정리한다.

★틀린 문제 : _____   ★다시 공부한 날 : _____

(1) 문제를 왜? 틀렸는지 곰곰이 생각하고 그 이유를 적어본다.

(2) 핵심 개념을 적는다.

(3) 자신이 몰랐던 단어와 숙어 표현이 있으면 정리한다.

(4) 해설집에서 필요한 부분을 골라 풀이 해법을 정리한다.

★틀린 문제 : _____   ★다시 공부한 날 : _____

(1) 문제를 왜? 틀렸는지 곰곰이 생각하고 그 이유를 적어본다.

(2) 핵심 개념을 적는다.

(3) 자신이 몰랐던 단어와 숙어 표현이 있으면 정리한다.

(4) 해설집에서 필요한 부분을 골라 풀이 해법을 정리한다.

1. 밑줄 친 부분을 강조하는 구문으로 바꾸어 쓸 때 빈 칸에 알맞은 말을 쓰시오.

> The famous Greek philosopher Diogenes went around the streets of Athens, lantern in hand, looking for an honest man.

→ _____ _____ the famous Greek philosopher Diogenes _____ went around the streets of Athens, lantern in hand, looking for an honest man.

오답노트

2. 다음 문장에서 생략할 수 있는 부분은?

> Ji-sung Park, who is the best soccer player in our school, is very tall.

❶ Ji-sung Park ❷ who
❸ who is ❹ soccer player
❺ is very tall

오답노트

3. 다음 밑줄 친 부분을 동격으로 고치시오.

> Seoul, which is the largest city in Korea, has old palaces.
> → _____

오답노트

4. 다음 빈칸에 들어갈 말로 가장 알맞은 것은?

> I can't cook, and my roommate _____.

❶ can, either ❷ can't, neither
❸ so can he ❹ neither can he
❺ can't, either

오답노트

5. 다음 중 밑줄 친 부분의 쓰임이 나머지와 다른 것은?

❶ I do want to eat out.
❷ You do look nice in that dress.
❸ She does laundry once a month.
❹ He does remember the accident quite well.
❺ We do hope you will enjoy your trip.

오답노트

6. 다음 두 문장이 같은 뜻이 되도록 빈칸에 알맞은 말을 쓰시오.

> I came to San Francisco when a boy of ten.
> =I came to San Francisco when _____ _____ a boy of ten.

오답노트

7. 다음 대화의 밑줄 친 부분과 용법이 같은 것은?

> A : Wow, he is a good player!
> B : Yeah, I think he plays basketball better than Jason <u>does</u>.

❶ She <u>does</u> like to have a chat.
❷ He always <u>does</u> his best.
❸ Believe me, I <u>do</u> love you.
❹ She speaks Chinese better than I <u>do</u>.
❺ What <u>do</u> you like to do in your free time?

오답노트

8. 다음 빈칸에 들어갈 알맞은 말은?

> The temple where I work stood on the hill.
> → On the hill _____.

❶ stood the temple where I work
❷ the temple stood where I work
❸ the temple where I work stood
❹ stood where I work the temple
❺ stood there the building.

오답노트

9. 다음 중 어법상 올바른 문장을 고르시오.

❶ Not only she reads English, but she speaks it very fluently.
❷ Little dreamed I such a terrible thing.
❸ Never were the students so scared of the teacher.

❹ Never he had seen such an efficiently run business.
❺ Hardly had fallen he asleep when the alarm went off.

오답노트

10. 다음 중 어법상 틀린 것은?

❶ Great was the sorrow of her parents.
❷ No matter how difficult it may be, you should finish it on time.
❸ So old was the document that it was barely decipherable.
❹ Not until the dawn I fell asleep.
❺ Little did I dream that I should meet her again.

오답노트

11. <보기>를 참고하여 빈칸에 들어갈 단어를 쓰시오.

> **보기** I'm tall and my sister is tall, too.
> → I'm tall and <u>so is my sister</u>.

> I like to fix things around the house and Ted likes to fix things around the house, too.
> → I like to fix things around the house and _____ _____ _____.

오답노트

12. 다음 중 밑줄 친 'It ~ that' 강조 용법이 아닌 것은?

❶ It is on Sunday that he enjoys listening to classical music.
❷ It was her mother that objected to their marriage.
❸ Where was it that you saw Bob an hour ago?
❹ It is a pity that Cindy hasn't been able to make any friends.
❺ It was last Saturday that I went fishing with my friends.

오답노트

13. 다음 중 밑줄 친 that의 쓰임이 나머지와 다른 것은?

❶ The belief that technology helps to relieve scarcities is a fact accepted by economists.
❷ The fact that most poor immigrants from India arriving in Canada make much money within just a few years shows their potential.
❸ I heard the news that Kevin was hospitalized.
❹ The opinion that the death penalty should be abolished will get stronger and stronger.
❺ He's one of the greatest novelists that Korea has ever produced.

오답노트

14. 밑줄 친 문장을 줄여 쓸 때 빈칸에 알맞은 것은?

> Birds, rain, and wind make a kind of music. The sea makes a kind of music, too.
> (→ _____ _____ the sea.)

❶ So do   ❷ So did   ❸ So does
❹ So have   ❺ So is

오답노트

15. 다음 밑줄 친 부분 중 생략할 수 있는 것은?

❶ The girl who was injured in the traffic accident was taken to the hospital.
❷ I have two teenage girls who are not very different from the girls in the report.
❸ Those who were present were almost all college students.
❹ Who is your favorite singer?
❺ I like a man who is tall and handsome.

오답노트

16. 빈칸에 들어갈 단어가 알맞게 짝지어진 것은?

> · Pasta is a famous Italian dish, and so _____ Pizza.
> · Jane came to this city a few years ago, and so _____ I.
> · You haven't been to a party for a long time, and neither _____ I.

❶ are – does – can   ❷ is – did – have
❸ have – is – did   ❹ can – have – had
❺ does – does – do

중간 · 기말고사 평가대비 단답형 주관식

A. 다음 밑줄 친 부분을 강조하는 문장을 「it ~ that」 구문을 사용하여 만드시오.

1. I started to write English books <u>in 2008</u>.

→ _____

2. <u>When</u> did you have the happiest moment of your life?

→ _____

B. 다음 문장에서 굵은 글씨로 처리된 부분을 강조하는 도치 구문을 만드시오.

On Christmas day, in the year of 1643, Isaac Newton was born. His mother little thought that he was destined to explain many matters which had been a mystery ever since the creation of the world.

→ _____

_____

C. 다음 빈칸에 알맞은 말을 넣어 도치 문장을 완성하시오.

1. We stayed not a single day in the hotel.

→ _____ a single day _____ _____ _____ in the hotel.

2. I little imagined that he would write such a good book.

→ _____ _____ _____ _____ that he would write such a good book.

3. He seldom thought that he was a great pianist.

→ _____ _____ _____ _____ that he was a great pianist.

D. 다음 문장에서 생략된 부분을 찾아 다시 쓰시오.

1. When in Rome, do as the Romans do.

→ _____

2. Though young, she has much experience.

→ _____

3. The girl playing the piano on the stage is my sister.

→ _____

실전 서술형 평가문제

출제의도 It is/was ~ that 강조 구문
평가내용 질문의 의도에 맞는 강조 구문 사용하기

A. 다음 대화를 읽고 「It is/was ~ that」 구문을 활용하여 질문에 알맞은 대답을 쓰시오.

[서술형 유형 : 6점 / 난이도 : 중하]

Kathy : What happened?
Jason : I saw that a thief broke the window last night.

(The police came to investigate the situation.)

The police : Who broke the window?

Jason   : **1.** _____

The police : What did a thief break last night?

Jason   : **2.** _____

The police : When did a thief break the window?

Jason   : **3.** _____

출제의도 도치를 통한 강조
평가내용 도치를 이용하여 강조 구문 만들기

_B_. ⟨보기⟩와 같이 밑줄 친 부분을 강조하는 문장으로 다시 쓰시오.　　　　[서술형 유형 : 14점 / 난이도 : 중]

보 기	I <u>little</u> dreamed that I should meet her again. → _Little did I dream that I should meet her again._

1. I have <u>never</u> stayed at such an expensive hotel.

　→ _____

2. I had <u>no sooner</u> walked through the door than the manager welcomed me.

　→ _____

3. He had <u>rarely</u> seen such a sunset.

　→ _____

4. We'd just got to the top of the hill when the rain came <u>down</u> and we got thoroughly

soaked.

　→ _____

5. She had <u>no sooner</u> seen the police than she ran away.

　→ _____

6. Everybody had <u>hardly</u> taken their seats when Dr. Smith began his lecture.

　→ _____

7. His surprise was <u>so great</u> that he almost ran away.

　→ _____

서술형 평가문제	채 점 기 준	배 점	나의 점수
A	표현이 올바르고 문법, 철자가 모두 정확한 경우	2점 × 3문항 = 6점	
B		2점 × 7문항 = 14점	
공통	문법, 철자가 1개씩 틀린 경우	각 문항당 1점씩 감점	
	내용과 전혀 일치하지 않거나 답을 기재하지 못한 경우	0점	

Memo

3-B

한국에서 유일한

중학영문법

알짜 3000제

📖 BOOK 정답 및 해설

idmbooks

중학교 3학년 영문법

3-B

한국에서 유일한

중학영문법

알짜 3000제

정답 및 해설

I am books

1-1 부사 만들기

p. 11

Challenge 1

01 quickly	02 clearly	03 slowly
04 quietly	05 suddenly	06 privately
07 happily	08 luckily	09 heavily
10 necessarily	11 gently	12 simply
13 nobly	14 terribly	15 truly
16 duly	17 fully	18 dully
19 basically	20 dramatically	

Challenge 2

01 lovely	02 friendly	03 ugly

1-2 형용사와 모양이 똑같은 부사

p. 13

Challenge 1

01 부사 / 높이	02 부사 / 열심히
03 형용사 / 빠른	04 형용사 / 이른, 빠른
05 형용사 / 어려운	06 형용사 / 가까운
07 부사 / 늦게	

Challenge 2

01 high	02 seriously	03 quickly
04 hard	05 near	06 heavy

Challenge 3

01 good	02 well	03 good

1-3 모양은 비슷하지만 뜻이 다른 부사

p. 15

Challenge 1

01 lately	02 hardly	03 hard	04 closely
05 near	06 nearly	07 most	08 mostly
09 shortly	10 short	11 high	12 highly

2-1 빈도부사

p. 17

Challenge 1

01 Elena sometimes writes a letter to her friend, Sofia.
02 Is Mary always worried about her dog?
03 The dog is always happy to see Mary when she comes home.
04 She usually doesn't drink coffee in the morning.

Challenge 2

01 sometimes take
02 always buy
03 seldom[rarely] finishes
04 never eats

2-2 too, so, either, neither

p. 19

Challenge 1

01 Jane doesn't play it, either (=Jane doesn't, either) / neither does Jane
02 Nancy has curly hair, too (=Nancy does, too) / so does Nancy

Challenge 2

01 So do I.	02 Neither did I.
03 So did I.	04 So would I.
05 Neither did I.	06 Neither can I.

2-3 too, very, enough

p. 21

Challenge 1

01 too heavy	02 too young
03 very hot	04 too noisy

Challenge 2

01 too much	02 enough
03 too many	04 too
05 enough	

Challenge 3

01 was too heavy to move

2-4 so, such

p. 23

Challenge 1

01 so	02 such a	03 such	04 so
05 such a	06 so / such	07 such	

Challenge 2

01 so rich that she can travel around the world
02 so foolish that I could trust him
03 so cold that we couldn't go swimming

2-5 still, yet, already, anymore

p. 25

Challenge 1

01 yet   02 already   03 already
04 yet / still 05 yet   06 anymore
07 anymore

Challenge 2

01 He's still hungry.
02 I don't eat at the cafeteria anymore.
03 Do you still live on Fifth Street?
04 She isn't here yet.

3-1 「타동사＋부사」의 어순

p. 27

Challenge 1

01 turn on the stove   02 put it out
03 take your shoes off   04 put them on
05 about my appearance

Challenge 2

01 looks at the wall clock 02 check it out
03 Put on your sweater 또는 Put your sweater on
04 dealing with it
05 took off her socks 또는 took her socks off
06 looking for a scapegoat
07 hand them in   08 throw it away

이것이 시험에 출제되는 영문법이다!

p. 28

Ex1 (c)
Ex2 Do you always watch TV in the evenings?
Ex3 (b)   Ex4 (d)   Ex5 (a)   Ex6 (d)
Ex7 (d)   Ex8 (a)

| 해설 |

Ex1 '세금 납기일이 시간상으로 가까이 다가오고 있다'라는 의미이므로 부사 near가 적합하다.
Ex2 의문문에서 빈도부사는 주어 뒤에 위치한다.
Ex3 형용사/부사를 강조할 때 so를 사용한다. 「so+형용사/부사+that～」의 구문이다.

Ex4 동의의 표현은 앞에 나온 (조)동사를 그대로 사용한다. 만약 be동사가 쓰였다면 동의의 표현에도 be동사를 사용한다. 여기서는 don't (have)가 나와 있으므로 ④ aren't를 이용한 동의의 표현은 올 수 없다.
Ex5 형용사는 enough 앞에 「형용사＋enough＋to ⓥ」의 어순이 된다.
Ex6 셀 수 있는 명사 앞에서 '너무 많은'을 뜻하는 것은 too many이다. 부정적인 결과나 문제를 암시하므로 a lot of 는 부적합하다.
Ex7 '벗다'라는 의미로 put out을 쓰지 않도록 주의하고, 특히 take off의 목적어가 대명사일 경우에는 반드시 동사와 부사 사이에 대명사를 넣어 take it off로 써야 한다.
Ex8 부정문에서 '아직'이란 의미의 yet이 올바르다.

기출 응용문제

p. 30

| 1 ② | 2 ④ | 3 ③ | 4 ③ |
| 5 ⑤ | 6 ② | 7 ④ | |

| 해설 |

1 형용사에 -ly를 붙이면 부사가 되고, 명사에 -ly를 붙이면 형용사가 된다. ①③④⑤는 모두 '형용사＋-ly'로 이루어져 있으나, ②는 '명사＋-ly'로 아루어져 있다.
2 '게임이 너무 폭력적이어서 함께 게임을 하지 않는다.'라는 의미이므로 never가 올바르다.
3 enough는 형용사 뒤에 써서 'kind enough to show'의 어순으로 쓴다.
4 ① '대개'라는 의미로 usually가 적절하고 ② 명사를 강조할 때에는 such를 쓴다. ④ '늦게'라는 의미로는 부사 late를 써야 하며 ⑤ '친근한'이란 의미의 형용사는 friendly로 써야 한다.
5 ⑤에서 과거의 상황이 현재 지속되지 않는 상태를 나타낼 때는 anymore(=any longer)를 쓴다.
6 셀 수 없는 명사 앞에서 '너무'의 의미인 too와 긍정문의 내용에 동의할 때 사용하는 too가 각각 쓰인다. 따라서 공통으로 알맞은 것은 too이다.
7 almost는 '거의'라는 뜻으로 nearly로 바꿔 쓸 수 있다. still은 '아직도, 여전히'라는 뜻이다.

중간 · 기말고사 100점 100승

p. 32

| 1 ④ | 2 ①, ⑤ | 3 ② | 4 ④ |
| 5 ④ | 6 ② | | |

7 Have you got enough money to buy an iPad? /
  I haven't got enough money to buy an iPad
8 Have you got enough gas to drive to Busan? /
  I haven't got enough gas to drive to Busan
9 Have you got enough eggs to make an omelette?
  / I haven't got enough eggs to make an omelette

10	⑤	11	⑤	12	①, ②	13	①

10 ⑤	11 ⑤	12 ①, ②	13 ①
14 ③	15 ④	16 ④	
17 too much time		18 too much coffee	
19 too many calories		20 too many people	
21 still	22 already	23 yet	
24 still	25 already		

26 Tina didn't know the answer to the question, either.

27 ③

28 Could you turn off the light (=turn the light off)

| 해설 |

1 부정의 내용에 동의할 땐 「neither+(조)동사+주어」를 쓴다.

2 ①의 late는 home 뒤, ⑤의 빈도부사는 의문문에서 주어 (you) 뒤에 위치해야 한다.

3 ② lovely는 형용사이고, 나머지는 모두 부사이다.

4 긍정문에서 already(벌써), 부정문에는 yet(아직), 지속되는 상태에는 still(아직도), 과거의 상황이나 행동이 더 이상 지속되지 않는 상태에는 anymore를 쓴다.

5 둘 다 여기에 오지 않겠다는 내용이므로 양자를 부정하는 Neither A nor B로 쓴다.

6 '너무'란 뜻으로 부정의 의미를 내포하고 있는 too를 쓴다.

10 ① neither를 either로 바꾸고 ② 부사 greatly로 쓴다. ③ 부사 late를 써야 하며 ④ '거의 ~하지 않다'라는 부정 의미의 부사 hardly를 쓴다.

11 well은 형용사로 '건강한'의 뜻으로 healthy로 쓸 수 있다.

12 ① enough는 형용사 old 뒤에 위치해야 하고 ② 대명사 가 「동사+부사」의 목적어로 쓰일 때는 반드시 동사와 부사 사이에 위치해야 한다.

13 명사를 강조할 때 'such a good book'으로 써야 한다.

14 부정문에서 '아직'이란 의미로 yet을 쓴다.

15 부정의 내용에 동의할 때 'Me, neither'로 줄여 쓸 수 있다.

26 부정의 내용에 동의할 때 Tina didn't know the answer to the question, either.로 쓴다. either 대신에 neither 를 쓰지 않도록 조심한다.

27 care about는 '~에 관심을 두다, ~에 신경 쓰다'의 의미로, 목적어는 care about 뒤에 위치해야 한다.

28 목적어가 명사이므로 turn off the light 또는 turn the light off 둘 다 가능하다.

중간·기말고사 평가대비 단답형 주관식   p. 36

A	1 very heavy	2 too heavy
	3 very tight	4 too big
B	1 Neither have I.	2 So do I.
	3 Neither am I.	4 So did I.
	5 Neither have I.	6 So would I.

| 해설 |

A 1~4 '어려움이 있어 불가능하다'라는 부정의 의미를 내포할 때는 too, '어려움은 있으나 가능하다'라는 긍정의 의미를 내포하고 있을 때는 very를 쓴다.

B 1 부정의 내용이고 조동사가 have이므로 have를 그대로 이 용하여 Neither have I.로 쓴다. 2 긍정의 내용이고 동사가 일반동사이므로 do를 이용하여 So do I.로 쓴다. 3 부정의 내 용이고 동사가 be동사이므로 인칭에 맞는 be동사 am을 이용 하여 Neither am I.로 쓴다. 4 긍정의 내용이고 동사가 과거 형이므로 did를 이용하여 So did I.로 쓴다. 5 부정의 내용이 고 조동사가 have이므로 have를 그대로 사용하여 Neither have I.로 쓴다. 6 긍정의 내용이고 조동사가 would이므로 would를 그대로 사용한 So would I.로 쓴다.

실전 서술형 평가문제 A   p. 37

모범답안

1 Steve doesn't always eat high-fat food at dinner, but Cindy sometimes doesn't eat high-fat food at dinner.

2 Steve usually goes to the movies, but Cindy often goes to the movies.

3 Steve never goes to school on foot, but Cindy usually goes to school on foot.

4 Steve is often late for school, but Cindy is always late for school.

실전 서술형 평가문제 B   p. 38

모범답안

1 Those T-shirts were so cheap that Kevin bought three of them. / Those T-shirts were cheap enough for Kevin to buy three of them.

2 This is such a difficult problem that I can't solve it.

3 Seoul is such a big city that we can't look around it in a day.

4 There were so many people on the bus that I couldn't find a seat.

5 Scott walked so fast that I couldn't keep up with him. / Scott walked too fast for me to keep up with.

6 Sally takes such a lot of photographs that she has to buy a new photo album every month.

Chapter 02 비교급과 최상급
p. 41~76

1-1 비교급 만드는 방법
p. 43

Challenge 1

01 larger than
02 smaller than
03 hotter than
04 more slowly than
05 wider than
06 bigger than
07 thinner than
08 more boring than
09 more interesting than
10 more shocked than
11 more comfortable than
12 more complicated than
13 heavier than
14 lazier than
15 more quickly than
16 more fluently than
17 prettier than
18 cheaper than
19 more pleasing than
20 more easily than
21 more amazing than
22 more energetic than

1-2 최상급 만드는 방법
p. 45

Challenge 1

01 more difficult – most difficult
02 higher – highest
03 more tired – most tired
04 heavier – heaviest
05 fatter – fattest
06 colder – coldest
07 hotter – hottest
08 larger – largest
09 more interesting – most interesting
10 shorter – shortest
11 funnier – funniest
12 luckier – luckiest
13 poorer – poorest
14 more popular – most popular
15 easier – easiest
16 more frequent – most frequent
17 more brightly – most brightly
18 sadder – saddest
19 more depressed – most depressed
20 more crowded – most crowded
21 more attractive – most attractive
22 healthier – healthiest

1-3 불규칙 변화형
p. 47

Challenge 1

01 better – best
02 better – best
03 worse – worst
04 worse – worst
05 older – oldest
06 elder – eldest
07 more – most
08 more – most
09 latter – last
10 farther – farthest
11 further – furthest
12 later – latest
13 less – least
14 fewer – fewest

Challenge 2

01 farther
02 better
03 better
04 further
05 farther
06 elder
07 best

Challenge 2

01 isn't as expensive as this car
02 don't speak Korean as fluently as Jason (does)
03 is longer than Cindy's

Challenge 3

01 as slowly as possible
02 four times as large as

4-2 알아두어야 할 기타 비교 표현 (1)   p. 61

Challenge 1

01 from   02 to   03 X   04 from
05 X   06 as   07 X

Challenge 2

01 A golf ball isn't the same size as a tennis ball.
02 A baseball player isn't the same height as a basketball player.
03 "Flour" has the same pronunciation as "flower".

Challenge 3

01 the same   02 different from
03 the same / as   04 similar [the same]

4-3 알아두어야 할 기타 비교 표현 (2)   p. 63

Challenge 1

01 alike   02 like   03 like / alike
04 like   05 alike   06 like
07 like

Challenge 2

01 like   02 like   03 alike
04 like / similar to   05 different from
06 alike / alike / different

이것이 시험에 출제되는 영문법이다!   p. 64

Ex1 (c)   Ex2 (d)   Ex3 (d)
Ex4 The harder / the better
Ex5 taller / other boy
Ex6 She is one of the most famous actresses in Korea.

| 해설 |

Ex1 little의 비교급은 less를 쓴다.
Ex2 주어진 문장은 '더 길지 않다'는 의미이므로 형용사 short의 비교급 shorter than으로 바꿔 쓸 수 있다.
Ex3 비교급이지만 부정어 nothing이 있으므로 의미는 최상급이다. 따라서 최상급 표현인 (d)가 올바르다.
Ex4 「the+비교급, the+비교급」으로 쓴다.
Ex5 비교급을 이용한 최상급 표현으로 「비교급+than any other+단수 명사」를 쓴다. 여기서 단수 명사를 복수 명사로 쓰지 않도록 조심한다.
Ex6 「one of the+최상급+복수 명사」로 actress를 복수 명사인 actresses로 써서 She is one of the most famous actresses in Korea.로 문장을 완성한다.

기출 응용문제   p. 66

1 ③   2 than   3 ③
4 far better than   5 a lot lighter than
6 she could
7 The smaller / the higher   8 ③   9 ③

| 해설 |

1 형태는 비교급이지만 의미는 최상급이므로 the fastest swimmer처럼 최상급 문장으로 만든다.
2 비교 대상 앞에는 than을 쓴다.
3 '~하면 할수록 더욱 더 ~하다'의 뜻인 「the+비교급, the+비교급」을 쓴다.
4 good의 비교급은 better이다. 따라서 비교급을 강조하는 far를 better 앞에 써서 far better than으로 문장을 완성한다.
5 light의 비교급은 lighter이다. 따라서 비교급을 강조하는 a lot을 lighter 앞에 써서 a lot lighter than으로 문장을 완성한다.
6 '가능한 ~한[하게]'의 뜻인 「as ~ as possible」 또는 「as ~ as+주어+can/could」를 쓸 수 있다. 따라서 빈칸에는 she could를 쓴다. 시제가 과거이므로 can이 아닌 could를 써야 한다.
7 '~하면 할수록 더욱 더 ~하다'의 뜻인 「the+비교급, the+비교급」을 쓴다.
8 〈보기〉의 내용을 보면 B가 D보다 비싸다. 따라서 ③은 B is more expensive than D로 써야 한다.
9 as ~ as 사이에는 원급을 쓰고, 두 번째 문장은 「the+비교급, the+비교급」 문장이므로 각각 old와 more가 들어가야 한다.

중간·기말고사 100점 100승
p. 68

1 the most / Nothing / important
2 one　　3 ②　　4 ④
5 so[as] fast as　　6 ③　　7 ⑤
8 ④　　9 ①　　10 ②　　11 ⑤
12 ④　　13 ④　　14 ④　　15 ②
16 No other / as / as
17 The higher / the less　　18 the　　19 ③
20 less sensitive / than　　21 ③　　22 ③

| 해설 |

1 최상급의 의미이므로 최상급을 이용한 the most important thing ~ 또는 원급을 이용한 Nothing is as important as ~로 쓸 수 있다.

2 '가장 ~한 것 중에 하나'라는 뜻인 「one of the+최상급+복수 명사」에서 one을 써주어야 한다.

3 '~만큼'이란 말은 동등비교를 뜻한다. 따라서 as big as a house가 알맞다.

4 ④ my hometown이라는 명사가 있으므로 alike가 아닌 전치사 like를 써야 한다. alike는 형용사 역할로 동사 뒤에 단독으로 쓴다.

5 동등비교의 부정은 not as[so] fast as로 쓴다.

6 동등비교이므로 '많은'을 나타내는 much를 이용하여 as much as you want로 문장을 완성한다.

7 첫 번째는 동등비교이므로 heavy, 두 번째는 최상급 문장이므로 highest, 마지막은 「the+비교급」 문장이므로 happier로 쓴다.

8 very는 비교급을 수식할 수 없다.

9 lots of는 비교급을 수식하지 않고, '많은'이란 뜻으로 명사를 수식한다. 비교급을 수식하는 a lot과 구별해야 한다.

10 ②에서 비교 범위를 정해 주는 표현인 of all the teachers가 있으므로 비교급이 아닌 최상급 the oldest로 써야 한다.

11 셀 수 있는 명사 앞에 쓰는 few의 비교급인 'fewer ~ than'으로 쓴다.

12 「as ~ as+주어+could」는 「as ~ as possible」로 바꾸어 쓸 수 있다. 따라서 he could 대신 possible을 쓴다.

13 ④의 비교급 앞에 있는 even이 '훨씬'이란 뜻의 비교급을 강조하는 단어로 〈보기〉와 같은 쓰임이다.

14 「the+비교급, the+비교급」을 이용한 구문이므로 알맞은 비교급 형태는 The cooler와 the better이다.

15 비교급을 이용한 최상급 표현이 되어야 한다. 따라서 '부정 주어(no other thing)+비교급'을 쓰면 된다.

16 원급 big이 있으므로 「부정 주어+as 원급 as」를 이용하여 최상급의 의미를 나타낸다.

17 '(가격이) 올라가면 올라갈수록 덜 (사게) 된다'라는 의미이므로 the higher와 the less를 쓴다.

18 「the+비교급」과 「the+최상급」이므로 공통 단어는 the이다.

19 「부정 주어(no one)~+비교급+than ~」은 '아무도 ~보다 더 ~하지 않다'는 최상급의 뜻이므로, ③의 의미와 같다.

20 '~보다 덜 하다'라는 뜻으로 less를 쓴다. 여기서 주의할 것은 형용사(sensitive)의 음절이 3음절이라 하더라도 more을 쓰지 않고 「less+형용사(부사)의 원급+than」으로 써야 한다.

21 63빌딩이 한국에서 가장 큰 건물이어야 하는데, ③은 not as tall as를 써서 최상급 의미가 되지 못하므로 질문에 대한 답으로 적절하지 않다.

22 ③ as ~ as(~만큼 ~한)는 동등비교이고 나머지는 모두 최상급의 의미이다.

중간·기말고사 평가대비 단답형 주관식
p. 72

A 1 smaller than　　2 larger than
　3 larger than　　4 the largest
B 1 is much younger than her father
　2 is a much better soccer player than me
　　(=I am)
　3 a little warmer than yesterday
C 1 the oldest　　2 as old as
　3 newer than　　4 the newest
D 1 the best　　2 better than any other
　3 No / better than　　4 No / as good as
E 1 The noisier / the angrier
　2 The faster / the more

| 해설 |

A 1 골프공은 야구공보다 작으므로 비교급 smaller than으로 문장을 완성한다. 2 축구공은 야구공보다 크므로 비교급 larger than으로 문장을 완성한다. 3 축구공은 골프공보다 크므로 비교급 larger than으로 문장을 완성한다. 4 축구공은 셋 중에 가장 크므로 최상급 the largest로 문장을 완성한다.

B 1 수잔의 엄마가 훨씬 더 젊으므로 형용사 young을 이용한 비교급 is much younger than her father로 문장을 완성한다. 비교급을 강조를 하는 much는 비교급 바로 앞에 쓴다. 2 피터가 훨씬 더 좋은 선수이므로 good의 비교급인 better를 이용하여 is a much better soccer player than me으로 문장을 완성한다. than me 대신 than I am을 써도 된다. 비교급을 강조하는 much는 비교급 바로 앞에 쓴다. 3 어제보다 조금 더 따뜻하므로 형용사 warm의 비교급인 warmer를 이용하여 a little warmer than yesterday로 문장을 완성한다.

C 1 호텔 A가 가장 오래된 호텔이므로 최상급 the oldest로 문장을 완성한다. 2 호텔 B와 D가 생긴 연도가 같으므로 동등비교를 이용한 as old as로 문장을 완성한다. 3 호텔 C는 호텔 B보다 나중에 지어졌으므로 비교급 newer than으로 문장을 완성한다. 4 호텔 C는 4개의 호텔 중 가장 늦게

지어졌으므로 최상급인 the newest로 문장을 완성한다.

D 「비교급＋than any other＋단수 명사」, 「부정 주어 ＋비교급」, 또는 「부정 주어＋원급」으로 최상급의 의미를 나타낼 수 있다.

E 「the＋비교급, the＋비교급」으로 '~하면 할수록 더욱더 ~하다'는 의미의 문장을 만든다.

실전 서술형 평가문제 A   p. 74

모범답안

1 Sofa B is more comfortable than sofa C.
2 Sofa C is the least comfortable of all.
3 Tom runs the fastest of all.
4 Mike runs faster than Jason.
5 John runs as fast as Jason.
6 Maria doesn't drive as carefully as Sunny (does). 또는 Maria drives less carefully than Sunny.
7 Cindy drives more carefully than Maria (does).
8 Sunny drives the most carefully of the three.
9 Maria drives the least carefully of the three.

실전 서술형 평가문제 B   p. 75

모범답안

1 louder and louder
2 colder and colder
3 more and more discouraged
4 more and more tired

실전 서술형 평가문제 C   p. 75

모범답안

1 the more she talked, the more bored I became
2 The longer I look at a computer screen, the more tired my eyes get.

실전 서술형 평가문제 D   p. 76

모범답안 : Answers will vary. Sample answers.

1 House 1 and House 3 are the same.
2 House 1 is different from House 2.
3 House 2 is different from House 3.
4 House 4 is similar to House 1 and House 3.
5 House 2 is different from all the other houses.
6 House 2 and House 1 are different.

Chapter 03 수동태
p. 77~102

1-1 수동태의 기본 개념 및 형태   p. 79

Challenge 1

01 The electric light bulb was invented by Thomas Edison.
02 The Eiffel Tower is visited by millions of tourists every year.
03 The door is being painted by Bob.
04 My purse has been stolen (by somebody).
05 The house will be painted by her.
06 The car is being repaired by him.
07 The letter is going to be sent by Tom.
08 The classroom has not been cleaned by them.
09 The work will have been finished by them by this time next week.
10 The Colosseum in Rome was built by the Romans.

1-2 by＋행위자(목적격) / 수동태를 쓰지 않는 경우   p. 81

Challenge 1

01 This house was built in 1920.
02 The office was cleaned yesterday.
03 Hundreds of people were injured in the accident.
04 My car was stolen a few days ago.
05 Soccer is played in most countries of the world.
06 How many languages are spoken in Canada?

Challenge 2

01 자동사   02 자동사
03 타동사 / The interview was conducted by the president of the company.
04 타동사 / A cure for AIDS will be discovered by research scientists someday.

1-3 4형식과 5형식 동사의 수동태

Challenge 1

01 Kathy was given the Best Actress award (by them). / The Best Actress award was given to Kathy (by them).
02 This birthday cake was bought for me (by my father).
03 The topic was explained to the children (by the teacher).
04 I was shown the bill by the waitress. / The bill was shown to me by the waitress.

Challenge 2

01 She was seen dancing like a mad person by me.
02 He was elected their leader by them.
03 I was made to stop smoking by the doctor.
04 I am always made happy by her.
05 We were forced to work over time everyday by the manager.

1-4 조동사의 수동태 / 준동사의 수동태 / get+p.p.

Challenge 1

01 Energy should be saved.
02 Our car must be fixed before we leave for Seattle.
03 Will the national anthem be sung by Kevin in the opening ceremony?
04 Bottles and paper should be recycled.
05 The village could be destroyed if the river floods.

Challenge 2

01 be disturbed   02 to be finished
03 being treated   04 to smoke
05 being seen

Challenge 3

01 got broken   02 gets irritated
03 got hurt   04 get asked

1-5 동사구의 수동태 / 명사절 목적어의 수동태

Challenge 1

01 He was laughed at (by people).
02 The dog was looked after by my sister.
03 My baby is taken good care of by her.
04 Our bank was taken over by a foreign company.

Challenge 2

01 It is said that she is a very sincere person. / She is said to be a very sincere person.
02 It is believed that the politician took a bribe. / The politician is believed to have taken a bribe.
02 It is believed that the company will lose money this year. / The company is believed to lose money this year.

1-6 by 이외의 전치사를 쓰는 수동태

Challenge 1

01 of   02 to   03 with
04 in   05 about

Challenge 2

01 satisfied with   02 made from
03 concerned about   04 married to

Challenge 3

01 is known for   02 known to
03 is made of   04 is made from

이것이 시험에 출제되는 영문법이다!   p. 90

Ex1 She was allowed to go
Ex2 will be put off   Ex3 (c)
Ex4 is said to work 12 hours a day   Ex5 (c)
Ex6 were made to finish our homework by the teacher

| 해설 |

Ex1 5형식 문장의 수동태는 목적어를 주어로 쓰고 동사는 be 동사+p.p.(was allowed) 형태로 쓰며 목적격 보어 to go는 수동태 뒤에 그대로 쓴다.
Ex2 조동사가 있는 수동태는 「조동사+be+p.p.」로 수동태를 만든다. put의 과거분사형은 put이므로 will be put off로 완성한다.
Ex3 '~로 구성되다'의 표현은 consist of, be made up of, be composed of 등으로 쓴다. 따라서 (c)의 is made up of 가 알맞다.
Ex4 that절의 주어를 수동태의 주어로 쓸 경우 that절 안에 있는 동사는 「to+동사원형」으로 바꾼다. 따라서 is said to

work 12 hours a day로 완성한다.

Ex5 the woman이 선출하는 것이 아닌 '선출된'이란 수동의 의미가 되어야 하므로 부정사의 수동태인 to be elected 로 완성한다.

Ex6 사역동사를 수동태로 만들 때 동사원형을 to부정사로 써야 한다. 따라서 We were made to finish our homework by the teacher.로 문장을 완성한다.

기출 응용문제   p. 92

1 ④	2 ⑤	3 ⑤	4 ⑤
5 ②	6 must not be thrown		7 ④
8 ③			

| 해설 |

1 동사 buy는 수동태가 되면 간접목적어 앞에 전치사 for를 쓴다.

2 빈칸 뒤에 행위의 대상이 되는 목적어가 없으므로 빈칸은 수동태가 되어야 한다. 따라서 is spoken이 알맞다. ④ will be spoken은 문법은 틀리지 않지만 '현재 스페인어가 사용되고 있다'는 의미가 되어야 하므로 미래시제는 적절하지 않다.

3 한 문장에 동사 are와 consider를 나란히 사용할 수 없다. 목적어가 없으므로 수동태 문장이 되어 are not considered 로 써야 한다.

4 진행형의 수동태는 「be being+p.p.」로 나타내고, 완료형의 수동태는 「have been+p.p.」로 나타낸다.

5 '~로 덮여 있다'는 be covered with로 쓴다.

6 조동사(must)가 있는 경우 「조동사+be+p.p.」로 수동태 문장을 만든다.

7 조동사(will)가 있는 경우 「조동사+be+p.p.」로 수동태 문장을 만든다.

8 동사 buy는 직접목적어만을 주어로 사용하여 수동태를 만든다. 따라서 ③는 A Nintendo DS was bought for the boy by his father.로 써야 한다.

중간 · 기말고사 100점 100승   p. 94

1 ④	2 ④	3 ③	4 ④
5 is believed to be		6 ③	
7 will be held		8 ⑤	9 ②
10 is made from		11 is known to	
12 ⑤	13 has been baked		14 ⑤
15 ⑤	16 ⑤	17 ⑤	18 ②
19 ③	20 ②		

| 해설 |

1 지각동사(heard)를 수동태로 바꿀 경우 목적격 보어인 동사원형 play는 to play로 바꿔 써야 한다.

2 진행시제 수동태 구문으로 「be being+p.p.」로 바꿔야 한다.

3 문맥상 '극장에 들어가는 것이 목격되었다'가 자연스러우므로 수동태 구문이 되어야 한다. 지각동사의 수동태는 「be동사+p.p.+to+동사원형」으로 하되, yesterday라는 과거표시어구가 있으므로 be동사는 과거형으로 쓴다.

4 take care of는 동사구로 항상 붙어 다니므로 수동태로 바꾸면 was taken care of가 된다.

5 that절 안의 주어를 수동태 문장의 주어로 쓸 때 that절 안의 동사는 반드시 「to+동사원형」 형태로 쓴다. 따라서 is believed to be가 되어야 한다.

6 '~에게 알려지다'는 be known to로 전치사 to를 쓰고 '~로 가득차다'는 be filled with로 전치사 with를 사용한다.

7 조동사가 있는 수동태 구문으로 「조동사+be+p.p.」의 형식으로 쓴다.

8 4형식을 3형식 문장으로 고칠 때 일반적으로 간접목적어 앞에 to를 쓴다. 단, 동사 ask는 of를 쓰고 buy, make 등과 같은 동사는 간접목적어 앞에 전치사 for를 쓴다.

9 ② they는 books를 대신하는 대명사로 write의 행위를 직접 할 수 있는 주체가 될 수 없으므로 수동태인 were all written 으로 써야 한다.

10-11 be made from은 '(화학적 변화로) 만들어지다,' be made of는 '(물리적 변화로) 만들어지다,' be known to는 '~에게 알려지다,' be known for는 '~으로 알려지다'이다.

12 목적어를 주어로 하여 수동태로 고치면 What the car is called가 되고, 여기서는 의문문이므로 be동사를 주어 앞으로 보내 What is the car called in English?로 만든다.

13 have+p.p.는 have been+p.p.로 수동태를 만든다.

14 has not seen의 수동태는 has not been+과거분사(seen)으로 쓴다.

15 조동사 must의 수동태는 must be+p.p.로 쓴다.

16 사역동사 make를 수동태로 만들 경우 목적격 보어인 동사원형을 'to부정사(to memorize)'로 고쳐 써야 한다.

17 지각동사를 수동태로 쓸 경우 목적격 보어인 동사원형은 'to부정사'로 쓰고 현재분사는 수동태 뒤에 그대로 붙여 쓴다. 따라서 You were seen talking on the phone.이 올바르다.

19 ③ it could cook은 it could be cooked가 되어야 한다.

20 명사절의 주어(Dokdo)를 수동태(be said) 문장의 주어로 하고 명사절 안의 동사(is)를 'to부정사(to be)' 형태로 써야 한다.

중간 · 기말고사 평가대비 단답형 주관식   p. 98

A 1 is being taught   2 must be sent
     3 has been cleaned
     4 our conversation was being recorded
     5 cannot be controlled

B 1 The telephone was invented by Alexander Graham Bell.

2 The Eiffel Tower was designed by Gustave Eiffel.

3 The office is cleaned every day.

| 해설 |

A 1 진행형의 수동태는 'be+being+p.p.'로 쓴다. 따라서 is being taught로 문장을 완성한다. 2 조동사가 있는 수동태 문장은 '조동사+be+p.p.'로 쓴다. 따라서 must be sent 로 문장을 완성한다. 3 완료시제의 수동태는 'have/has been+p.p.'로 쓴다. 따라서 주어가 3인칭 단수이므로 has 를 이용한 has been cleaned로 문장을 완성한다. 4 과거 진행시제의 수동태는 'was/were being+p.p.'로 쓴다. 따라서 목적어 our conversation을 주어로 하여 our conversation was being recorded로 문장을 완성한다. 5 조동사가 있는 수동태 문장은 '조동사+be+p.p.'로 쓴 다. 따라서 cannot be controlled로 문장을 완성한다.

B 1 행위자는 Alexander Graham Bell이다. 따라서 주어를 The telephone으로 하여 The telephone was invented by Alexander Graham Bell.로 수동태 문장을 완성한다. 시제는 과거(was invented)라는 점에 유의한다.

2 행위자는 Gustave Eiffel이다. 따라서 the Eiffel Tower를 주어로 하여 The Eiffel Tower was designed by Gustave Eiffel.로 문장을 완성한다. 역시, 시제는 과거(was designed) 이다. 3 행위자가 없으므로 the office를 주어로 하여 The office is cleaned every day.로 쓴다. '매일 청소가 된다' 라는 의미이므로 시제는 현재시제인 is cleaned로 쓴다.

실전 서술형 평가문제 A   p. 99

모범답안

1 was/is cooked by Nancy

2 was/is washed by Scott

3 was/is cleaned by the children

4 were/are watered by Tiffany

실전 서술형 평가문제 B   p. 100

모범답안

1 The word "hamburger" is believed to have appeared in 1834 on the menu of Delmonico's restaurant in New York.

2 The first McDonald's restaurant was opened by the McDonald brothers in California in 1949.

3 Only three things were served by the restaurant: hamburgers, French fries, and milkshakes.

4 The restaurant was bought by Ray Kroc.

5 Since then, over 25,000 McDonald's restaurants have been opened around the world (by the company).

6 More than 40 million hamburgers are eaten every day (by people).

7 No change

실전 서술형 평가문제 C   p. 101

모범답안

1 A dictionary can be used during the test.

2 You must pay your phone bill.

3 The president has been seen on TV many times.

4 The teacher does not allow you to use your books during a test.

5 When do the bride and groom open wedding gifts?

6 You are expected to learn English in the U. S.

7 The teacher has told you to write a composition.

8 It is thought that the prisoner escaped by climbing over a wall. 또는 The prisoner is thought to have escaped by climbing over a wall.

실전 서술형 평가문제 D   p. 102

모범답안

1 Is the car going to be repaired?

2 Are the witnesses going to be interviewed by the police?

3 The people are going to be rescued by the firefighters.

4 The cars are going to be removed.

5 The fire is going to be put out.

1-1 and, but, or, so   p. 105

Challenge 1

01 and	02 or	03 but
04 and	05 and	06 or

Challenge 2

01 so	02 yet	03 for

Challenge 3

01 so	02 but	03 but
04 so	05 so	06 but

2-1 상관접속사의 종류   p. 107

Challenge 1

01 both / and	02 Neither / nor
03 either / or	

Challenge 2

01 The scientist is famous not only in Korea but (also) in foreign countries.
02 The gift shop gave away small souvenirs as well as offered discounts.
03 Not only the United states but (also) some other countries use English as their first language.

Challenge 3

01 both / and	02 not only / but (also)

3-1 명사절로 쓰이는 that   p. 109

Challenge 1

01 That drug abuse can damage a person's health is a widely known fact. / It is a widely known fact that drug abuse can damage a person's health.
02 That he won the frist prize is hardly surprising / It is hardly surprising that he won the frist prize.

Challenge 2

01 dreamed √ I	02 notice √ Wilson
03 out √ a labor	

Challenge 3

01 (don't) think that computers will have emotions

3-2 의문사로 시작하는 명사절(간접의문문)   p. 111

Challenge 1

01 why the sky is blue
02 how old my grandfather is
03 how often the bell rings at a time

Challenge 2

01 did Tom go / you said / Tom went

Challenge 3

01 Where do you think I can park my car?
02 Who do you think will be the next president?
03 What do you think the most typical Korean dish is?

3-3 if와 whether로 시작하는 명사절   p. 113

Challenge 1

01 if / whether I turned off the gas
02 if / whether Tiffany is here today
03 if / whether Kevin went to work yesterday
04 if / whether the passengers come out here

Challenge 2

01 if you can drive the car
02 if you are going to be
03 if Kelly has already left

3-4 그외 자주 사용하는 명사절 that   p. 115

Challenge 1

01 I'm sorry that I missed class yesterday.
02 I was disappointed that the peace conference failed.
03 It is a fact that women live longer than men.
04 I was not aware that men laugh longer, more loudly, and more often than women.

Challenge 2

01 I believe that rice is the chief food for half the people in the world.
02 I hope that my flight won't be canceled because of the bad weather in Seoul.
03 I hope that Brian is going to be at the meeting.
04 I believe that the library is open on Sunday.

4-1 시간을 나타내는 부사절(1)   p. 117

Challenge 1

01 while   02 when   03 As soon as
04 since   05 until

Challenge 2

01 I made some friends while I was staying in Seattle.
02 As we got closer to downtown, the bus became more crowded.
03 By the time we reached home, it was quite dark.
04 While she was listening to the radio, someone knocked on the door.

4-2 시간을 나타내는 부사절(2)   p. 119

Challenge 1

01 When seeing the police, the thief turned and ran away.
02 I shut off the lights before leaving the room.
03 After meeting the movie star in person, I understood why she was so popular.
04 After graduating from university, my daughter is going to get a good job.

Challenge 2

01 After she finishes her homework, she's going to go to the movies.
02 When I call Kevin tomorrow, I'll ask him to come to my party.
03 After Nancy gets home tonight, she's going to read the history book.
04 When I am 25 years old, I will get married.

4-3 원인과 결과의 부사절   p. 121

Challenge 1

01 Because they didn't have time, they didn't go for

a drive. / They didn't have time, so they didn't go for a drive.
02 Because I was sick, I went to bed early last night. / I was sick, so I went to bed early last night.

Challenge 2

01 Having no food at home, we decided to go out to eat.
02 Being tired, Brian went to bed early last night.

Challenge 3

01 Due to   02 because of   03 Thanks to

4-4 조건의 부사절   p. 123

Challenge 1

01 If my parents need help, I'll take care of them.
02 If I don't have money, I will get help from the government.

Challenge 2

01 in case   02 if   03 in case   04 if

Challenge 3

01 We can start the project only if our boss approves it.
02 The alligator will attack you only if you move suddenly.

4-5 양보와 대조를 나타내는 부사절   p. 125

Challenge 1

01 because of   02 Though
03 whereas   04 In spite of
05 because

Challenge 2

01 Even though ostriches have wings, they can't fly.
02 He looks about forty, whereas his wife looks about twenty.
03 Despite living on the same street, we hardly ever see each other.
04 He didn't get the job in spite of being extremely qualified.
05 Some children are spoiled, while others are well-behaved.

06 Although we had planned everything carefully, a lot of things went wrong.

이것이 시험에 출제되는 영문법이다! p. 126

Ex1	(b)	Ex2	(d)	Ex3	(d)

Ex4 visited Germany as well as France

Ex5	(b)	Ex6	if/whether Sunny is here today	

Ex7 how can people be poor → how poor people can be

Ex8	on finishing	Ex9	(d)	Ex10	(b)
Ex11	(d)	Ex12	(a)	Ex13	(c)	Ex14	(c)
Ex15	(d)				

| 해설 |

Ex1 등위접속사 앞뒤에는 같은 문장 성분이 와야 한다. 따라서 앞에도 과거분사, 뒤에도 과거분사형인 written을 쓴다.

Ex2 대등하게 연결되는 내용이므로 and를 쓴다.

Ex3 either는 or과 함께 쓴다.

Ex4 as well as로 문장을 전환할 때 but also 뒤에 있는 Germany가 앞으로 나가서 visited Germany as well as France로 쓴다.

Ex5 명사절 접속사 that은 동사 dreamed 뒤에 있는 that이다. (a)의 that은 that 앞에 명사가 있는 것만 봐도 관계사 that이라는 것을 알 수 있다.

Ex6 의문사가 없는 의문문을 간접의문문으로 바꿀 때는 if 또는 whether를 사용한다. 어순은 「주어+동사」이므로 if / whether Sunny is here today로 문장을 완성한다.

Ex7 문장 중간에 나온 「how+형용사 / 부사」는 뒤에 '주어+동사'의 어순으로 써야 한다. 즉, how poor를 한 단어의 의문사로 보고 뒤에 '주어+동사'의 어순인 people can be로 쓴다.

Ex8 「as soon as+주어+동사」는 '~하자마자'의 뜻으로 「on+V-ing」로 바꿔 쓸 수 있다.

Ex9 '네가 돌아올 때까지'는 동작이 계속됨을 나타내고 있으므로 접속사 until이 적절하다.

Ex10 동사 뒤에 오는 if는 '~인지 아닌지'의 명사절 if이다. 따라서 명사절 if 안에는 미래시제를 쓴 will accept가 알맞다.

Ex11 시간의 부사절 before 안의 시제는 비록 그 뜻이 미래를 나타내더라도 현재시제를 써서 미래를 표현한다. 따라서 leaves를 쓴다.

Ex12 원인을 나타내고 빈칸 뒤에는 명사 weather가 있으므로 '~때문에'의 표현인 due to가 알맞다.

Ex13 명사 efforts가 있으므로 despite를 쓴다.

Ex14 since가 완료시제와 함께 쓰일 때는 '~이래로, 이후로'의 뜻이 된다. 이때는 과거의 어느 시작점을 나타내므로 since절 안에는 반드시 과거시제를 써서, since he was a student가 되어야 한다.

Ex15 when절이 과거시제이므로 주절에는 과거 또는 과거진행

시제가 와야 한다. 걷고 있던 동작이 먼저 행해지고, 나중에 비가 오기 시작했으므로 주절에는 과거진행형인 were walking을 써야 한다.

기출 응용문제 p. 130

1	⑤	2	②	3	③
4	not only / but also	5	③	6	⑤

7 In case it rains

| 해설 |

1 주절의 내용이 모두 예기치 못한 결과를 나타내므로 '~임에도 불구하고'의 뜻인 접속사 although가 알맞다.

2 not only는 but also와 항상 짝을 이루어 사용된다. also를 생략하고 but만 쓰기도 한다.

3 첫 번째 문장은 「명령문+or ~」로 '~해라 그렇지 않으면'의 뜻이고, 두 번째 문장은 「Which ~, A or B?」로 정해진 것 중 하나를 선택하는 의문문이다. 따라서 공통으로 들어갈 접속사는 or이다.

4 「as well as」는 「not only ~ but also」와 같은 뜻이다. 단, your talents와 your interests의 자리를 바꿔 not only your interests but also your talents로 써야 한다.

5 「unless+주어+동사」는 「If+주어+don't / doesn't~」로 바꿔 쓸 수 있다. 따라서 if you don't have other plans가 알맞다.

6 that 앞에 명사가 위치할 때는 관계사 that으로 보면 된다. 따라서 ⑤는 관계사로 쓰였고 나머지는 모두 문장 맨 앞이나 동사 뒤에 위치한 명사절을 이끄는 접속사 that이다.

7 whether가 문장 맨 앞에 와서 쉼표로 분리되고 완전한 주절이 나올 때 whether는 명사절 접속사가 아닌 부사절 접속사가 되어 '~이든 아니든 간에'라는 뜻이 된다. 따라서 '비가 오든지 안 오든지 만일에 대비해서 (우산을 가지고 가라)'는 의미인 In case it rains로 바꿔 쓸 수 있다.

중간·기말고사 100점 100승 p. 132

1	⑤	2	⑤	3	④	4	④
5	as well as	6	②	7	①	8	②
9	①	10	whether 또는 if			11	③
12	Whether	13	Since	14	until	15	③
16	③	17	⑤				

18 how many day's vacation people get

19 how many people you are going to interview for this job

20 Who do you think is in the restroom?

21	neither / nor	22	③	23	②

| 해설 |

1 「both A and B」는 복수 취급하므로 동사는 has가 아닌

have를 써야 한다.

2 '~인지 어떤지'는 'whether ~ or'를 쓰므로, 첫 번째는 whether가 알맞고, 두 번째는 명사절을 이끄는 접속사 that이 알맞다.

3 두 문장 모두 주절에 예상치 못한 결과의 내용이 나오므로 '~임에도 불구하고'란 표현이 필요하다. 첫 번째 문장은 빈칸 뒤에 명사 plans라는 명사가 있으므로 in spite of를 쓰고 두 번째 문장은 주어와 동사가 있으므로 접속사 although가 필요하다.

4 risks는 명사이므로 because of를 쓰고, 두 번째 문장은 '~하지 않으면'의 의미인 unless를 쓰는 게 적절하다.

5 「not only A but (also) B」는 「B as well as A」와 같은 뜻이다.

6 '~할 때까지'라는 완료의 기한을 나타내므로 by the time이 적절하다.

7 「as soon as+주어+동사」는 「on+V-ing」로 바꾸어 쓸 수 있다.

8 ② in case는 조건을 나타내는 부사절이다. 따라서 미래시제 (will drop)가 아닌 현재시제 drops를 써서 미래를 나타낸다.

9 ①은 '언제'라는 의미의 의문사가 간접의문이 되어 명사절 접속사로 쓰였고, 나머지는 모두 '~할 때'라는 의미의 부사절 접속사다.

11 ③의 that은 「so ~ that 구문」으로 부사절을 이끄는 접속사이다. 나머지는 모두 명사절을 이끄는 접속사 that이다.

15 주어진 문장의 as는 '~함에 따라'라는 뜻으로 두 가지 동작이 동시에 이루어지고 있음을 나타낸다. 따라서 ③의 as와 의미가 같다.

16 ③의 that은 접속사가 아닌 명사 girl을 꾸며주는 지시형용사로 쓰였다.

17 '~인지 아닌지'의 의미인 명사절 접속사 if가 알맞다.

18 how many day's vacation을 한 단어의 의문사로 보고 「의문사+주어(people)+동사(get)」로 문장을 완성한다.

19 how many people을 하나의 의문사 덩어리로 보고 are you~를 '주어+동사'의 어순으로 바꿔서 간접의문문을 만든다.

20 동사 think는 의문사를 문장 맨 앞으로 보내고 '주어+동사'의 어순으로 쓴다.

21 양자를 부정하는 상관접속사 neither A nor B를 쓴다.

22 ③ not only는 반드시 but (also)와 짝을 이룬다.

23 although는 '비록 ~일지라도'의 뜻으로, 양보의 부사절을 이끈다. 따라서 ②는 '교통 체증이 있었지만 정시에 도착했다'라는 의미이므로 서로 상반되는 내용의 접속사 but을 쓰는 게 적절하다.

중간·기말고사 평가대비 단답형 주관식 p. 136

A 1 Why did Bob leave?
  2 what time he will return
  3 How far is it to his house?
B 1 I couldn't sleep despite being tired.
  2 Because the street is covered with snow, it is slippery.
  3 I'm going to major in either sociology or economics.
  4 Though Kevin is very famous, he is not satisfied.
  5 Some forms of radiation can be dangerous unless they are handled properly.
  6 Neither Alice nor Janet told the truth.
  7 Are you studying not only Korean but (also) Japanese?

| 해설 |

A 1 시제가 과거이므로 did를 이용한 의문문 Why did Bob leave?로 문장을 완성한다. 2 what time을 하나의 의문사 덩어리로 보고 will he return의 어순을 바꿔 what time he will return으로 문장을 완성한다. 3 be동사를 주어 앞으로 보낸 의문문 How far is it to his house?로 문장을 완성한다.

B 1 despite 뒤에는 명사가 와야 하므로 despite 뒤에 '주어+동사' 형태로 쓰면 틀린다. 따라서 be동사인 was를 동명사 being으로 바꿔 I couldn't sleep despite being tired.로 문장을 완성한다. 2 길에 눈이 덮여 있는 것이 원인이므로 Because the street is covered with snow로 문장을 완성한다. 3 「either A or B」의 형태로 A를 sociology로, B를 economics로 하여 I'm going to major in either sociology or economics.로 문장을 완성한다. 4 'Kevin은 매우 유명한데도 불구하고'의 의미이므로 Though Kevin is very famous로 문장을 완성한다. 5 '방사능 물질을 올바르게 다루지 않는다면'의 의미이므로 'unless they are handled properly'로 문장을 완성한다. 6 양자 부정 「neither A nor B」이므로 A를 Alice, B를 Janet으로 하여 Neither Alice nor Janet told the truth.로 문장을 완성한다. Neither ~ nor 자체가 부정의 의미를 내포하고 있으므로 동사를 부정형으로 쓰지 않는다. 7 「not only A but (also) B」이므로 A를 Korean, B를 Japanese로 하여 Are you studying not only Korean but (also) Japanese?로 문장을 완성한다.

모범답안

1 When the e-mail arrived, Karen was eating the hamburger.
2 Everyone was dancing when Janet arrived at the party.
3 While Alice was driving to the bank, her cell phone rang.
4 We were having dinner when somebody knocked on the door.

모범답안

1 If they don't come in ten minutes, I'll leave. / Unless they come in ten minutes, I'll leave.
2 If he doesn't apologize, I won't speak to him again. / Unless he apologizes, I won't speak to him again.
3 If Karen doesn't like her new dress, she can return it. / Unless Karen likes her new dress, she can return it.

모범답안

1 I feel[don't feel] that smoking in public places should be prohibited.
2 I doubt[don't doubt] that there will be peace in the world soon.
3 I wonder[don't wonder] why the world exists.
4 I would like to know[wouldn't like to know] when I will die.
5 I am afraid[am not afraid] that someone may make unwise decisions about my future.
6 I know[don't know] what I want to do with my life.

모범답안

1-3

if / whether you had many boyfriends
if / whether you like to watch soccer game
if / whether you have lived in other countries
if / whether you want me to call
if / whether you are thinking about me

4-6

if / whether you like to go to the movies
if / whether you studied Korean in school
if / whether I should call you
if / whether you can ski
if / whether you have done volunteer work
if / whether you are neat and tidy

Chapter 05 관계사

1-1 명사를 구체적으로 설명하는 형용사절   p. 143

Challenge 1

01 where we met yesterday / 우리가 어제 만났던 장소
02 who was playing tennis / 테니스를 치고 있던 소녀
03 in the restaurant / 레스토랑에 있는 여자
04 to drink / 마실 커피
05 to learn a foreign language / 외국어를 배우는 유일한 방법
06 reading a newspaper / 신문을 읽고 있는 한 소녀
07 that I didn't know / 내가 모르는 것
08 when we first met / 우리가 처음 만났던 날
09 where we had dinner last night / 우리가 어젯밤에 저녁을 먹었던 식당
10 to take care of / 돌볼 아이들

11 which I want to live in / 내가 살고 싶은 나라
12 that lives in Australia / 호주에 사는 동물
13 repaired by the man / 그 남자에 의해 수리된 차

2-1 주격 관계대명사　　　　　　　　　　p. 145

Challenge 1

01 who　　　　02 who　　　　03 which

Challenge 2

01 The girl who was injured in the accident is now in the hospital.
02 A building which was destroyed in the fire has now been rebuilt.
03 The bus which goes to the airport runs every half hour.
04 A passport is a special paper which permits a citizen to travel to other countries.
05 Ginny works for a company which makes washing machines.

Challenge 3

01 was　　　　02 is　　　　03 is
04 were　　　　05 was

2-2 목적격 관계대명사　　　　　　　　　p. 147

Challenge 1

01 That's the woman who(m) I met a few times last year.
02 Albert Einstein is a name which everybody knows.
03 This is a new 3D game which I want to buy.
04 She is the author who(m) the prosecutor accused of a crime.
05 The hard drive which you bought yesterday doesn't have a warranty.

Challenge 2

01 X　　　02 which　　03 who　　04 that
05 X　　　06 whom　　07 X　　　08 that

2-3 소유격 관계대명사　　　　　　　　　p. 149

Challenge 1

01 I know a man whose brother is a guitarist in a pop group.
02 I met a pretty girl whose parents run a big bakery downtown.
03 I know a man whose daughter is a professional wrestler.
04 We're going to buy a car whose color is very beautiful.
05 The woman whose purse was stolen called the police.
06 I apologized to the woman whose coffee I spilled.

Challenge 2

01 who　　　　02 whose　　03 whose
04 which　　　05 which　　06 whose

2-4 전치사와 관계대명사　　　　　　　　p. 151

Challenge 1

01 The woman with whom he fell in love left him after a few weeks. / The woman who(m) he fell in love with left him after a few weeks. / The woman that he fell in love with left him after a few weeks. / The woman he fell in love with left him after a few weeks.
02 This is the book about which we talked yesterday. / This is the book which we talked about yesterday. / This is the book that we talked about yesterday. / This is the book we talked about yesterday.

Challenge 2

01 you told me about　　02 we were invited to

2-5 관계대명사 what의 용법 / that만 사용하는 경우　　　　　　　　　　　　　　　p. 153

Challenge 1

01 What I told you at the meeting is really important.
02 I can't believe what she said.
03 Show me what is in your bag.
04 Do you believe what he said last month?

Challenge 2

01 What　　　　02 That　　　　03 that

Challenge 3

01 what you want　　　　02 what Kathy saw

Challenge 2

2-6 관계대명사의 계속적 용법 p. 155

Challenge 1

01 for she 02 but / it 03 but he 04 and it

Challenge 2

01 The new stadium, which can hold 100,000 people, will be opened next week.
02 My English teacher, who comes from Texas, loves us.
03 Wilson, who(m) I've known for a very long time, is one of my closest friends.
04 I'll introduce our new program, which will help you lose weight.

3-1 관계부사 when, where p. 157

Challenge 1

01 where 02 which 03 when

Challenge 2

01 The White House is the place where the President of the United States lives. / The While House is the place in which the President of the United States lives. / The White House is the place which the President of the United States lives in. / The White House is the place that the President of the United States lives in. / The While House is the place the President of the United States lives in.
02 2002 was the year when the World Cup was held. / 2002 was the year in which the World cup was held. / 2002 was the year which the World Cup was held in. / 2002 was the year that the World Cup was held in. / 2002 was the year the World Cup was held.

Challenge 3

01 This is the building where the Japanese tortured out people.
02 2007 was the year when they got married.

3-2 관계부사 why, how p. 159

Challenge 1

01 why 02 how 03 that
04 that 05 in which 06 for which

Challenge 2

01 Do you know the reason why she moved to Chicago?
02 Can you tell me how you learned English?

Challenge 3

01 the reason why 02 the reason why
03 how

3-3 관계부사의 독특한 특징 p. 161

Challenge 1

01 The hotel (where) Tom / 관계부사 생략
02 The album (that) he recorded / 목적격 관계대명사 생략
03 The documentary (that) we saw / 목적격 관계대명사 생략
04 summer vacation (when) we first / 관계부사 생략
05 that shop (where) Nancy bought / 관계부사 생략
06 a sponsor (that) you must / 목적격 관계대명사 생략

Challenge 2

01 This is why she became so excited. / This is the reason she became so excited. / This is the reason that she became so excited.
02 I remember when I took my first airplane ride. / I remember the day I took my frist airplane ride. / I remember the day that I took my first airplane ride.

4-1 복합 관계대명사 / 복합 관계부사 p. 163

Challenge 1

01 Whenever 02 Whoever
03 Whoever 04 Whichever
05 However

Challenge 2

01 No matter who comes to the office, don't bother our important meeting.
02 No matter how much you give them, it's never enough.
03 There are times when you can't do anything that you like.
04 Mother Teresa was welcomed at any place where she went.
05 Anyone who arrives first will be the winner.

06 You can talk to her at any time when you want.

이것이 시험에 출제되는 영문법이다! p. 164

Ex1 (b)　　Ex2 (c)　　Ex3 (d)　　Ex4 (c)

Ex5 who(m) I wanted to see

Ex6 What happened last night　　Ex7 (b)

Ex8 (b)　　Ex9 (b)　　Ex10 (d)

Ex11 when my boyfriend proposed to me

Ex12 (a)　　Ex13 (a)　　Ex14 Whenever

Ex15 However expensive it may be

| 해설 |

Ex1 선행사가 old furniture이므로 관계대명사 which를 쓴다.

Ex2 선행사 the house만 보면 where도 답이 될 것 같지만 buy의 목적어가 없기 때문에 목적격 관계대명사 which 가 알맞다.

Ex3 who는 people을 대신하는 관계대명사이다. 따라서 주어 가 복수이므로 관계사절 안에도 복수형 use를 쓰고 본동 사인 be동사도 are를 써야 한다.

Ex5 the woman과 her가 공통 명사이다. 따라서 her를 문장 을 연결할 수 있는 대명사 who(m)로 고쳐 The woman who(m) I wanted to see ~로 문장을 완성한다.

Ex6 the thing that에서 선행사 the thing을 포함하고 있는 관 계사는 what이다. 따라서 What happened last night was ~로 문장을 완성한다.

Ex7 said의 목적어가 없는 불완전한 문장이므로 관계사 What 을 쓴다.

Ex8 (b)는 의문사로 쓰인 what이고 나머지는 관계사 what이다.

Ex9 빈칸 뒤에 「주어(I)+자동사(worked)+전치사(as)+전치 사의 목적어 (a waitress)」의 완전한 문장이 나오고 빈칸 앞에는 장소를 나타내는 선행사(coffee shop)가 있으므 로 관계부사 where가 알맞다.

Ex10 a book을 선행사로 하는 계속적 용법의 관계대명사 which는 「접속사(and)+대명사(it)」로 풀어 쓸 수 있다.

Ex11 부사구 on the day를 대신하는 시간의 관계부사 when 으로 바꿔 when my boyfriend proposed to me로 문장을 완성한다.

Ex12 (a) the way와 how는 한 문장에서 함께 쓰지 않는다. 둘 중 하나를 생략해야 한다.

Ex13 explain 뒤에 선행사 the reason이 생략되어 있는데 이 때는 관계부사 why를 쓰고 that으로 바꿔 쓸 수 없다. that을 쓰려면 선행사가 있을 때만 가능하다.

Ex14 시간을 나타내는 복합관계부사 Whenever를 쓴다.

Ex15 「However+형용사+주어+동사」의 어순으로 쓰므로 However expensive it may be로 문장을 완성한다.

기출 응용문제 p. 168

1 ⑤	2 ⑤	3 ①
4 in which	5 ④	6 ②
7 What	8 ⑤	

| 해설 |

1 관계부사는 '전치사+관계대명사'로 바꾸어 쓸 수 있다. 여기 서 where는 장소의 관계부사이므로, 전치사 in이 가장 적절 하다. 관계대명사 that은 전치사와 함께 쓸 수 없다.

2 선행사가 사람이고 관계사절 안의 문장이 완전하므로 소유 격 관계대명사를 쓴다.

3 전치사 to 뒤에 목적어가 없으므로 목적격 관계대명사가 필 요하다. 선행사가 사람이므로 who(m) 또는 that을 쓸 수 있다.

4 선행사가 장소이므로 where 또는 in which로 쓴다.

5 ④ that 뒤에 동사 sailed가 바로 나오므로 주격 관계대명 사이다. 주격 관계대명사는 생략할 수 없다. 나머지는 모두 목적격 관계대명사이므로 생략할 수 있다.

6 첫 번째 문장은 선행사가 사람(woman)이고 fell in love with의 목적어이므로 with whom을 쓴다. 두 번째 문장은 선행사가 사물(money)이고 목적격 관계대명사이므로 which 또는 that을 쓸 수 있다.

7 선행사를 포함한 관계대명사 what이 공통으로 들어간다.

8 「However+형용사+주어+동사」의 어순으로 쓴다.

중간·기말고사 100점 100승 p. 170

1 ④	2 ①	3 ④	4 ⑤
5 ④	6 ⑤	7 ①	8 ④
9 ②	10 ②	11 ⑤	12 ④

13 What　　14 who[that] served us

15 when they got married

16 why FMD spreads at varying speeds in different areas

17 ②

18 the way how → the way 또는 how

19 where → when　　20 what → why

21 whose　　22 ①　　23 ①

24 on which I first rode my bike / when I first rode my bike

| 해설 |

1 '~하는 사람 모두'의 의미인 whoever가 적절하다.

2 '~하는 사람들'의 뜻인 those who를 쓴다.

3 선행사를 포함한 복합관계사 whichever가 알맞다.

4 '어느 것이(을)~한다 할지라도'의 no matter which를 쓴다.

5 선행사가 각각 이유, 장소, 방법, 시간이므로 why, where, how, when을 쓴다.

6 ⑤ next to는 '~옆에'의 의미로, 관계사 who는 전치사 to의

목적격 관계대명사이므로 생략 가능하다.

7 선행사가 장소이므로 in which는 where, 선행사가 이유이므로 for which는 why, 마지막으로 선행사가 시간이므로 at which는 when으로 바꿔 쓸 수 있다.

8 빈칸은 등위접속사 and로 연결되어 장소의 areas를 공통의 선행사로 하는 관계부사 where가 들어갈 자리이다.

9 선행사가 사물(planet)인 경우이므로 관계대명사 which 또는 that을 쓸 수 있다. 또, 선행사는 (a part) of의 목적어이므로 of which we are a part 또는 which we are a part of가 되어야 한다.

10 선행사를 포함한 관계대명사는 ②이다. ①④는 의문사, ③은 '어떤, 무슨'을 뜻하는 의문형용사, ⑤는 감탄문에 사용된 what이다.

11 ⑤ 관계사 that은 전치사와 함께 쓸 수 없다. that을 쓰려면 전치사는 뒤로 보내야 한다.

12 no matter how는 「however+형용사+주어+동사」로 바꿔 쓸 수 있다.

13 '내가 가장 좋아하는 것'이란 말은 선행사를 포함하는 관계대명사 what을 이용한다.

14 she를 관계대명사 who 또는 that으로 바꿔 선행사 the waitress 뒤에 who[that] served us를 붙여 쓴다.

15 시간을 나타내는 부사 then을 관계부사 when으로 고쳐 선행사 the year 뒤에 when they got married를 붙여 쓴다.

16 선행사가 이유를 나타내므로 why 또는 the reason why FMD spreads ~로 쓴다.

17 ② where는 asked의 목적어절을 이끄는 명사절 접속사이다. 나머지는 모두 관계부사절을 이끄는 where이다.

18 선행사 the way와 관계부사 how는 함께 사용하지 않는다. the way만 쓰거나, the way를 생략한 how만이 가능하다.

19 시간을 나타내는 선행사는 관계부사 when이다.

20 선행사가 이유를 나타내므로 관계부사 why를 쓴다.

21 his의 소유격을 대신하고 문장을 연결할 수 있는 관계대명사 whose를 쓴다.

22 선행사가 all과 같은 부정대명사인 경우 관계대명사는 that만 쓴다.

23 시간과 장소를 나타내므로 관계부사 when과 where를 쓴다.

24 시간을 나타내는 관계부사 when은 on which로 바꿔 쓸 수 있다.

중간·기말고사 평가대비 단답형 주관식   p. 174

A 1 No matter how loud I shout, he wouldn't look over.
　2 No matter how boring the class may be, you have to stay until it is over.
　3 No matter how bad the weather may be, they will not postpone the game.

B 1 I'll never forget the time when I was speaking in public for the first time.

　2 Let's meet in the lecture room where we took the English class last semester.

C 1 A building which is now being built was destroyed in the fire.
　2 I thanked the man who helped me move the refrigerator.
　3 The firefighters whose department has won many awards are very brave.
　4 I watched a little girl whose dog was chasing a ball in the park.

| 해설 |

A 1 'However+형용사+주어+동사'는 'No matter how+형용사+주어+동사'로 바꿔 같은 의미를 나타낸다. 따라서 However loud I shout를 No matter how loud I shout로 쓰고 나머지는 그대로 쓴다. 2 However boring the class may be를 No matter how boring the class may be로 쓰고 나머지는 그대로 쓴다. 3 However bad the weather may be를 No matter how bad the weather may be로 쓰고 나머지는 그대로 쓴다.

B 1 선행사가 시간(the time)이므로 관계부사 when 또는 that을 이용하여 the time when(=that) I was speaking in public for the first time으로 쓴다. 따라서, I'll never forget the time when I was speaking in public for the first time.으로 문장을 완성한다. 2 선행사가 장소(the lecture room)이므로 관계부사 where 또는 that을 이용하여 the lecture room where we took the English class last semester로 쓴다. 따라서, Let's meet in the lecture room where(=that) we took the English class last semester.으로 문장을 완성한다.

C 1 대명사 it을 대신하면서 문장을 연결시킬 수 있는 관계대명사 which로 바꾼다. which is now being built를 선행사 A building 뒤에 붙여 A building which is now being built was destroyed~로 쓴다. 2 the man과 He가 공통 명사이다. 따라서 대명사 He를 대신하면서 문장까지 연결시킬 수 있는 관계대명사 who로 바꾼다. who helped me move the refrigerator를 선행사 the man 뒤에 붙여 I thanked the man who helped me move the refrigerator.로 문장을 완성한다. 3 소유격 their를 대신하면서 문장을 연결시킬 수 있는 관계대명사 whose로 바꾼다. whose department has won many awards를 선행사 the firefighters 뒤에 붙여 쓴다. 4 소유격 her를 대신하면서 문장을 연결시킬 수 있는 관계대명사 whose로 바꾼다. whose dog was chasing a ball in the park를 선행사 a little girl 뒤에 붙여 쓴다.

실전 서술형 평가문제 A

모범답안

1 A woman asked me for directions. / She was wearing a gray suit.
2 The people who(m) Kathy visited yesterday were French.
3 Two people walked into the classroom. / I didn't know them.
4 The girl who broke the vase apologized to Mrs. Cook.
5 I know a man. / His daughter is a pilot.
6 The reporter whose articles explained global warming won an award.

실전 서술형 평가문제 B

모범답안

1 The thing which we saw was shocking. / What we saw was shocking.
2 The picture which she drew is very interesting. / What she drew is very interesting.
3 We are polluting the water and air which all life needs. / We are polluting what all life needs.
4 That isn't the thing which we ordered last night. / That isn't what we ordered last night.

실전 서술형 평가문제 C

모범답안

1 whose mother is an English teacher
2 whose sister writes detective stories
3 whose parents bought her an iPhone
4 whose ambition is to climb Mt. Everest

실전 서술형 평가문제 D

모범답안

1 That is the cafeteria where we ate lunch.
2 That is the island where you spent your vacation.
3 That is the year when I was born.
4 That is the day when the space flight to Mars is scheduled to leave.
5 That is the country where the earthquake occurred.
6 That is the room where the examination will be given.
7 That is the time when you felt the happiest.

Chapter 06 가정법

1-1 현재와 미래를 나타내는 1차 가정문
p. 181

Challenge 1

01 If we go to London, we will[can] see Buckingham Palace.
02 If we go to New York, we will[can] see the Statue of Liberty.
03 If we go to Sydney, we will[can] see the Sydney Opera House.
04 If we go to Rome, we will[can] see the Coliseum.
05 If we go to Tokyo, we will[can] see the Imperial Gardens.

Challenge 2

01 close
02 will tell
03 doesn't freeze
04 exercise
05 grows
06 comes
07 will return

1-2 가능성이 거의 없는 2차 가정문(1)
p. 183

Challenge 1

01 won
02 rains
03 studied
04 will cancel
05 were

Challenge 2

01 What would you do if you lost your cell phone?
02 What would you do if there was[were] a fire in the building?

Challenge 3

01 would call / didn't have / would walk / were / would wait
02 woke / heard / would go / were / would lock

1-3 가능성이 거의 없는 2차 가정문(2)   p. 185

Challenge 1

01 If I had a job   02 If she worked
03 If we had a car   04 If he studied hard
05 If you heard her speak English
06 If he lived in a rich country

Challenge 2

01 As she is lazy, she can't get a job.
02 If I knew her address, I could write to her.
03 I don't know her well, so I can't invite her to the party.
04 If I had enough time, I would take a long trip.

1-4 가능성이 0%인 3차 가정문   p. 187

Challenge 1

01 might have turned   02 had had
03 had been   04 would have been

Challenge 2

01 had known / would have gone
02 wouldn't have gotten / had remembered
03 had known / wouldn't have voted

Challenge 3

01 If Kevin had not lent me the money, I wouldn't have been able to buy the car.
02 If I had known that Alex had to get up early, I would have woken him up.

2-1 현재의 소망을 나타내는 「wish+과거시제」   p. 189

Challenge 1

01 I wish I knew Brian's phone number.
02 I wish I could see her more often.
03 I wish I were allowed to go out after 8 o'clock.
04 Nancy wishes she had a cell phone.
05 Susan wishes she didn't have to finish her assignment by tomorrow.

Challenge 2

01 I wish you would send me a copy of the document.
02 I wish you wouldn't waste your time.
03 I wish you wouldn't play the radio so loud.
04 I wish you would be creative and (would) think of a horse of another color.

2-2 과거에 대한 소망 「wish+과거완료」/ 혼합 가정문   p. 191

Challenge 1

01 I wish I had studied harder when I was a student.
02 I wish I hadn't told the secret to him.
03 Kevin wishes he hadn't eaten
04 I wish I had read many good books in my school days.

Challenge 2

01 If I had finished my report yesterday, I could begin a new project today.
02 If I had eaten lunch, I wouldn't be hungry now.
03 If I hadn't received a good job offer from the oil company, I would seriously consider taking the job with the electronics firm.

3-1 as if[though]+가정법 / It's time+가정법 과거   p. 193

Challenge 1

01 as if[though] she knew everything about the accident
02 as if[though] he were rich
03 as if[though] she had been a famous painter
04 as if[though] she had known everything about the accident
05 as if[though] he had been rich

06 as if[though] he had seen a ghost
07 as if[though] I were her younger brother

Challenge 2

01 returned   02 started   03 to get up
04 were   05 to have

3-2 if를 사용하지 않는 가정법 p. 195

Challenge 1

01 Had I not realized you need help, I couldn't have helped you.
02 Should I see her, I'll give her the message.
03 Were I you, I wouldn't go.
04 Had I known the mixer was broken, I would never have bought it.

Challenge 2

01 If it weren't for this horrible weather
02 If it had not been for her help
03 If it weren't for protection
04 If it had not been for your wise advice

이것이 시험에 출제되는 영문법이다! p. 196

Ex1 (b)   Ex2 (d)   Ex3 (b)   Ex4 (d)
Ex5 (a)
Ex6 as if he had been a famous soccer player
Ex7 (a)

| 해설 |

Ex1 if절의 동사가 과거(were)이므로 주절에도 조동사 과거로 일치시킨 would be를 써야 한다.
Ex2 주절의 형태가 조동사 과거(would)인 가정법 과거이다. 따라서 If절은 과거 동사가 와야 하는데 be동사의 경우에는 주로 were가 온다. if를 생략해서 쓸 때는 동사와 주어가 도치되어 Were I rich로 쓸 수 있다.
Ex3 주절의 형태가 「조동사 과거+have+p.p.」이다. 따라서 If절의 시제도 had known을 써서 3차 가정문(가정법 과거완료)으로 만든다.
Ex4 직설법을 가정법으로 바꿀 때 시제가 현재면 과거로, 그리고 긍정은 부정으로, 부정은 긍정으로 표현한다. 따라서 과거형의 긍정인 knew와 could를 쓴다.
Ex5 현재와 미래의 소망을 나타낼 때 「wish+가정법 과거」를 쓴다. 따라서 과거시제인 were가 올바르다.
Ex6 말하는 시점(현재)보다 앞선 시제를 나타내므로 'had+p.p.'를 이용하여 as if he had been a famous soccer player로 쓴다.

Ex7 주절의 형태가 「조동사 과거+have+p.p.」이므로 if절에도 'had+p.p.'를 써야 한다. (b)는 if가 없어서 정답이 될 수 없고 if를 생략하여 도치된 Had I known이 올바르다.

기출 응용문제 p. 198

1 had had enough time to read   2 ④
3 ①   4 ③   5 had worked
6 had / could buy   7 ③
8 as if[though] she were Canadian   9 ①

| 해설 |

1 과거에 대한 유감을 나타내므로 「wish+과거완료」를 쓴다.
2 if 가정법 과거에서 be동사가 올 때는 인칭과 수에 관계없이 were를 쓴다.
3 1차 가정문에서 if절의 시제가 현재나 미래를 나타낼 경우 현재시제를 쓴다. 긍정을 부정으로 고친 don't leave가 알맞다.
4 '내가 너라면'이란 표현으로 If I were you를 쓴다. be동사는 were를 주로 쓴다. if절의 시제가 과거이므로 주절의 시제도 과거시제인 would (not)를 써야 한다.
5 주절의 동사 would have passed로 보아, 이 문장은 가정법 과거완료 구문임을 알 수 있다. 직설법 과거를 가정법 과거완료로 나타낼 경우에는, 과거 사실에 대한 유감을 뜻한다. 가정법 과거완료에서 조건절의 동사는 과거완료(had+p.p.)로 나타낸다.
6 직설법 현재는 가정법 과거로 나타낼 수 있다. 가정법 과거는 「If+주어+were(혹은 과거동사) ~, 주어+would(혹은 could, should, might)+동사원형」으로 표현한다.
7 ③은 if절과 주절의 시제가 일치하지 않는다. had를 have로 고치거나 want를 would want로 써야 한다.
8 말하는 시점과 시제가 같으므로 as if 뒤에는 과거시제를 쓴다.
9 주절의 형태가 '조동사 과거+have+p.p.'이므로 if절도 'had+p.p.'를 써야 한다. 보기에는 'If+주어+had+p.p.'의 표현이 없으므로 if를 생략한 Had it not been for가 알맞다.

중간 · 기말고사 100점 100승 p. 200

1 ③   2 ④   3 ⑤
4 had   5 were   6 ③
7 As 또는 Because / helped
8 I didn't have so much assignment
9 Mom hadn't found out about my bad behavior at school
10 you hadn't broken up with him
11 If it were not for oxygen, all animals would disappear.
12 If it had not been for his skill, the bridge would

have never been built.

13 ⑤	14 ①, ⑤	15 ③	16 ④
17 ⑤	18 ③	19 as if[as though]	
20 were	21 knew / could		
22 answered / could [would]			23 ⑤
24 ②	25 ③		

| 해설 |

1 그녀는 집안일을 안 하면서 마치 하는 것처럼 말한다는 의미가 되어야 하므로 「as if+주어+동사의 과거형」 형태의 as if 가정법 과거로 써야 한다.

2 가정법 과거완료를 직설법으로 고칠 때 시제는 과거, 그리고 부정은 긍정, 긍정은 부정문으로 고친다.

3 과거의 일이고 현재의 가능성이 전혀 없으므로 가정법 과거완료를 쓴다.

4 I wish는 가정법 과거를 이끈다는 사실을 꼭 기억하라. 가정법 과거에서는 과거동사를 사용한다.

5 가정법 과거에서는 인칭과 관계없이 be동사는 were를 쓴다.

6 가정법 과거를 직설법 현재로 고칠 때 시제는 현재로, 그리고 긍정은 부정, 부정은 긍정문으로 고친다.

7 3차 가정문인 가정법 과거완료를 직설법으로 고칠 때 시제는 과거로 고치고 부정은 긍정으로, 긍정은 부정문으로 바꾼다. 따라서 '그가 나를 도와줬기 때문에...'라는 의미가 되므로 접속사 Because나 As를 이용한 As[Because] he helped me, I ~로 쓴다.

8 현재의 소망을 나타내므로 「wish+가정법 과거」를 쓴다. 따라서 I didn't have so much assignment로 문장을 완성한다.

9 과거의 상황에 대한 유감이나 과거의 사실과 다른 소망은 「wish+가정법 과거완료」를 쓴다. 따라서 Mom hadn't found out about my bad behavior at school로 문장을 완성한다.

10 과거의 상황에 대한 유감, 과거의 사실과 다른 소망은 「wish+과거완료」를 쓴다. 따라서 you hadn't broken up with him으로 문장을 완성한다.

11 '~이 없다면'은 If it were not for, Were it not for 또는 But for로 바꿔 쓸 수 있다. 주절의 시제가 과거이므로 If it were not for oxygen, all animals ~로 바꿔 쓴다.

12 주절의 시제가 「조동사 과거+have+p.p.」이므로 But for를 If it had not been for ~로 바꿔 쓴다.

13 직설법 과거는 가정법 과거완료로 바꿀 수 있다.

14 주절의 시제가 「조동사 과거+have+p.p.」이므로 Without은 But for, If it had not been for 또는 if를 생략한 Had it not been for로 바꿔 쓸 수 있다.

15 주절의 시제가 과거이므로 if절에도 과거를 쓴다. be동사는 인칭에 상관없이 were를 쓴다. 대답 또한 가능성이 현저히 떨어지는 조동사 과거를 이용한다.

16 현재와 미래의 소망을 나타낼 때 「wish+과거시제」로 나타낸다.

17 말하는 시점과 같은 상황이므로 as if 뒤에는 '과거시제'를 쓴다. 말하는 시점보다 더 이전의 일을 가정하고 있으면 과거완료를 쓴다. 따라서 '현재 말하는 시점에 미국인처럼 말한다'라는 의미이므로 과거시제인 were를 쓴다.

18 ③ 시제만 보면 맞는 문장인 것 같지만 의미상 혼합가정문이다. 따라서 if절에 가능성 0%인 과거완료를 쓰고 주절에 약간의 가능성을 염두에 두고 말하는 '조동사 과거+동사원형'을 써야 한다. 따라서 would have been을 would be로 고쳐야 한다.

19-20 as if ~ 가정법 문장에서 be동사의 경우는 항상 were가 온다. 「as if+가정법 과거」는 '마치 ~인 것처럼'의 뜻이다.

21 직설법 현재를 가정법으로 고칠 때 시제는 현재를 과거로, 부정은 긍정문으로 고친다. 따라서 knew와 cannot의 과거 긍정인 could를 쓴다.

22 직설법 현재를 가정법으로 고칠 때 시제는 현재를 과거로, 부정은 긍정으로 고친다. 따라서 빈칸에는 각각 answered, could[would]가 온다.

23 '진작 ~ 했어야 했는데 지금 하고 있지 않다'라는 의미를 내포한 「It's time+주어+과거시제」를 쓴다. 따라서 첫 번째 문장은 과거시제인 had를 쓰고, 두 번째 문장은 '~이 없다면'의 표현인 Without을 쓴다.

24 빈칸 주변의 정보만으로 시제를 알기 어렵다. 여기서 정보는 And we wouldn't have enjoyed이다. 따라서 빈칸의 시제 역시 가정법 과거완료가 되어야 한다.

25 가정법 과거완료를 직설법으로 고칠 때 시제는 과거시제를 쓰고, 긍정은 부정으로 바꾼다.

중간·기말고사 평가대비 단답형 주관식 p. 204

A 1 had eaten / wouldn't be
  2 hadn't been shining / wouldn't have gone
  3 weren't closing / wouldn't have to leave
B 1 Were I you   2 Had I been offered
C 1 had come with us, she would have seen the wonderful concert
  2 had not skipped breakfast in the morning, I would not be hungry
  3 had had the opportunity, he would have learned Korean

| 해설 |

A 1 '점심을 먹지 않은 것'은 이미 지난 과거, '배고픈 것'은 현재이므로 가능성 0%와 가능성 20%의 혼합 가정문을 만든다. 따라서 3차 가정문 if절 형태인 had+p.p와 2차 가정문 주절의 형태인 「조동사 과거+동사원형」을 쓴다. 2 두 개의 시제 모두 과거이므로 현재의 가능성이 0%인 3차 가정문을 쓴다. 3 현재 가능성이 전혀 없지만 어느 정도 염두에

두고 말하는 2차 가정문을 쓴다.

B if를 생략한 가정법 문장은 주어와 (조)동사가 서로 바뀌는 도치현상이 일어난다.

C 1 현재 Jane이 함께 와서 콘서트를 볼 가능성은 0%이므로 3차 가정문인 가정법 과거완료로 문장을 만든다. 2 아침식사를 거르지 않을 가능성은 현재 0%, 그리고 지금 현재는 배가 고프므로 가능성 20%인 혼합가정법을 써야 한다. 따라서 If절에 가정법 과거완료인 had not skipped를 쓰고 주절에는 2차 가정문인 가정법 과거 would not be hungry로 문장을 완성한다. 3 두 가지 시제 모두 과거이므로 현재와 아무런 관련이 없는 가능성 0%인 가정법 과거완료를 써야 한다.

실전 서술형 평가문제 A p. 205

모범답안

1 I wish newspapers didn't write untrue stories about me.
2 I wish moviegoers didn't touch me and pull my clothes.
3 I wish I didn't have to sign autographs all the time.
4 I wish I didn't have to smile all the time.
5 I wish I could wear anything I want.
6 I wish I could go to the restaurant to get food.
7 I wish I had privacy.

실전 서술형 평가문제 B p. 206

모범답안

1 If he had gone to the coffee shop yesterday, he would have seen his friends.
2 If she knew Peter's phone number, she could call him.
3 If she hadn't walked in the rain yesterday, she wouldn't have caught a bad cold.

실전 서술형 평가문제 C p. 207

모범답안 : Answers will vary.

1 If I were you, I'd buy her a new one.
2 If I were you, I'd apologize to him.
3 If I were you, I would paint it blue.
4 If I were you, I would go to the shopping center.
5 If I were you, I would wake up earlier in the morning.

실전 서술형 평가문제 D p. 208

모범답안 : Answers will vary.

1 If all the lights suddenly went out, I'd get my candle and turn it on.
2 If I saw a strange person breaking into my neighbor's house, I'd call the police.
3 If I smelled smoke in my house, I'd call the fire department and leave right away.

실전 서술형 평가문제 E p. 208

모범답안

1 I wish I had asked her to dance with me.
2 I wish I hadn't told him I was tired.

Chapter 07 일치와 화법

1-1 주어와 동사의 일치(1)

p. 211

Challenge 1

01 eat	02 makes	03 is	04 provides
05 is	06 vary	07 becomes	

Challenge 2

01 is	02 is	03 has	04 have
05 uses	06 serves	07 consists	08 needs

1-2 주어와 동사의 일치(2)

p. 213

Challenge 1

01 are	02 is	03 is	04 are
05 are	06 is	07 are	08 is
09 is	10 was	11 has	12 are
13 has	14 was	15 is	16 are

1-3 주어와 동사의 일치(3)

p. 215

Challenge 1

01 is	02 is	03 are	04 are
05 is	06 is	07 are	08 is
09 is	10 speak and understand		
11 are	12 confirms	13 are	14 are
15 seeks	16 has		

1-4 주어와 동사의 일치(4)

p. 217

Challenge 1

01 is	02 want	03 were	04 have
05 are	06 is	07 are	08 am
09 is	10 wants	11 is	12 is
13 are	14 is	15 is	16 was

1-5 시제의 일치

p. 219

Challenge 1

01 would study	02 had been
03 had gone	04 had to win

Challenge 2

01 goes	02 rises	03 rotates	04 is
05 makes	06 invented		

Challenge 3

01 gets up at 6 every morning
02 water boils at 100℃
03 was over in 1865

2-1 평서문의 화법 전환

p. 222

Challenge 1

01 She said that she could walk to the shops from the house.
02 Steve says that he loves swimming.
03 They said that they had looked for a long time.
04 Kelly says that she can't swim, but she can ride a bicycle.
05 He told me that it would rain the next day.
06 He tells me that he is studying hard to pass the bar exam.
07 He told me that he had met that boy three years before.
08 He said that he was going to do the work.
09 Tony said that he had gone to the gym the day before.
10 Paul said that he had been to the gym that week.

Challenge 2

01 It was raining hard, but I went there / it had been raining hard, but he had gone there
02 I met this girl two years ago / me that he had met that girl two years before
03 I will return this comic book to you tomorrow / me that he would return that comic book to me the next day

Challenge 3

01 The winds may reach 170 miles per hour.
02 There will be more rain tomorrow.

2-2 의문사가 있는 의문문의 화법 전환 p. 225

Challenge 1

01 why she was practicing it
02 where I was going
03 why my brother was late for school
04 where his office was

Challenge 2

01 She asked me where I was from.
02 My mom asked Jina where she had been.
03 The reporter asked me when the train would arrive.
04 He asked me how long it took to get there.

2-3 의문사가 없는 의문문의 화법 전환 p. 227

Challenge 1

01 if[whether] I had met Cindy before
02 if[whether] I was happy then
03 if[whether] I liked to play basketball
04 if[whether] we can go to the moon someday for a field trip

Challenge 2

01 He asked me if[whether] I had gone to the park the previous night.
02 I asked her if[whether] she was angry then.
03 He asked me if[whether] I had gone to the meeting the night before.
04 Wilson asked us if[whether] we had had a chance to talk to Johnson.

2-4 요청과 명령의 화법 전환 p. 229

Challenge 1

01 She asked him to lend her some money.
02 The doctor advised him to stop drinking.
03 My mom ordered me to do my homework at once.
04 My father told me to clean the car the next day.

Challenge 2

01 She asked us to put all our books and papers away.
02 She asked us not to try to copy our classmates' work.
03 She told us not to talk.

04 She advised us to check the answers carefully before handing in our papers.

이것이 시험에 출제되는 영문법이다! p. 230

Ex1 are   Ex2 are / is   Ex3 imitates / vote
Ex4 me not to be late for school

| 해설 |

Ex1 관계사절 who ~ world를 가리고 보면 주어는 복수인 people이다. 따라서 이에 알맞은 복수 동사 are를 쓴다.
Ex2 부분을 나타내는 말 some of는 of 뒤에 있는 명사의 단/복수에 따라 동사를 결정한다. books는 복수 명사이므로 be동사는 are를 쓴다. / each는 단수 취급하여 항상 단수 동사를 써야 한다.
Ex3 「not only A but also B」는 B에 동사의 수를 일치시킨다. B에 해당하는 것은 대명사 it이므로 단수 동사 imitates를 쓴다. / percent of 뒤에 복수 명사(the people)가 있으므로 동사도 복수형인 vote를 쓴다.
Ex4 부정 명령은 목적격 보어에 「not to+동사원형」을 써서 me not to be late for school로 문장을 완성한다.

기출 응용문제 p. 232

1 ⑤   2 ④   3 ④
4 what he liked to do   5 ④   6 ②
7 she can't swim, but she can ride a bicycle
8 ⑤

| 해설 |

1 명령문의 간접화법은 동사를 'to부정사'로 만들어 목적격 보어에 쓴다. 따라서 Do를 to do로 쓴다.
2 간접화법 전환 시 전달동사의 시제가 과거(said)이면 과거진행시제는 과거완료 진행시제로 바뀐다.
3 ④ 전달동사의 시제가 과거(told)라 하더라도 매일 아침 6시에 일어나는 것은 현재의 습관이므로 시제의 영향을 받지 않는다. 따라서 got up이 아닌 gets up으로 써야 한다.
4 직접화법을 간접화법으로 바꿀 때는 전달자의 시점에 특히 유의하여 시제, 주어, 부사어 등을 알맞게 전환해야 한다. 주절의 시제가 과거(asked)이므로 like는 liked로, you는 Bob을 가리키므로 he로 바꾸어야 한다. 이때 뒤에 오는 간접의문문은 「의문사+주어+동사」의 어순으로 쓴다는 데 주의한다.
5 의문사가 없는 의문문이므로, 「if[whether]+주어+동사」를 사용한다. 주어는 he가 되고, 시제는 주절의 시제(과거)와 일치시킨다.
6 Neither A nor B에서 동사의 수는 B에 일치시켜야 한다. 따라서 B에 해당하는 the teacher가 단수이므로 단수 동사인 knows를 써야 한다. 두 번째 문장은 the students의

복수 명사이므로 복수 동사인 know를 써야 한다.

7 평서문의 화법에서는 접속사 that을 이용한다. 전달자의 시점으로 바꿔야 하므로 주어 I는 she로 바꾸고 전달동사(says)의 시제가 현재이므로 조동사는 그대로 can't로 쓴다.

8 학문을 나타내는 명사는 단수 취급한다. 하지만 두 개의 학문이 and로 연결되어 있으므로 복수 취급한다.

중간 · 기말고사 100점 100승   p. 234

1 ④	2 ②	3 ③	4 ②
5 ⑤	6 is → am	7 ④	8 ④
9 ⑤	10 ②	11 ①	12 ②
13 ③	14 ⑤	15 ④	

16 asked me to open the door
17 have got → got / before → ago   18 ⑤
19 asked / if I liked   20 she had   21 ⑤

| 해설 |

1 의문사가 없는 의문문을 간접화법으로 고칠 때 접속사 if나 whether를 쓴다. 피전달동사인 want를 과거시제 wanted로 고친다.

2 학문명을 나타내는 명사는 -ics로 끝이 나더라도 단수 취급하여 동사는 단수인 is를 쓴다.

3 ③ 직접의문의 주어 you는 간접의문문으로 바꿀 때 목적어에 일치시키므로, she was doing이 아니라 I was doing이 되어야 한다.

4 a number of는 복수 취급하고, the number of는 단수 취급한다.

5 「both A and B」가 주어 자리에 올 때 주어는 복수 취급하여 동사도 복수형을 써야 한다.

6 「neither A nor B」는 B에 동사의 수를 일치시켜야 한다.

7 의문문의 간접화법 전환 시 전달동사 said to는 asked로 바꾸고, 의문문은 「의문사+주어+동사」의 어순을 취해야 한다. 시제가 과거이므로 의문문 안의 동사 live는 lived가 되어야 한다.

8 부정 명령문의 간접화법은 「not+to부정사」를 목적격 보어에 써서 warned the patient not to smoke anymore로 문장을 완성한다. 전달동사는 명령을 나타내는 5형식 동사 ask, tell, advise, warn 등을 자유롭게 쓸 수 있다.

9 ⑤ Neither A nor B에서 수 일치는 B에 일치시킨다. 따라서 the students가 B에 해당하므로 동사는 are로 써야 한다.

10 현재의 습관, 매일 반복되는 행위는 전달동사의 시제와 상관없이 현재시제를 써야 한다.

11 the United States는 하나의 나라이고 객관적 사실을 나타내고 있으므로 현재형 단수 동사인 is를 쓴다.

12 ② 형용사구(about kings and queens)를 제거하면 주어는 단수 명사인 the story이므로 동사는 is를 써야 한다.

13 ③ 동사는 said를 그대로 쓰고, his son은 직접화법에서 my son이 되며, be동사 was는 현재시제 is가 된다.

14 의문사가 없는 의문문은 직접화법을 간접화법으로 바꿀 때 전달동사는 ask를 쓰고 접속사는 if나 whether를 이용한다.

15 피전달문의 내용이 불변의 사실이므로 주절의 시제와는 상관없이 현재시제로 써야 한다.

16 명령문의 간접화법에서 전달동사 said to는 asked로 바꾸고, 피전달문의 동사(open)는 to부정사(to open)로 쓴다.

17 직접화법으로 바꿀 때 과거완료 시제(have got)는 과거시제 got으로, before는 ago로 바꾼다.

18 ⑤ 'one of ~'는 '~의 하나'라는 의미의 단수 주어로 쓰인다. 따라서 동사 were를 was로 써야 한다.

19 said to는 asked로 바꾸고, 의문사가 없으므로 「if[whether]+주어+동사」를 사용한다. 주어 you는 I가 되고 동사는 주절과 같은 시제인 liked가 알맞다.

20 주어 I는 알맞은 인칭대명사 she로 바꾸고, 현재형 동사 have to는 과거시제인 had to로 바꾼다.

21 매일 반복되는 일상이므로 동사의 시제와 상관없이 현재시제 drinks를 쓰고 before 뒤에는 「주어(she)+동사(goes)」에서 she가 생략되었으므로 동사 goes를 going으로 바꾼다.

중간 · 기말고사 평가대비 단답형 주관식   p. 238

A 1 Seo-yoon said that she liked listening to music.
   2 She asked me what time it was then.
   3 My teacher told[ordered] us to be quiet.
   4 Tom asked me who had written that book.
   5 She told me not to open the door.

B 1 She said to him, "Where do you live?"
   2 I said to the woman, "Do you know Mr. Smith?"
   3 I said to her, "Where were you last night?"

C 1 Either David or Kim will help you.
   2 Either my mother or my father drives me to school.
   3 Neither John nor Fiona has been to Spain.
   4 Both Tom and I are learning Korean this year.
   5 Neither Emma nor Kathy won the race.

D 1 are   2 has   3 were   4 believes
   5 are   6 was   7 is   8 is

| 해설 |

A 1 전달동사 said는 said로 그대로 쓰고 인용문의 동사는 과거인 liked로 일치시켜야 한다. 따라서 접속사 that과 함께 Seo-yoon said that she liked listening to music으로 쓴다. 2 의문사가 있는 문장을 간접화법으로 전환할 때는 의문사를 그대로 이용하여 '의문사+주어+동사'의 어순으로 그대로 쓴다. 따라서 전달동사 said to는 asked로 바꾸고

인용문의 동사 is의 시제는 과거 was로 고쳐 쓴다. 따라서 She asked me what time it was then. 으로 쓴다. 부사 now는 전달하는 시점에 맞게 then으로 고치는 것도 잊지 말아야 한다. 3 명령과 충고 등의 간접화법은 인용문의 동사를 to 부정사로 바꾼다. 전달동사 said to는 의미에 따라 told 또는 ordered로 바꿀 수 있다. 부정사를 이용하여 '명령동사＋목적어＋to 부정사'의 5형식 명령문장과 똑같은 어순인 My teacher told[ordered] us to be quiet.로 쓴다. 4 인용문의 의문사가 주어인 경우 '의문사＋동사'의 어순으로 쓴다. 따라서 전달동사 said to를 asked로 바꾸고, 인용문의 동사 wrote는 과거완료인 had written으로 고쳐 쓴다. 따라서 Tom asked me who had written that book. 으로 쓴다. this를 that으로 고치는 것도 잊지 말아야 한다. 5 부정명령문은 인용문의 동사를 to부정사로 쓰고 부정사 앞에 not을 쓴다. 따라서 said to를 told로 바꾸고 don't open을 not to open으로 바꾼 She told me not to open the door.로 문장을 완성한다.

B 1 전달동사 asked는 said to로 고치고 인용문의 시제는 과거를 현재로 고쳐 직접 의문문인 where do you live?로 쓴다. 따라서 She said to him, "Where do you live?" 로 문장을 완성한다. 2 전달동사 asked는 said to로 고친다. 접속사 if를 보아 인용문에는 접속사가 있는 직접 의문문임을 알 수 있다. 따라서 인용문의 과거시제 knew를 현재시제 know로 고쳐 I said to the man, "Do you know Mr. Smith?"로 문장을 완성한다. 3 전달동사 asked는 said to로 고친다. 인용문의 과거완료시제 had been은 과거시제 were로 고쳐 I said to her, "Where were you last night?"로 문장을 완성한다. the night before도 last night 으로 고쳐 쓴다.

C 1 Either A or B이므로 Either David or Kim will help you.로 쓴다. 2 엄마 또는 아빠 중에 한 명이 차로 학교에 데려다 주므로 Either my mother or my father drives me to school.로 문장을 완성한다. 동사의 수 일치는 Either A or B에서 B에 일치시키므로 주어가 단수 my father이므로 3인칭 단수형인 drives를 써야 한다. 3 양자 부정을 나타내는 Neither A nor B이므로 각각 John과 Fiona를 A와 B에 넣어 Neither John nor Fiona has been to Spain.으로 쓴다. 동사의 수 일치는 B에 일치시키므로 단수 주어(Fiona)이므로 단수형인 has를 쓴다. Neither가 부정의 의미이므로 동사를 has not으로 쓰면 안 된다. 4 Tom과 I 둘 모두를 의미하므로 Both Tom and I are learning Korean this year.로 문장을 완성한다. Both A and B가 주어로 쓰일 때 복수가 되므로 동사는 복수형인 are를 써야 한다. 5 양자부정의 의미이므로 Neither Emma nor Kathy won the race.로 쓴다. Neither가 부정의 의미이므로 동사를 didn't won으로 쓰면 안 된다.

D 1 부분을 나타내는 '분수＋of'는 of 뒤에 오는 명사에 수를 일치시킨다. 복수 명사(books)이므로 동사 are를 쓴다. 2 The number of cars가 주어로 쓰이면 동사는 단수형을

써야 하므로 has로 쓴다. 3 there be의 주어는 be동사 뒤에 나온다. 따라서 주어가 복수 lots of people이므로 be 동사 복수형인 were을 쓴다. 4 '~의 하나'라는 의미의 one of＋복수명사에서 one이 who 이하의 선행사이다. 따라서 선행사가 단수이므로 단수동사형인 believes를 써야 한다. 5 the와 함께 쓰여 국민 전체 또는 사람들을 나타낼 때는 the English는 복수 취급한다. 따라서 복수형인 are를 써야 한다. 6 and로 연결되더라도 하나의 사물을 나타내므로 단수 동사인 was를 써야 한다. 7 Europe은 여러 나라가 모인 하나의 덩어리를 나타내는 말이므로 단수 취급하여 is 를 써야 한다. 8 학문분야는 -ics로 끝나 복수형처럼 보이지만 단수 취급한다. 따라서 단수형인 is를 써야 한다.

실전 서술형 평가문제 A　　p. 240

모범답안

1 A number of people / are
2 One of the people(＝One of them) / is
3 None of the people
4 Each of the women / is

실전 서술형 평가문제 B　　p. 240

모범답안

1 Either Peter or his sister takes the dog out for a walk.
2 They say vitamin C not only prevents heart disease but also prevents colds. 또는 They say vitamin C prevents both heart disease and colds.
3 Neither Lisa nor James told the truth.

실전 서술형 평가문제 C　　p. 241

모범답안

1 her granddaughter played the piano beautifully
2 she and her husband had enjoyed the movie the night before
3 he was going to buy a new cell phone the following month
4 he had been washing the car all morning

실전 서술형 평가문제 D
p. 242

모범답안

1 asked Peter if[whether] he would go to the soccer game on Saturday / told Bob that he wouldn't because he was going camping at the weekend
2 asked Kathy why she hadn't bought the blue dress / told Cindy that she had liked the pink one better
3 asked the boys if[whether] they had bought any new CDs / said that they had, but they hadn't listened to them all yet
4 asked Philip if[whether] he had watched the movie the night before / told Susan that he hadn't, because he had been reading a very interesting book

실전 서술형 평가문제 E
p. 243

모범답안

1 Tom told his wife to stop eating.
2 Karen's husband told her not to drive so fast.
3 She asked him(=her brother) to lend her five dollars.

실전 서술형 평가문제 F
p. 244

모범답안

1 she and her husband were planning to go there the following evening
2 she had heard that it was quite expensive
3 she knew that, but it was her birthday the following day and she wanted to do something special
4 it was the right place to go to
5 the chef was from Paris and that the service was excellent
6 she was sure she[they] would have a delicious meal

Chapter 08 특수구문
p. 245~267

1-1 도치가 이루어지지 않는 강조(1)
p. 247

Challenge 1

01 It was in London that I met Susan last month.
02 It was the money that Tom returned last night.
03 It was last night that she saw the man break into the house.
04 It was on the road that Bob picked up a coin yesterday.

Challenge 2

01 does like
02 did forgive
03 do remember
04 did eat
05 did finish

1-2 도치가 이루어지지 않는 강조(2)
p. 249

Challenge 1

01 the very
02 in the least

03 at all
04 and
05 and
06 on earth
07 in the world
08 at all

Challenge 2

01 When did you see Kelly in front of the bank?
02 What was it that you bought at the store?
03 When is it that the winter vacation begins?
04 When did you have the happiest moment of your life?
05 What was it that Kelly saw in front of the bank an hour ago?

2-1 도치를 통한 강조(1)
p. 251

Challenge 1

01 stood her mother
02 she is
03 fell the girl
04 stood an old woman
05 he walked
06 he was

Challenge 2

01 Great was the joy of Columbus.

02 Great was the performance yesterday.

03 In New York is Thomason now.

04 The trip to Australia with my family I will remember forever.

2-2 도치를 통한 강조(2)   p. 253

Challenge 1

01 Never have I seen such a beautiful girl.

02 No sooner had I gone to bed than I got a phone call.

03 Hardly can I believe what she said.

04 No sooner had she heard the word than she turned pale.

05 Hardly had they started watching the movie when the power went out.

06 Never had I seen so many people in one room.

Challenge 2

01 Neither am I.   02 So do I.

03 Neither have I.   04 So would I.

05 So am I.   06 So did I.

3-1 생략   p. 255

Challenge 1

01 (they were)   02 (which was)

03 (I was)   04 (come)

05 (speak English)   06 (she was)

07 (studying is)   08 (come to the party)

09 (late for school)

Challenge 2

01 She pretended to be pleased, but she wasn't pleased.

02 He was very healthy when he was young.

03 He is far better than he was yesterday.

04 The first commercial film which[that] was made in California was completed in 1907.

3-2 삽입, 동격, 무생물 주어   p. 257

Challenge 1

01 surprisingly   02 so to speak

03 we have learned   04 I thought

05 if ever

Challenge 2

01 I had no idea that he would fail in the exam.

02 The news of her death was a great shock to me.

03 Graham Bell, an American scientist, invented the telephone.

04 We heard the news that he had entered Harvard.

Challenge 3

01 His father's sudden death

02 A few minutes' walk

03 The noise in the street

04 Twenty minutes' walk

이것이 시험에 출제되는 영문법이다!   p. 258

Ex1 It is an adventurous spirit that makes people invent things.

Ex2 (d)   Ex3 (c)   Ex4 had he gone out

Ex5 (b)   Ex6 (b)

| 해설 |

Ex1 시제가 현재이므로 It is ~ that 사이에 an adventurous spirit을 넣어 강조 구문을 만든다.

Ex2 동사를 강조할 때는 인칭과 시제에 따라 do/does/did를 쓴다. 시제가 과거 seemed이므로 did로 동사를 강조한다.

Ex3 의문사를 강조하기 위해 「의문사+is/was+it that ~?」의 형태로 쓴다. 여기서는 의문사 who를 그대로 쓰고 시제는 과거이므로 Who was it that ~으로 강조하는 문장을 완성한다.

Ex4 부정어 Hardly를 문두에 쓸 때 주어와 동사는 도치된다. had가 주어 앞으로 이동하여 had he gone out으로 쓴다.

Ex5 전치사구(near my house)가 문두에 나올 때 주어와 동사는 도치된다. 따라서 (b)는 is a tiny dry-cleaning shop의 어순으로 써야 한다.

Ex6 동사가 일반동사 like이므로 do 또는 does를 쓴다. 여기서는 주어(Nancy)가 단수이므로 does를 써야 한다.

기출 응용문제   p. 260

1 ⑤   2 ③   3 ②

4 It was Wilson that I met at his birthday party last month.

5 Never do I do things I don't like to do.

6 was Tom that[who]   7 ④   8 ④

9 ②

1 동사의 과거형을 강조할 때는 조동사 did를 본동사 앞에 쓰고 본동사는 원형으로 쓴다.

2 조동사가 있는 문장에 동의할 때는 조동사를 그대로 이용하여 「So / Neither + 조동사 + 주어」로 쓴다. 여기서는 긍정에 대한 동의이므로 So will I가 되어야 한다.

3 ② 상대방의 말에 동의하는 표현은 「So + be동사[조동사] + 주어」의 형태로 쓴다. 주어(Kelly)가 단수이므로 동사는 has를 쓴 ②번이 정답이다.

4 목적어 Wilson을 It was ~ that 사이에 두어 It was Wilson that I met at his birthday party last month.로 쓴다. 시제가 과거(met)이므로 「It ~ that 강조 구문」의 be동사도 과거인 was를 써야 한다.

5 부정어가 문두에 위치할 때 「부정어 + 조동사 + 주어 + 동사」의 어순으로 바뀐다. 이 문장에서 동사는 do이므로 일반동사의 조동사 역할을 하는 do를 이용하여 Never do I do things I don't like to do.로 쓴다.

6 「It is / was ~ that」 강조구문에서 It is / was와 that 사이에 강조하고자 하는 말을 넣는다. 사람일 때는 that 대신 who도 쓸 수 있다. 여기서 시제는 과거 broke이므로 be동사 또한 과거 was를 써야 한다.

7 의문사를 강조하기 위해 「의문사 is / was it that ~?」의 형태로 쓴다. 시제가 과거이므로 was it that으로 빈칸을 완성한다.

8 〈보기〉의 do는 일반동사(worry)를 강조하는 조동사 do이다. 반면 ④는 '~하다'의 의미인 일반동사이다.

9 While I was staying에서 주어와 be동사가 생략되어 있는 문장이다.

쓰였다.

6 주어와 시제를 일치시킨 I was를 쓴다.

7 접속사로 연결되어 반복되는 어구를 생략한 ④번이 알맞다.

8 전치사구가 문두에 위치할 경우 「전치사구 + 동사 + 주어」의 어순으로 도치된다.

9 ① she reads → does she read, ② dreamed I → did I dream, ④ he had seen → had he seen, ⑤ had fallen he → had he fallen으로 고쳐야 한다.

10 ④ 부정어가 문두에 나와 도치되면 「부정어 + 조동사 + 주어 + 동사」의 형태로 쓴다. 따라서 I fell을 did I fall로 고쳐야 한다.

11 긍정의 내용에 동의할 때 「so + do동사 / 조동사 / be동사 + 주어」로 쓴다. 주어가 3인칭 단수 Ted이고 동사가 일반동사이므로 so does Ted로 빈칸을 완성한다.

12 ④는 강조의 구문이 아니라 가주어 / 진주어 구문이다.

13 ⑤는 관계대명사로 사용된 that이고, 나머지는 모두 동격의 that절이다.

14 긍정문에 대한 동의의 표현은 「so + do동사 / be동사 / 조동사 + 주어」로 쓴다. 여기서는 동사가 일반동사(makes)이므로 does를 이용하여 So does the sea.로 완성한다.

15 「주격 관계대명사 + be동사」는 생략해도 문법과 의미에 큰 영향을 끼치지 않으므로 생략할 수 있다.

16 동의의 표현은 긍정일 때 「so + do동사 / 조동사 / be동사 + 주어」, 부정일 때 「Neither + do동사 / 조동사 / be동사 + 주어」이다. 첫 번째 문장은 주어가 단수이고 be동사이므로 is를 쓰고, 두 번째 문장은 동사가 일반동사의 과거이므로 did, 마지막 문장은 조동사 have를 쓴다.

중간 · 기말고사 100점 100승   p. 262

1	It was / that[who]		2	③
3	Seoul, the largest city in Korea		4	⑤
5	③	6 I was	7 ④	8 ①
9	③	10 ④	11 so does Ted	
12	④	13 ⑤	14 ③	15 ①
16	②			

| 해설 |

1 시제가 과거(went)이므로 be동사 과거 was를 이용하여 It was ~ that[who]으로 빈칸을 완성한다.

2 계속적 용법의 who와 is는 생략해도 문법과 내용에 큰 영향을 끼치지 않으므로 who is를 생략할 수 있다.

3 쉼표 뒤에 있는 which is를 없애면 두 개의 명사(구)가 나란히 연결되는 동격 구문이 된다.

4 부정의 내용에 동의할 때 「주어 + (조)동사의 부정형 + either」 또는 「Neither + (조)동사 + 주어」로 쓴다.

5 나머지는 동사를 강조하는 강조 용법의 do인데, ③의 do laundry는 '세탁하다'라는 뜻으로 여기서 do는 일반동사로

중간 · 기말고사 평가대비 단답형 주관식   p. 265

A 1 It was in 2008 that I started to write English books.

  2 When was it that you had the happiest moment of your life?

B Little did his mother think that he was destined to explain many matters which had been a mystery ever since the creation of the world.

C 1 Not / did we stay

  2 Little did I imagine

  3 Seldom did he think

D 1 When you are in Rome, do as the Romans do.

  2 Though she is young, she has much experience.

  3 The girl who is playing the piano on the stage is my sister.

| 해설 |

A 1 시제가 과거이므로 「It was ~ that」 강조구문을 만든다.

  2 의문사를 강조하기 위해 '의문사 + is / was + it that...?'의

어순으로 쓴다. 시제가 과거이므로 be동사 was를 사용한 When was it that you had the happiest moment of your life?로 쓴다. When did you have ～에서 동사 have는 과거를 표시하는 조동사 did가 없어지므로 과거시제인 had로 바꾸는 것도 잊지 말아야 한다.

B 부정어구 little을 문장 맨 앞에 쓰면 「Little+조동사+주어+동사」의 어순으로 도치된다. 여기서는 시제가 과거이므로 조동사 did를 이용하여 Little did his mother think that ～으로 도치 구문을 완성한다.

C 「부정어구+조동사+주어+동사」의 어순으로 도치된다.

D 1 일반인을 지칭하는 you are가 생략되었다. 2 접속사 뒤에 주어와 동사가 생략되었다. 주어는 주절의 주어(she)와 같고 동사는 주절의 동사가 현재이므로 현재형 is를 쓴다. 3 the girl과 playing 사이에 「주격 관계대명사+be동사」가 생략되었다.

실전 서술형 평가문제 A p. 266

모범답안

1 It was a thief that broke the window last night.
2 It was the window that a thief broke last night.
3 It was last night that a thief broke the window.

실전 서술형 평가문제 B p. 267

모범답안

1 Never have I stayed at such an expensive hotel.
2 No sooner had I walked through the door than the manager welcomed me.
3 Rarely had he seen such a sunset.
4 We'd just got to the top of the hill when down came the rain and we got thoroughly soaked.
5 No sooner had she seen the police when she ran away.
6 Hardly had everybody taken their seats when Dr. Smith began his lecture.
7 So great was his surprise that he almost ran away.

중학영문법 3-B

한국에서 유일한 중학영문법

 정답 및 해설